Books by Joe David Bellamy

Fiction
Suzi Sinzinnati
Atomic Love
Sohio and Other Stories

Nonfiction
The New Fiction
American Poetry Observed
Literary Luxuries: American Writing at the End of the Millennium
The Bellamys of Early Virginia
The Lost Saranac Interviews (with Connie Bellamy)
New World Extra

Poetry
Olympic Gold Medalist
The Frozen Sea

Anthologies
Apocalypse: Dominant Contemporary Forms
Superfiction or the American Story Transformed
Moral Fiction
New Writers for the Eighties
Love Stories/Love Poems

KINDRED SPIRITS

Four Hundred Years of an American Family

Joe David Bellamy

PublishingWorks, Inc.

2011
Exeter, NH

Epigraph opposite dedication page is from lyrics to the song, "Rise Again," by Leon Dubinsky. Reprinted with permission.

First Edition

PW

PublishingWorks, Inc.
151 Epping Road
Exeter, NH 03833
603-778-9883

Distributed to the trade by Publishers Group West.

Designed by: Anna Pearlman

LCCN: 2010932476
ISBN-13: 978-1-935557-72-2

KINDRED SPIRITS

Four Hundred Years of an American Family

Joe David Bellamy

When the waves roll on over the waters
And the ocean cries
We look to our sons and daughters
To explain our lives
As if a child could tell us why
That as sure as the sunrise
As sure as the sea
As sure as the wind in the trees

We rise again in the faces of our children
We rise again in the voices of our song
We rise again in the waves out on the ocean
And then we rise again
And then we rise again

for my mother
Beulah Zutavern Bellamy

for my grandmothers
Harriet Kagy Zutavern and Sarah Edith Lawhorn Bellamy

and for my great grandmothers
Alice Whipple Clark, Hannah Siple, and Alveda Spalding

CONTENTS

Beulah Pearl Bellamy

1.

The Most Beautiful Woman in the World

After the death of my mother made me an orphan in middle age—my father had died twenty-four years earlier—I developed a sudden interest in genealogy that was close to an obsession. I realized, fairly quickly, that this obsession was probably a certain form of bereavement, but that did not lessen its intensity. Suddenly I was overwhelmed with the feeling that my mother's life and the immediate past of my whole extended family was in danger of being lost forever, as the far past was already lost. I was perhaps the first person in my lineage, a lineage that was undoubtedly ancient—as ancient as everyone else who is alive today—with the opportunity to discover whatever past was there, and I felt I had to take a stand about it. In spite of all the usual distractions, I was simply going to do it. I felt it as an important responsibility.

I was not interested in genealogy in order to prove that I was *somebody*, the legitimate heir to the English throne perhaps, or a descendant of the Pilgrims. The fact is I had come from a rather large extended family, and now—with the death of my mother— most of them were gone. I remembered them all vividly, mostly with affection, but no doubt I was feeling lonely. I had had children of my own, a daughter and a son, but they were out of the nest starting their own families now, living far away. I wanted to reclaim the sense of having a family once again.

Who were we anyway? We were, I supposed, an ordinary middle class family from the American Midwest, a family of white people, vaguely English (or Irish, I thought) with a little bit of German and Swiss from my mother's side. We were basically standard white-bread Americans, just plain folks, people somehow without ethnicity or real history, yet people who had been lucky and privileged enough that, in the latter part of the twentieth century, we had been taught to feel a little bit guilty about being so white and so bland, so lacking in any specific cultural identity, as if we had reached whatever middling level of economic security we had attained through almost no effort at all, simply because we were white and ordinary.

In a tangible sense, I didn't know who we were. I felt we needed to identify ourselves more clearly and fully, find out where we came from, when and under what circumstances we arrived in the places we called home, and pass this information on to future generations of descendants. This information was perishable, after all—some of it had surely perished already. It would be ignorant and careless of me not to do what I could to find out what was left and make it permanent, if possible—put it on a CD or bury it somewhere deep in the bowels of the Library of Congress—so that it might survive. Of course, I wouldn't have minded if my ancestors all turned out to be decent and accomplished. But if there were horse thieves or worse, I wanted to know that too. I was determined to be ruthless—I wanted to know the truth, even if it might be unpleasant.

The last time I saw my mother, about two months before she died suddenly from a heart attack in 1998, we had spent an afternoon going through boxes of old photographs from her attic, many of which she had inherited from her own mother. She had pictures of herself as a child that I had never seen before—she was an adorable little girl—and as a ravishingly beautiful young woman, or so she seemed to me. At one point, marveling at the pictures, I blurted out something about her having been "the most beautiful woman in the world," and I felt at the time that I probably should not have said it in spite of the fact that she seemed pleased and I felt it was true. It seemed a little silly and self-indulgent saying something like that to this sweet, wizened 79-year-old woman with age-spots on her forehead who was hardly a beauty of any kind at the time. What immoderately well-loved son does not believe his mother is beautiful? Still, after she died, I was more grateful that I had made that one rash statement than anything else I may have said that day.

She showed me pictures that afternoon that amazed me. For the first time in my life, I saw a photograph of my great grandmother, Hannah Siple, my mother's mother's mother. She was so far away in time; she had died long before I was born, and her life had been tragically sad. But I felt so close to her at that moment. Her life had made my life possible. I was certain we would have been close friends, if only because she resembled my mother so completely. I don't quite know how to express this, but I wanted to speak to Hannah Siple. I wanted to be able to tell her that her misery had not been entirely in vain, that life she had set in motion had gone on and was going on still. That photograph of Hannah Siple was a revelation for me and led to a search for many other photographs—as many as I could find of all my missing family members.

Why did it take me so long to learn about Hannah Siple's life and to come to a point in my own life that I could focus on her and come to include her in my idea of the family I had inherited? My family, like so many others, seemed to accept the tacit conviction that there was no way to know, finally, who our ancestors were. If our immediate relatives could not tell us about them, we assumed we would never know. When they did try to tell us what little they remembered, perhaps we were too young and preoccupied to listen.

Perhaps our ancestors had been so engaged in simply living their lives, of hacking their way through the wilderness, they forgot their history—or they never knew it—or they died before they could pass it on. It takes only one lost generation to engender oblivion. Perhaps because so many of them were living on the very edge of civilization, without the resources of civilization—including, in some cases, literacy itself—and perhaps suffering too from a kind of permanent homesickness, having left behind their own extended families—they let it slide away. Americans are, after all, the offspring of banished peoples—revolutionaries, renegades, rebels, and rabble-rousers—nonconformists, adventurers, indentured servants, slaves, religious fanatics, the offspring of murdered martyrs, and opportunists—the dispossessed from every corner of the world. Certainly my ancestors were exactly that sort of people—people, in some cases, who might have wanted to forget their pasts.

Or—as in the case of Rolla and Harriet, my mother's parents—each inherited lovely, thick family histories, Rolla Zutavern for his mother's family, the Spaldings, Harriet for her father's family, the Kagys. There is evidence that they did read these genealogies. But perhaps, for them, the contents of these volumes seemed a little abstract and musty, something very far away. And the family histories they did inherit, though valuable, were hardly perfect. The Kagy genealogy listed my grandmother (the owner of the book when I discovered it) as dying when she was nine days old! Actually, she lived to be 89. The Spalding genealogy listed Mercy Mary Adams as if she were just any little Adams hausfrau who happened to marry a Spalding, and it said nothing about her incredible lineage (more about that to come)—because her lineage was not known to the collator (or to anyone else in the family).

Perhaps there are any number of plausible excuses for the muddle we had gotten into as a people apparently without a knowable past. But now all that has changed.

What I didn't know at the time was that my sudden interest in genealogy coincided with a revolution, and that revolution is even bigger than the popular phenomenon that struck in the late seventies with Alex Haley's *Roots*. Twenty years after *Roots*, family history hit the internet. All over the world, websites were launching, and they still are. The Mormons, with their enormous repository of genealogical data kept safe inside the Granite Mountain Vault in Utah—nuclear-bomb-proof and climate-controlled—were about to go on-line. Then they did!

Suddenly, through the Church of the Latter Day Saints (LDS) at familysearch.org, it was possible to access information on more than a *billion-and-a-half* of the seven to eight billion humans who ever lived on the planet and who left names or records behind. Suddenly there was the U.S. Genweb Project, which made it possible to access a great many county birth/death/marriage/ probate/land and court records from almost any county in the U.S. in the comfort of your home via the internet. Suddenly there was Ancestry.com for census information and for archived family histories on-line. Suddenly the vast record holdings of the New England Historic Genealogical Society were available on the internet.

Suddenly it was possible to join a user group on-line where everyone involved was a cousin you never knew you had and the avowed purpose was to discover more about your common ances- tors. Suddenly everyone and his uncle had a family history site on the web that listed the several trees within that family—with regular updates as new information was discovered and recorded. According to several sources, genealogy is now the second most popular subject area on the internet after pornography!—and if you try to access the LDS site on a Sunday afternoon, you will find out just how true this is. You can almost feel their huge servers straining under the torrent of hits.

With the help of the access to multiple worlds of knowl- edge made possible by the internet and the computer, genealogy might become the human equivalent of the genome project or constructing the first replica of the DNA molecule. Instead of looking at the two or three immediate generations of a family or a person—only those living or those whom the living remember— what if we could stand back at some greater distance from the teeming, then lost, lives within a family and examine ten genera- tions or twenty generations or thirty generations? Not just one line of twenty or thirty generations but multiple lines or every single line—the whole picture. What giant patterns might emerge? What genetic tendencies might become clearer? If one could accom- plish such a study within one's own family, what better path to greater self-knowledge could one possibly find? What better way to understand one's own inclinations and aptitudes?

What I am here to report is that such a thing is now possible, and I have done it—with unexpected results. It is a humbling experience to uncover and then to understand and to come to terms with the hundreds, the thousands, whose lives preceded one's own. I started out by wondering how I could have made the choices I did that defined my modest life in my peculiar field, given that my immediate ancestors seemed so unlikely—and *so unlike me*. I ended up seeing exactly why I had made so many of the decisions that defined my life. I wish I had known sooner just where I came from. It might have made the choices easier.

Of course, it is one thing to find out and prove the names of one's ancestors, and quite another to learn something worth knowing about the lives they lived. The names themselves seem valuable to me, and I still want to find more of them; but the names have little interest to anyone not in the immediate family, and sometimes not even to them. But *the lives*—if they can be learned—can be revelations. To discover the lives, if possible, became my goal; and what an enormous effort it took.

It's true—one of the pleasures of genealogy is in solving mysteries—in finding where all the bodies are buried—and another is the purely clerical enjoyment in the working out of a gigantic crossword puzzle, filling in all the little boxes. But these are boxes that count *for all time* once you get them right, and the satisfaction of resurrecting some long forgotten soul, whose life was absolutely necessary to your own, and restoring them to their rightful place in the historical record, is gratifying.

Of course, some of what one finds out there is not all it seems—even the Mormon researchers are fallible. Their belief in the importance of the family and the sheer grandeur of their vision is admirable, and the work they have done to preserve records is an incalculable service to humankind. But their genealogy program is, after all, an arm of their missionary effort. Each church member is admonished to seek out his ancestors in order to perform various religious rites that will assure all can meet again in the Celestial Kingdom. Such motives coupled with the fact that even the uneducated among them must perform the same rituals may not be the best prescription for accuracy. Some observers are simply suspicious of any motivation that is not purely scientific. Genealogical research is like any other research—its quality depends upon the experience, intelligence, care, and unbiased attitude of the researchers.

There are other good reasons why, up until now, genealogy has had a dubious reputation—somewhere between pseudoscience and fanaticism. In the early part of the twentieth century in America many fraudulent genealogies were prepared for the nouveau riche who wished to prove they were descended from European aristocracy. If you could afford to pay a "genealogist," you could receive impressive "proof" of such descent, and the Mormons had nothing at all to do with it. Unfortunately, some of these fictitious trees are still in circulation, and their presence, like bad science, mucks up the whole and sullies the reputation of the enterprise

Also, there is the age-old problem of paternal descent. Even if one finds good evidence from the record that so-in-so's parents were Mr. and Mrs. So-in-So, how could anyone ever know with certainty it was true? You could be relatively certain that the child's mother was actually the correct mother—if the record said so. But what about the father? Certainly you could never know that part with scientific exactitude. Therefore, why bother? Genealogy seemed to its detractors nothing more than an excuse for self-deception, wishful thinking, or self-aggrandizement. But now we have DNA testing! A father's link to the next generation can be proven scientifically.

Even with the immense resources the internet makes possible— and the many breakthroughs and leads it may generate—there comes a time when there are no new sites to find, no one with good information you haven't already talked to, and every new FamilyTreeMaker CD is just another dead end. You are in *terra incognita*, and that is when you are on your own and you have to start doing the original research yourself—traveling long days to distant courthouses and libraries, filling out National Archives forms and waiting for weeks for some tiny tidbit, making dopey phone calls to bewildered elderly cousins residing in nursing homes. And that is when you find out just how full of holes, lies, and not-so-inspired suppositions everything else you have found up until then may have been. It turns out there is an incredible lot of junk on the internet, too—and sometimes in people's recollections.

Nevertheless, in a few short years of working in the new world of information access and internet genealogy—plus taking my research to several remote courthouses in Virginia, to the LDS Library in Salt Lake City and the Daughters of the American Revolution Library in Washington, DC, to family reunions, to Jamestown, to Plymouth Rock, to the New York Public Library, to FamilyTreeDNA.com, to ancient houses and graveyards, including the site of the oldest brick house in America—I can now say with absolute surety: I know more than I ever thought I would know about my family and its history. In fact, I know more about my family than any member of my family has ever known before in the history of the world—and more than all but a handful of contemporaries have ever known about *any* family. I've located over 2000 direct ancestors and tens of thousands of others, and I know their names and, for some, I know about their lives.

This book is a family saga, and the saga of many, many families. It is not just about finding one's great grandmother. It's also about finding *her* great grandmother, and hers, and hers, and hers—back into time farther than you could have imagined—and grandfathers and great great great grandfathers too—with a degree of accuracy never before achieved. The acquisition and salvage of these lost generations is now attainable.

My parents near the time of their elopement in 1938

2.

A Magical Relationship

Sometimes the barest genealogical details seem to suggest a story. I started to appreciate that when I first came across my relation to the Bulkeley family in sixteenth-century England.

Frances Bulkeley, born in 1568, had died in 1610 at age 42, and her sister Sarah Bulkeley, born in 1580, had died a year later at age 31. Yet both had lived long enough, according to the record, to bear children who outlived them, who carried on and bore children of their own. I immediately started to wonder what might have caused these sisters to die so young; perhaps they had died in childbirth or from the plague. I imagined that Sarah, the younger sister, who was my father's ancestor, must have been devastated when Frances died and probably had no inkling that she would be dead herself within a year.

I imagined the sisters as very close—I imagined that Frances, who was twelve years older than Sarah, had been like a mother to her; and I imagined Sarah grieving for her, in particular, for that reason, grieving more than the others and grieving for a longer time.

I felt lucky to have scraped by myself, because if Sarah had not married Mr. Oliver St. John in 1597 and given birth to a son in London in 1604, I would not be here today to tell about it. I felt astonished to realize that I had had ancestors who were contemporaries of Shakespeare. But, of course, everyone who is alive today had ancestors who were contemporaries of Shakespeare. Of course they did.

The day I discovered the Bulkeley sisters was a red letter day at the LDS site. The line I was following went all the way back to 1300 with incredibly detailed documentation. The Bulkeley sisters were descendants of William De Bulkeley, born after 1300, and Maude Davenport, daughter of Sir John Davenport and Margery Brereton. Sir John Davenport and Lady Margery sounded like the kind of people I wouldn't mind claiming as members of my family, even if they did live seven hundred years ago.

In 1938, my father, a direct descendant of Sir John Davenport and, later, of Sarah Bulkeley, turned down a humped back country road near Bloomville, Ohio. He was a lonely, divorced 30-year-old vacuum cleaner salesman from the Ohio River town of Portsmouth, a branch manager with a new car and a rakish reddish mustache. He turned in the driveway at my grandmother's farm and knocked on the door. While he was attempting to sell my grandmother an Airway vacuum cleaner, he noticed my mother's picture in a gilt frame on top of the piano and he said, without hesitation, that she was the most beautiful woman he had ever seen.

My grandmother informed him that the woman was not a woman at all but only her eldest daughter Beulah, who was not yet twenty years old. My father replied that her daughter had the loveliest eyes he had ever seen on a human face, including any movie star she would care to name. She might not realize it yet, he said, but her daughter was indeed a woman. Half an hour later, my grandmother bought the vacuum cleaner.

My father was an affable, persuasive man who was not above flattery, but he seldom lied about his true feelings. A few weeks later he stopped by unexpectedly at the Zutavern farm—to see how the vacuum cleaner was performing, he said. My 19-year-old mother, who had returned from college in the meantime, was on the phone when he walked into the room, accepting a blind date. After she hung up, he said spontaneously: "It's really too bad you accepted that date because I was going to ask you out myself."

"Oh, that's all right," she said. "I can break it." There was a kind of instant recognition between them that the attraction they felt for each other was serious.

After they had been out a few times, my father tried to coax my mother to return with him to his hotel room. But she wouldn't go. My father said it was very discouraging to him that she didn't trust him. My mother said: "Oh, I trust you, Jim, but my mother always told me that I should never do anything that might have the appearance of evil." (I never heard her say anything even faintly like this again.) Two weeks later, they eloped!

My parents were deeply, romantically, in love their whole lives together; and they stayed in love for the better part of four decades—until my father died—and, of course she never stopped loving him after he was gone. They held hands in public like teenagers, even in their sixties.

Now here comes the scary part of the story. One day while I was working on my mother's Spalding line, I found that Benjamin Spalding, her gggggg grandfather had married a woman named Olive Farwell, born in 1647 in Concord, Massachusetts. Olive's father was Henry Farwell, an Englishman, and her mother was named Olive Welby, born in 1604 in England. Olive Welby was the daughter of Richard Welby and Frances Bulkeley.

When I hit upon the name Frances Bulkeley, it didn't register at first. I had been plowing through hundreds of names, and I remembered that I had seen the name Bulkeley, a possible precursor of "Buckley," before. But it had been a while since I had been working on my father's line, and I was not sure where I had seen it.

The truth came to me in the middle of the night, and I got out of bed to compare the genealogical lines on my various printouts. The connection caused the hair to stand up on my arms and on the back of my neck as if a chilly wind had blown in through an open window. My father was a direct descendant of Sarah Bulkeley, who died in 1611. My mother was a direct descendant of her sister Frances Bulkeley, who died in 1610, and who, I imagined, had been so deeply mourned by her younger sister Sarah.

In other words, roughly 400 years earlier, two daughters of Rev. Edward Bulkeley and Olive Irby, Frances (1568-1610) and Sarah (1580-1611), married, gave birth, and died in England.

Their respective descendants were born, grew up, moved from place to place, married into several different families, had children, and died. Roughly 375 years after their births, my father (Sarah's gggggggggg grandson) married my mother (Frances' gggggggggg granddaughter). Need I add that, during their lifetimes, my parents had absolutely no idea about this connection, though, had they known, I think it would have delighted them.

If it is true that—in some respects—we are born to fulfill the unrealized dreams of our ancestors, then was there something of Sarah's longing to be reunited with her departed sister Frances in my father's love of my mother? and something of Frances' almost maternal love for Sarah in her love for him? Who can say?

Rev. Edward Bulkeley (1540-1619/20) + Olive Irby (1547-1613/14)

/ \

Frances Bulkeley + Richard Welby	Sarah Bulkeley + Oliver St. John
Olive Welby + Henry Farwell	Matthias St. John + Sarah Mary
Olive Farwell + Benjamin Spalding	Mercy St. John + Ephraim Lockwood
dward Spalding + Mercy Mary Adams	Daniel Lockwood + Sarah Benedict
Thomas Spalding + Abigail Brown	Rebecca Lockwood + Nathan Barnum
William Spalding + Mary Dunham	Nathan Barnum + Lois Wheeler
Thomas Spalding + Elizabeth Ayres	Relief Barnum + John Clark
Samuel Spalding + Mary Ann Trail	Barnum Clark + Lucy Whipple
Alveda Spalding + Paul Zutavern	Benjamin Clark + Marietta Broadhurst
Rolla Zutavern + Harriet Kagy	Alice Whipple Clark + John Lawhorn
	Sarah Lawhorn + Judge Bellamy

\ /

Beulah Zutavern + Orin Bellamy

|

Joe David Bellamy

My maternal grandfather Rolla Harrison Zutavern
and my grandmother Harriet Kagy

3.

THE MISSING

In 1938, after their elopement, my parents returned to Bloomville for a few days—to make up with her parents—then they left for Cincinnati, where my father lived in those days. For my grandmother, it was too quick. My father had met and married my mother all within a few weeks' time. There was no wedding—no wedding that Gram was a part of, at any rate—and then Beulah was simply absent from her life.

After my parents had been gone for a few weeks, my grandmother started to worry about my mother, her eldest daughter. Coincidentally, my grandmother read an article about White Slavery in *Reader's Digest,* and too many of the details seemed identical to just the way Beulah had met Jim and then suddenly left them. *She was only nineteen years old! Except for a few months at college, she had never been out of Bloomville! She was so trusting and innocent!* She was just exactly the kind of person who would be taken advantage of, just exactly the kind of person described in the article.

Just as in the article, Beulah had gone off and married this complete stranger, an older man who was a little bit slick, and they hadn't had a proper wedding at all. How did she even know they were married? Maybe they weren't! Then he had quickly taken her away to Cincinnati, or God knows where? Maybe she wasn't even in Cincinnati! Jim and Beulah didn't have their phone installed yet, and that was suspicious in itself. She had written to the address Beulah had given her and had not received a reply in over a week. It wasn't like Beulah to wait so long to write. Maybe Jim Bellamy had sold her into White Slavery and she was already in Istanbul or some god awful place half way around the world and unable to communicate! If Beulah had been sold down the river, wouldn't she want her mother to come looking for her?

Rolla said she was just being ridiculous, just getting herself upset for no good reason. Everything was just as it appeared. They had fallen in love. Jim was a perfectly good, honest, hard-working man who just happened to live in Cincinnati. She would be getting a letter soon, he was sure of it. Oddly, their opinions of my father had both changed. Before the wedding, Rolla had been the suspicious one, and Gram had liked him. But when the newlyweds returned to Bloomville after their elopement, Rolla had welcomed them (in July) with an exclamation of, "Merry Christmas!" He was grateful they had tied the knot!

Then he had gotten to know Jim quite a bit better, and he found that my father was a man's man. They had hit it off. But my father had not hit it off with Gram. Gram had wanted a tradi-tional wedding for her first daughter, an occasion that she would forever be deprived of now, and she resented it. She had been taken in by him once, when she bought the god-damned vacuum cleaner, but she was not going to be taken in again! Every time she swept the floor, she thought of him and it made her mad. She never should have let him in the door!

The more my grandmother dwelled on the White Slavery problem and reread the article and the longer she waited for the letter to arrive and it didn't, the more her imagination went wild. Beulah could be suffering now! They could be torturing her and doing unspeakable things to her, and here they were sitting around like dodos and not doing anything about it! They had already waited too long. It might be too late already. Rolla would have to drive down to Cincinnati and find out if everything was okay! That was the only way to be sure. He would have to leave this afternoon and drive straight through and find out if Beulah was still there and how Jim was treating her. And if he wasn't treating her well, Dad should bring her home immediately! And if she had been sold into White Slavery, Jim Bellamy should be arrested and thrown into jail, and they would have to do everything in their power to find her and bring her back.

Rolla didn't want to go. It was a six-hour drive in those days, and he had pressing matters to attend to on the farm and at the bank. But he had been married to Harriet Kagy long enough to know that the only way he was going to have any peace was to do exactly what she wanted him to—except he was damned if he was going to leave that afternoon. It was already five o'clock. Tomorrow morning would have to be good enough. He would get up first thing tomorrow morning and drive to Cincinnati, if she wanted him to, and pay a visit to the love birds. He wouldn't mind doing that, in any case.

"Tomorrow morning might be too late!" my grandmother insisted.

"It takes half a day to drive down there," Rolla said. "If I leave right now, I won't get there until after dark! They'll be in bed, for Christ's sake!"

"Well, you shouldn't be driving after dark. It's too dangerous."

"Then I'd better leave tomorrow morning."

"Oh, I'm so worried about her I don't know what to do!"

"I'll drive down there tomorrow morning, and we'll settle it. We'll find out how she is, and everything will be all right."

"All right. If you can't leave now, then tomorrow morning *early.*"

"I'll leave before sun-up. Will that suit you?"

"I guess it will have to, but I doubt if I'll get a wink of sleep tonight—just worrying about it."

Rolla gave her a hug and rubbed her back and said, "What's for dinner?"

First thing after breakfast the next morning, Rolla climbed into his 1937 maroon Chevrolet and started on the long road from Bloomville to Cincinnati, watching the sun come up over his left shoulder. Two days later he was back. (He hadn't called because there were very few public phones in those days, and, of course, cell phones had not yet been invented.)

"Where's Beulah?" were the first words out of my grandmother's mouth, as soon as he got out of the car.

"Why, she's in Cincinnati with her husband, just as I said she was," Rolla said. "They live in a nice little bungalow on a nice little street, and they're getting their telephone installed later this week. Things like that take a little longer in the big city."

"And she's all right?" Gram seemed almost disappointed.

"She's happier than I've ever seen her."

"Oh, Dad."

"It's true."

"She's not pregnant, is she?"

"She's not now, but she will be."

"How do you know?"

"Just a hunch."

He was right about that, of course. But he did not live long enough to see me. Rolla died of a massive heart attack a few months before I was born, three years later. I was born in December of that year, the day after my mother's birthday, so I was almost a birthday present. But I entered a world where my grandfather had recently died and my father was about to go to war. I was born the same month that the Japanese bombed Pearl Harbor.

When I was small I knew I had one father, one mother, one grandfather and one grandmother, so I thought that's the way it was for everyone. It made some goofy sense really. The grandfather was on my father's side, and the grandmother was on my mother's side, and no one informed me at that early stage that, actually, my father had a mother—*had* to have—and my mother, of course, had to have a father. The mystery of my missing grandparents assumed a somewhat larger place in my imagination than it might have because even after I found out about them, found out they existed, no one showed me any photographs of them. There *weren't* many photographs of them, and the photographs there were were not very satisfactory, were not the sort of photographs that would suggest character and personality. Both had died young, in their fifties; and both had been very important to their families.

I have seen the photographs now, and dug up some lost ones on my own, and I have quizzed every living person who ever knew them about my missing grandparents. But I miss not having known them. I know now I'll never be able to replace not having known them, no matter what I do.

I could tell by the respectful way my father always talked about Rolla Zutavern that he thought my grandfather was quite a man, and I'm grateful for that—because my father was a good judge of people.

This is what I know about my grandfather, Rolla Harrison Zutavern:

"Rolla H. Zutavern, 52, prominent Bloom township farmer, died in the Christian-Holmes hospital in Cincinnati at eight o'clock Friday morning [1941]. His death was caused by cardiac hypertrophy. He had been seriously ill since last November and had been confined in the Cincinnati hospital for the last five weeks. Every method known to science was used in trying to combat his illness, but although he was given every care, his life could not be saved.

"Mr. Zutavern was born on December 10, 1888, to Paul and Alveda Spalding Zutavern in the Zutavern homestead in Bloom township where he lived at the time of his death. Following his education in Bloom township public schools, he took up special work at Ohio Northern University. Upon completion of this and a further agricultural course at Ohio State University, he joined his father in operating the farm at home.

"On October 22, 1915, he was united in marriage to Miss Harriet A. Kagy and to this union were born three daughters: Mrs. Beulah Bellamy of Cincinnati, and Dorothy and Margaret at home, who are left to mourn together with his wife. He is also survived by a brother, Harry of Tiffin, who is the only remaining member of his immediate family.

"Keen, alert, and forward-looking in managing his farm operations, he was a leader in the community in which he lived. Seeing the benefit of more cooperation among farm neighbors, he was one of the pioneers in organizing the Farm Bureau, and he further served the community as township trustee and bank director. He was one of the directors of the Bloomville Exchange State Bank at the time of his death. He will long be remembered as an industrious, honest, stalwart and dependable friend and neighbor.

"Funeral services were held in the family residence Monday afternoon."

He was born, lived, and had his funeral in the same house! It was the house where my grandmother lived, the house where I visited her on the farm. In the middle of the front walk, my grandfather had embedded an Indian arrowhead made of chiseled pink rock he had found while plowing. As a boy, I used to sit on the end of that sidewalk and run my fingers over the arrowhead and wish that I could find another arrowhead on the farm the way he had that was half as beautiful. I associated my grandfather with that artifact and with the mysterious power to embed stone into concrete so that it would stay that way forever.

What my mother said about his death was that he knew he had heart trouble, but he insisted on sawing a log in the wood house; and it was while he was sawing the log that he suffered the heart attack that eventually killed him. He rolled his own cigarettes and smoked too many of them at a time when no one knew of the connection between smoking and heart disease.

The expression on his face in all the pictures I have of him is pleasant but unsmiling. He was not a man who mugged for the camera. He is dignified and calm but his eyes are intense. His jawline and his forehead are shaped like mine, and the pictures of Rolla as a young man could almost be me. Though he was a farmer by occupation, he is well-dressed for all the pictures I have of him. In them, he always wears a white shirt and a tie and a fine-looking coat, and he seems comfortable in that attire. He looks more like the bank director he was than the farmer he also was.

I have a difficult time imagining how he and my grandmother related to one another because he is so obviously a strong, dominant personality, yet I never met anyone who dominated my grandmother. I think he did. I asked my cousin Margie (Gram's niece) about this and she said, "Well, he was a German, you know!" which I thought was comical, coming from a ninety-four-year-old who is every bit as much a German as he was. Rolla's paternal grandfather was born in 1809 in Eppingen, Baden, Germany, though the Zutaverns, like so many of my other maternal ancestors, were from Switzerland, just as cousin Margie's mother's ancestors were. Rolla's mother's family, the Spaldings, on the other hand, were nothing but English all the way back to the beginning of time.

Rolla's great grandfather, Conrad Zutavern, and his wife Anna Maria Schwemle sailed down the Rhine River, crossed the Atlantic, and landed in Baltimore, Maryland, in 1817. The Zutaverns were Lutherans, but with surnames like Kessler, Zimmerman, Rieger, Alberts, and Roth farther back in the gene pool, it's a lucky thing they got out of Germany in the nineteenth century, or Hitler's henchmen might have come looking for them in the twentieth.

It is not known why they left, but Europe suffered from severe crop failures in 1816-17 that led to wider immigration for a few years afterwards. These Zutaverns started for Ohio by wagon. For a month the family halted at Pittsburgh. Anna Maria and the children stayed there while Conrad proceeded on foot to Ohio and purchased their land on Sugar Run in Tuscarawas County. Then he returned to Pittsburgh and collected his family. They broke ground at Sugar Run and lived there and farmed the rest of their lives. Today their graves may be seen in the Zutavern Church Cemetery, Lawrence Twp., Tuscarawas Co. (south of Canton), Ohio.

Conrad and Anna Maria's son Jacob Henry Zutavern, who was eight years old when he came to this country, married Margaret

Geiger, from another Eppingen family, and moved to Bloomville, Ohio, in Seneca County and pioneered a farm there. They had eleven children, three sons and eight daughters. They are both buried in the Reformed Church Cemetery, on the west side of Rt. 19 at the north edge of Bloomville. So when their son Paul married the girl next door, Alveda Spalding, daughter of Samuel Dunham Spalding and Mary Ann Trail, the two family's farms were eventually joined into one. No one remembered, of course, but Sam Spalding's English ancestors had been in the New World since 1619 at Jamestown.

I am quite certain that neither Rolla nor Harriet knew it, but, in fact, their distant ancestors must have known one another—in Germany. The Zutavern family lived in the villages of Richen and Eppingen before Conrad Zutavern, the immigrant, sailed down the Rhine River with his wife Anna Marie and children, crossed the Atlantic, and landed in Baltimore in 1817. I have records for the Zutaverns and the families they married into in the same area of Germany from which they departed going back to the 1600s.

The village of Gemmingen, where the Gemmingen family origi-nated, and the Dammhof at Adelshofen, where my grandmother's ancestor Ludwig Welck von Gemmingen was born in 1729, are roughly five kilometers from Richen, where the Zutaverns lived. The road from Gemmingen to Adelshofen passes through Richen, and Eppingen is also a neighboring village. Though some of Rolla's ancestors were prominent lawyers, judges, and mayors, mostly they had been farmers. Still, the von Gemmingens probably knew of them. On the other hand, it would have been inconceivable for the Zutaverns not to have known of the von Gemmingens, who were members of the aristocracy.

In other words, if their ancestors had never left Germany, it would not have been all that surprising if Rolla and Harriet had met and married there (if class distinctions had not prevented it). Possibly it would have been more likely for a Zutavern to have married the daughter of the von Gemmingen's dairy master than to have married into the noble family itself. That Rolla (a Zutavern) and Harriet (a von Gemmingen) did, in fact, marry half a world away without knowing of this ancient connection, is all the more remarkable.

Paul Zutavern and Alveda Spalding, Rolla's parents, my great grandparents

4.

THE SPALDINGS AND THE ADAMS CONNECTION

I was lucky to have inherited a tree of Spaldings directly from *A Genealogical History of Edward Spalding of Virginia and Massachusetts and His Descendants* by Charles Warren Spalding, 1897, that was passed down to me from my grandmother. The brown leather cover was still in good shape, though the binding was loose and many of the pages were falling out or crumbling. It had belonged to the grandfather I never met, Rolla Zutavern, whose mother was a Spalding—Alveda Spalding. I had Alveda's line all the way back to her 5th great grandfather, my 8th, the immigrant Edward Spalding, who arrived at Jamestown in 1619 with Sir George Yardley's group, according to the book. I checked that line against all the sources I could find, including the Mormons, and found that it was still sound.

It was in the year 1607 that the first English emigrants to successfully form a permanent colony in the New World landed in Virginia. For twelve years after its settlement it languished under the government of Sir Thomas Smith, Treasurer of the Virginia Company in England. According to Charles Warren Spalding, "The Colony was ruled during that period by laws written in blood; and its history shows how the narrow selfishness of despotic power could counteract the best efforts of benevolence. The colonists suffered an extremity of distress too horrible to be described." Recently, the author David A. Price proved less squeamish than Charles Spalding and described this period quite brilliantly in his riveting book *Love and Hate in Jamestown*.

Of the thousands of emigrants who had been sent to Virginia at great cost, not one in twenty remained alive in April, 1619, when Sir George Yardley arrived. He brought certain commissions and instructions from the company, for the "better establishing of a commonwealth heere"; and the prosperity of Virginia began from this time, when it received, as a commonwealth, the freedom to make laws for itself. The first meeting of the new government was held July 30, 1619—more than a year before the *Mayflower*, with the Pilgrims, left the harbor of Southhampton.

However, on March 22, 1622, at mid-day, Indians fell upon the English population in Virginia. "Children and women, as well as men, the missionary, the benefactor—all were slain with every aggravation of cruelty. In one hour, 347 persons were massacred. However, the night before the massacre, the plan had been revealed to an Englishman by a converted Indian who wished to rescue him." Thus, Jamestown and the nearest settlements had made some hurried preparations against the attack. "The savages, as timid as they were ferocious, fled at the appearance of wakeful resistance; and the larger part of the colony was saved," according to Charles Warren Spalding.

After the massacre, it was ordered that a census be taken of the living and dead in Virginia. The names of Edward Spalding and his family are recorded, together with the names of all persons then living in the colony. But sickness prevailed among the dispirited survivors, as well as continuing fear of the Indians. Some returned to the mother country. The number of inhabitants had exceeded 4000. A year after the massacre there remained less than one-half of that number.

By what means Edward Spalding and his family reached Massachusetts Bay—whether they took passage on a trading vessel, or went on a ship returning to England—is not positively known. It is possible that the family lived for a number of years in Bermuda (then called the Somers Islands). Nor do we know precisely when they arrived in the Massachusetts Bay Colony, but the first permanent settlement of Braintree, Massachusetts, can be traced to 1634. "Previous to this time, those who came were adventurers," according to Charles Warren Spalding, "who had neither sympathy nor interest with the civil or ecclesiastical ideas of the permanent settlers of the Massachusetts Colony." It is probable that Edward and his family arrived about this time, or very soon afterwards.

Records show that it was in Braintree, Massachusetts, that his first wife Margaret and his daughter Grace died, and where one of his children, Benjamin, my ancestor, was born. Edward Spalding was made a Freeman May 30, 1640, from which fact we know that he was a member of the established church of the colony, as no person could be made a Freeman, or be entitled to any share in the government, or be capable of being chosen a magistrate, or even of serving on a jury, who was not a member of one of the churches established in the colony.

The next mentions of Edward Spalding in the public records of the time have to do with the acquisition of land in the creation of various towns: the first, in 1645, the successful petition (along with twenty other Freemen) for 10,000 acres; the next, in 1653, for an area of about six miles square in connection with the founding and settlement of Chelmsford, Massachusetts, where in 1654 he was chosen one of seven Selectmen, to "officiate in ordering the Public Affairs of the Place by the Consent of the Major Part of the Town."

At the time, Chelmsford did not extend to the Merrimack River, but May 3, 1656, on petition of the inhabitants, the northeast boundary was extended to the river. Among the signers of the petition was Edward Spalding. In this enlargement was some of the best land in the town, and a portion of some 214 acres was fenced in 1669 and called the "New Field." The names of the proprietors are given, and among them are Edward Spalding, Sr., Edward Spalding, Jr., and John Spalding.

Edward Spalding was also elected Selectman in 1656, 1660, and 1661. In 1663, he was "the Surveyor of the Highways," and, later, "Surveyor for the Newfield."

The attention of the first settlers was early given to the culture of apple trees, and special mention is made of the orchard of Edward Spalding in 1664. Edward, Sr., died February 26, 1670.

Having established original documentation for the life of the progenitor Edward Spalding, one of the few colonists to have been a member of both the Jamestown Colony and the Massachusetts Bay Colony, I went to work trying to expand the female lines attached to the Spaldings. I prefer female lines, actually, because they are the keys to unlocking the mysteries of many new families.

The surname of Edward's wife Rachel is not known, so I couldn't start with that one. But his son Benjamin married Olive Farwell. Benjamin's son Edward married Mercy Mary Adams. Edward's son Thomas married Abigail Brown, and four generations later my great grandmother, Alveda Spalding, was born. It was Alveda Spalding who broke the untrammeled line of English blood and in the hothouse atmosphere of Bloomville, Ohio, in 1882, married a German! Alveda's Spaldings came from the village of Spalding in Lincolnshire, which was founded in 732 AD!

Paul Zutavern made a related decision when he married Alveda. His Zutavern and allied lines were nothing but Swiss-Germans all the way back to at least 1389 when the first Taverna appeared in Davos, Switzerland. But in the blooming aura of Bloomville in 1882 he forgot 500 years of history and tradition and married the English! By all accounts, Paul and Alveda were very happily married, I might add—in spite of their defiance of ethnic taboos—or maybe such differences were completely irrelevant.

Not mentioned at all in the Spalding genealogy was the fact that my mother's 5th great grandmother in the Spalding line, Mercy Mary Adams, was a direct descendant of Henry Adams and Edith Squire of Braintree, great grandparents of both John Adams, our second president, and Samuel Adams, Governor of Massachusetts and one of our most important revolutionaries. Coincidentally, one of my father's 7th great aunts was Abigail Baxter, daughter of Gregory Baxter and Margaret Paddy, who were also the great grandparents of John and Samuel Adams. To put it another way, of the eight great grandparents of John and Samuel Adams, I am a direct descendant of four of them, two on each side. This was a little hard to believe at first because I can hardly think of anyone I would rather be related to, and how often does one usually get one's choice of relatives? Not often. This Adams tree also includes, of course, our 6th president John Quincy Adams; the eminent diplomat and historian Charles Francis Adams, President of the Massachusetts Historical Society; and the great Henry Adams of *The Education of Henry Adams* and the nine-volume *History of the United States of America During the Administrations of Thomas Jefferson and James Madison*, which Gary Wills has recently described as "the nonfiction prose masterpiece of nineteenth century America."

An interesting genealogical fact about these Adamses is that they are *not* the descendants of the ancient baronial family of Ap Adam of Beverstone and Tildenham, Gloucester, England, as had originally been supposed when President John Adams went searching for his ancestors. Each subsequent Adams generation tried to locate the key to their ancestry in England—without success. Perhaps the thread had been lost because the earliest Adams generations in Massachusetts were so caught up in the stern struggle for survival in such a wild, uncivilized location.

It was not until 1925 that it was finally proven beyond doubt that Henry Adams of Braintree was the son of John Adams of Barton St. David, Somersetshire. "Barton" is a name for a certain kind of farm, and the evidence is that this family had been in Barton St. David for at least four generations for well over a century, and probably much longer, before Henry Adams immigrated to Massachusetts in 1638. They were essentially farmers, just sturdy yeomen, which J. Gardner Bartlett describes as, "derived most largely from the ancient pre-Norman stock of England whose blood was mainly of so-called Anglo-Saxon origin mingled with smaller strains of Danish and Briton ancestry." Incidentally, this was true of about ninety percent of the colonial emigrants from Old England to New England.

Henry's wife was Edith Squire, the daughter of Henry Squire, the granddaughter of Rev. William Squire, who was Rector of Charlton Mackrell as early as 1545. During the reign of Bloody

Mary (1553–1558) a list was made of all the married clergy in England, and they were ordered to divorce their wives in order to conform to the Roman Catholic law regarding clerical celibacy! At the annual ecclesiastical visitation of Charlton Mackrell in 1554, the church wardens presented that "William Squyer was marryed and doth minister ageyne, not separated."

It is not exactly clear what further nonsense Rev. Squire had to endure until Bloody Mary was deposed, but whatever it was, it did not persuade him to leave his wife. Since his son Henry, Edith's father, was not born until about 1563, we are very happy the Rev. Squire defied Queen Mary's edict—not only because if he had not, we would not be here, but also, if Henry Squire had not been born and Edith Squire therefore had not been born and had not married Henry Adams, and the two of them had not emigrated to Braintree, Massachusetts, in 1638 and become the great grandparents of John and Samuel Adams, there might never have been a United States of America! Seldom has a humble man's defiance of a queen had more lasting and momentous consequences.

Consider this: When the British army marched to Lexington and Concord to arrest Samuel Adams (my mother's relative) on that fateful day in April, 1775, six members of the Bacon family (my father's relatives) from the nearby area joined the Minutemen at the North Bridge and along the road to defend him. The North Bridge itself was adjacent to a corn field owned by my relative David Brown. My cousin, Capt. Phineas Cooke, led a company of Minutemen "which did good service in the battles of Lexington and Concord, and for their brave conduct received the thanks of General Warren." If you read the sermons of Rev. William Emerson, who was minister at the Congregational Church in Concord and whose ancestor Rev. Peter Bulkeley (my parents' common relative through the Bulkeleys) had founded Concord a century and a half earlier, you will know why some of those men were there that day at the North Bridge—because Rev. Emerson was preaching Revolution from the pulpit!

1. Henry Adams (1582/83–1646) + Edith Squire (1587–1672/73)
2. Thomas Adams (1612–1688) + Mary Blackmore (1612–1693/94)
3. Pelatiah Adams (1646/47–1725) + Ruth Parker (1655–1719)
4. Mercy Mary Adams (1676–1754) + Edward Spalding (1672–1740)
5. Thomas Spalding (1719–) + Abigail Brown (1717–)
6. William Spalding (1754–1829) + Mary Dunham (1759–1836)
7. Thomas Spalding (1783–1850) + Elizabeth Ayers (1789–1852)
8. Samuel-Dunham Spalding (1814–1881) + Mary-Ann Traill (1823–1864)
9. Alveda Spalding (1864–1932) + Paul Washington Zutavern (1859–1929)
10. Rolla Harrison Zutavern (1888–1941) + Harriet Alvaretta Kagy (1892–1981)
11. Beulah Pearl Zutavern (1918–1998) + Orin Ross Bellamy (1908–1974)
12. Joe David Bellamy (1941–)

❧ ❧

1. Henry Adams (1582/83–1646) + Edith Squire (1587–1672/73)
2. Joseph Adams (1625/26–1694) + Abigail Baxter (1634–1672)
3. Joseph Adams (1654–1737/38) + Hannah Bass (1662/63–1705)
4. John Adams (1690/91–1761) + Susannah Boylston (1698/99–1797)
5. John Adams (1735–1826)

❧ ❧

1. Henry Adams (1582/83–1646) + Edith Squire (1587–1672/73)
2. Joseph Adams (1625/26–1694) + Abigail Baxter (1634–1672)
3. John Adams (1661–1702) + Hannah Webb (1665–1694)
4. Samuel Adams (1689–1747/48) + Mary Fifield (1692–)
5. Samuel Adams (1722–1803)

1. Gregory Baxter (–1659) + Margaret Paddy (–1661)

2. John Baxter (1639–1719) + Hannah White (–1723/24)

3. Samuel Baxter (1666–1744) + Mary Beale (1668–1744)

4. Thomas Baxter (1701/02–) + Deliverance Marshall (1703–)

5. Ruth Baxter + John Clark (1725–)

6. John Clark (1753–) + Relief Barnum (1753–1837)

7. Barnum Clark (1774–1837) + Lucy Whipple (1777–1863)

8. Benjamin Whipple Clark (1812–1880) + Marietta Broadhurst (1820–1890)

9. Alice Whipple Clark (1846–1899) + John Brown Lawhorn (1803–1892)

10. Sarah Edith Lawhorn (1876–1934) + Townley Hannah Bellamy (1873–1959)

11. Orin Ross Bellamy (1908–1974) + Beulah Pearl Zutavern (1918–1998)

12. Joe David Bellamy (1941–)

1. Gregory Baxter (–1659) + Margaret Paddy (–1661)

2. Abigail Baxter (1634–1672) + Joseph Adams (1625/26–1694)

3. John Adams (1661–1702) + Hannah Webb (1665–1694)

4. Samuel Adams (1689–1747/48) + Mary Fifield (1692–)

5. Samuel Adams (1722–1803)

❧ ❧

1. Gregory Baxter (–1659) + Margaret Paddy (–1661)

2. Abigail Baxter (1634–1672) + Joseph Adams (1625/26–1694)

3. Joseph Adams (1654–1737/38) + Hannah Bass (1662/63–1705)

4. John Adams (1690/91–1761) + Susannah Boylston (1698/99–1797)

5. John Adams (1735–1826)

EDWARD I.

King Edward the First

5.

The American Society of the Descendants of Ancient Peasants and Oppressed Minorities

Frances and Sarah Bulkeley were among my 9th and 10th great grandmothers, and yet Frances was *but one* of the 2048 great grandparents I had in the 9th generation, and Sarah was *but one* of the 4096 great grandparents I had in the 10th generation. (This is not even counting all the great grandparents in the generations between the 9th and 10th and the present.) Most of the others from the 9th and 10th I know nothing about and will never know anything about—because their histories are forever lost. If records about them were ever kept—of their births, deaths, or offspring—they are now gone. But, of course, for a certain branch of humanity at that age of the world—the *majority*—there were no records ever kept. They were illiterate, and they were surrounded by illiteracy. They did not worry about such things. They simply worried about survival, and it was a full-time occupation. According to Alex Shoumatoff, "Of all the people ever alive, between eighty-five and ninety-two percent lived, died, and slipped into oblivion without even leaving their names. The loss of their identities, like the extinction of a species, is irreparable."

There are no societies made up of the Descendants of Medieval and Renaissance Peasants because, even if someone wanted to create such a group, no one would have any proof to substantiate membership, though it is a fair guess that every one of us would qualify—if the facts could be known. We are all stuck with finding only those ancestors who were a little more "civilized" than the rest. We all had some of those too. But just in case this should lead us to a certain puffery, to believing that we spring from only the cream of society, from kings and lords and ladies, from princes who ruled wisely and knights who slew other knights for good reason, it is important to remember the majority who lived at the bottom of the social scale, who may have been more virtuous, in some cases, all things considered, than the "upper" classes, but who shall forever remain anonymous.

Like most Americans, just about all of my ancestors—except a few like Edward Plantagenet, the Bulkeley sisters, the von Gemmingens, Sir John Davenport, and a few other members of the ancient English aristocracy—were members of oppressed minorities. The early Bellamys and Lawhorns I unearthed on my father's side were white slaves in the tobacco fields of Virginia. The early Puritans and Pilgrims in my trees came to the New World because powerful elites in the Old World wanted to eradicate them. The early Swiss and German Mennonites on my mother's side were imprisoned, bludgeoned, and burned at the stake simply because they had a different view of religious worship and the determination to adhere to their beliefs in the face of whatever befell them. Their holocaust was terrible and long, though not as large in numbers as the Jewish holocaust that took place in the same vicinity a few centuries later.

The oppression that my ancestors suffered was longer ago than that of the oppressed minorities of the last two centuries, far enough in the past that much of it has been forgotten. But it existed—it was real. It is as much a part of my DNA as that of others whose ancestors have suffered similar fates.

So many of my ancestors were rebels or refugees, I can't help wondering if they were simply victims of circumstance, victims of their principles and stubbornness, or worse. Was there something about them—other than their unwillingness to yield—that caused others to want to drive them away? Were they too proud, too committed to the truth when they could have lied their way out of a problem, too irritable, too pugnacious? Was there something about them that caused others to spread unfounded, malicious rumors about them that poisoned their lives and forced them to move on?

I have very good evidence that I am a direct descendant of Edward the First of England, who died in 1307 A.D. In fact, I am a direct descendant on both sides. Edward (b.1239, reigned 1272-1307) is described by several sources as one of the most successful of the medieval monarchs. In *A Chronicle of the Kings of England*, Sir Richard Baker says of him: "He had in him the two wisdoms, not often found in any, single; both together, seldom or never: an ability of judgment in himself, and a readiness to hear the judgment of others." In his time, Edward acquired acres of valuable real estate for England and held onto it. He was described as "the best lance in all the world" by a contemporary at the time of his coronation at Westminster Abbey in 1274. He was a veteran of the Crusades by then, a hardened warrior, and a leader with energy and vision and with a formidable temper, it was said. But maybe this was just the spin from his PR Director. I suppose, if you had to be related to a king, he isn't a bad choice—he isn't the worst—though it does mean you probably had some cousins you might rather avoid talking about.

The genealogical evidence on Edward the First is based on investigations by some of the most eminent genealogists in the world, and it has been worked over, refined, and validated numerous times for centuries, with the experts trying to poke holes in each generation. So there is a fair chance that it may be true. I can look at the names in the actual line of descent in a wonderful book entitled *The Royal Descents of 500 Immigrants to the American Colonies or the United States Who Were Themselves Notable or Left Descendants Notable in American History* and try to imagine the lives of each member of my line back to Edward and try to feel gratitude that they lived and bred. Joan Plantagenet, for example, or Sir Piers Hildyard.

However, I am not alone. The highly regarded genealogist Gary Boyd Roberts, author of the aforementioned volume, estimates that over sixty percent of Americans of English descent are, in fact, related, to British royalty! Chances are high that if you are reading this book, you are related to British royalty too. My question is: Why would you want to be? Was there ever a more conceited, tyrannical group in human history? This is an identity problem that many Americans might have to deal with, once they learn more fully of their true ancestry.

The cause of this royal legacy, you see, is that Edward lived so long ago and that he had so many children, sixteen by his first wife Eleanor of Castille before her death in 1290, three more with his second wife Margaret, Princess of Norway, and who knows how many illegitimate children? His genealogy and that of his offspring has been carefully preserved, of course, and it has been growing exponentially all this time.

But what does it really mean to be a direct descendant of someone who lived in the thirteenth century? Edward the First, for example, was my ancestor Olive Welby's eleventh great grandfather, and she was my eighth great grandmother. So King Edward would be my twenty-first great grandfather. In other words, he was twenty-three generations ago. Twenty-three generations ago, just like everyone else, I had approximately 8-million, 388-thousand, 6-hundred-and-eight great grandparents in that generation alone, i.e, not even counting all the ancestors from the twenty-third generation on down. So even if Edward may have been the progenitor of more than two of the lines that produced me, which is quite probable, each line makes up a very small fraction of the inheritance I have now. Do I even have *any* of the one eight-millionth of my genes from my mother's side that Edward contributed? Are the early genes more powerful? Do they lay down a bed rock of genetic material that resists change? Who knows? My guess would be that Edward the First is all but obliterated from my DNA, and, if so, I really don't mind at all.

MOTHER'S LINE

1. Edward Plantagenet (1239–1307) + Eleanor of Castile (1240/41–1290)

2. Joan Plantagenet (1272–1307) + Gilbert de Clare (1243–1295)

3. Margaret de Clare (1292–1342) + Piers de Gaveston (–1312)

4. Amy de Gaveston + John de Driby

5. Alice de Driby + Sir Anketil Malory

6. Sir William Malory (1375–1445)

7. Margaret Malory (1387–1437/38) + Robert Corbet (1383–1440)

8. Mary Corbet (1418–) + Robert Charlton (1430–1471)

9. Richard Charlton (1450–1522) + Anne Mainwaring (1452–)

10. Anne Charlton (1482–1560) + Randall Grosvenor (1480–1559)

11. Elizabeth Grosvenor (1515–1591) + Thomas Bulkeley (1515–1591)

12. Edward Bulkeley (1540–1619/20) + Olive Irby (1547–1613/14)

13. Frances Bulkeley (1567/68–1610) + Richard Welby (1563/64–)

14. Olive Welby (1604–1691/92) + Henry Farwell (1601–1670)

15. Olive Farwell (1647–) + Benjamin Spalding (1643–1708)

16. Edward Spalding (1672–1740) + Mercy Mary Adams (1676–1754)

17. Thomas Spalding (1719–) + Abigail Brown (1717–)

18. William Spalding (1754–1829) + Mary Dunham (1759–1836)

19. Thomas Spalding (1783–1850) + Elizabeth Ayers (1789–1852)

20. Samuel-Dunham Spalding (1814–1881) + Mary-Ann Traill (1823–1864)

21. Alveda Spalding (1864–1932) + Paul Washington Zutavern (1859–1929)

22. Rolla Harrison Zutavern (1888–1941) + Harriet Alvaretta Kagy (1892–1981)

23. Beulah Pearl Zutavern (1918–1998) + Orin Ross Bellamy (1908–1974)

24. Joe David Bellamy (1941–)

FATHER'S LINE

1. Edward Plantagenet (1239–1307) + Eleanor of Castile (1240/41–1290)
2. Edward Plantagenet (1284–1327) + Isabella of France
3. Edward Plantagenet (1327–1377) + Philippa of Hainault (1311–1369)
4. Lionel Plantagenet (1338–1368) + Elizabeth de Burgh (1332–1363)
5. Philippa Plantagenet (1355–aft 1378) + Edmund Mortimer (1352–1381)
6. Elizabeth Mortimer (1371–1417) + Sir Henry Percy (1364–1403)
7. Elizabeth Percy (–1437) + John Clifford (–1421/22)
8. Mary Clifford + Sir Philip Wentworth (–1464)
9. Elizabeth Wentworth + Sir Martin de la See
10. Joan de la See + Sir Piers Hildyard
11. Isabel Hildyard + Ralph Legard
12. Joan Legard (1530–) +Richard Skepper (1500–1556)
13. Edward Skipper (1552–1629) + Mary Robinson (1575/76–1630)
14. William Skepper (1597–1640) + Sarah Fisher (1617–)
15. Sarah Skipper (1640–1710) + Walter Fairfield (1631–1723)
16. William Fairfield (1662–1742) + Esther Batcheler
17. Mary Fairfield + John Whipple (1690–)
18. Joseph Whipple (1711–1771) + Mary Whipple (1716/17–1807)
19. Samuel Whipple (1749–1782) + Lucy Brown (1747–1814)
20. Lucy Whipple (1777–1863) + Barnum Clark (1774–1837)
21. Benjamin Whipple Clark (1812–1880) + Marietta Broadhurst (1820–1890)
22. Alice Whipple Clark (1846–1899) + John Brown Lawhorn (1803–1892)
23. Sarah Edith Lawhorn (1876–1934) + Townley Hannah Bellamy (1873–1959)
24. Orin Ross Bellamy (1908–1974) + Beulah Pearl Zutavern (1918–1998)
25. Joe David Bellamy (1941–)

Robert Spencer of Althorp

6.

Princess Di Stole My Pedigree!

One of the families I am related to—through the Bulkeleys—is the ancient Despencer family of Gloucestershire. Although they are now extinct, that is, there are no survivors from the ancient family of that name *who still bear the name*, some of us still do carry around some of the genes of the Despencers because their inheritance was preserved through female lines. I had no idea of the significance of this fact until I learned in John Pearson's *Blood Royal* the history of Princess Di's family, the Spencers.

During the period in the early seventeenth century when James I was on the throne, Princess Di's ancestor, Robert Spencer, was a prosperous sheep farmer. King James' attitude toward *honors* during his regime was very different from that of his predecessor Queen Elizabeth and much more akin to the attitude of the U.S. Congress towards *votes*—he considered them saleable commodities. I am speaking here of honors such as knighthoods, baronetcies, earldoms, etc. Robert Spencer was a good businessman, and because he must have had an instinct for spotting a bargain (and because he could afford it), he purchased a barony for £3000.

Although he had no scruples regarding the purchasing of a peerage, the new Lord Spencer apparently did not appreciate the continuing snobbery he had to endure from members of more ancient aristocratic families in the kingdom who considered him an upstart. Pearson recounts a story of an encounter between Robert Spencer and Lord Arundel in the House of Lords.

During one speech, Robert was referring to earlier times, when Lord Arundel abruptly interrupted him with the loud comment: "When these things were doing, the noble Lord's ancestors were keeping sheep."

Robert replied: "When my ancestors were keeping sheep, the noble Lord's ancestors were plotting treason," which was a little too close to the truth.

Such an uproar followed that Arundel was briefly committed to the Tower for contempt of Parliament.

Robert Spencer seems to have been adept at dealing with insults from snobs such as Arundel, but he had no appetite for it and he retired to his country estates and concentrated on the wholesale meat trade, amassing an even larger fortune. When the King offered Robert an earldom some years later for a piddling L10,000, he turned it down, content with his humble barony. He preferred the country life in pastoral Althorp, where, as one historian described it, he busied himself "making the countrie a virtuous court where his flocks and fields brought him more calm and happie contentment than the various and mutable dispensations of court."

Robert's father, John Spencer III, had already done his part to try to avert any taint attached to the parvenu status of the Spencer family by hiring a bureaucrat of the College of Heralds to concoct a spurious genealogy. This intricate tree linked the Spencers to a far older and more distinguished family whose name was similar to theirs—the Despencers of Gloucestershire. The Despencers had come to England with William the Conqueror and had been one of the great families during the Middle Ages.

With this fabricated ancestry established as part of the record, the Spencers were permitted by the College of Heralds to bear the Despencer coat-of-arms, which they did with regularity and with aplomb. They masqueraded as one of the ancient aristocratic families for the next two centuries, and were gradually accepted as such. So that in 1901, when the eminent genealogist, Prof. J. H. Round, scrutinized the Spencer connection to the Despencers and pronounced it an elaborate error—showing that there was absolutely no connection at all between the Althorp Spencers and the ancient Despencers of Gloucestershire, there was barely a ripple. By then, the Spencers had married into so many other aristocratic families that their claim to be members of the plutocracy was no longer in doubt. Even if they were not Despencers, they had long since arrived.

THE MAGNA CARTA SURETIES

One of the curiosities in the history of genealogical study is the attention paid to the descendants of the barons who signed the Magna Carta. You may or may not remember from your eighth-grade history class that the Magna Carta was a seminal document in English history because it became one of the foundations of English law, and it has been called a cornerstone of democracy as well. In fact, the ancient document contains few sweeping statements of principle but is rather a list of concessions wrung from the unwilling King John by his rebellious barons in 1215. The Magna Carta is important because it established for the first time that the highest governmental or administrative power—in this case, the absolute power of the king—could be limited or abridged by a written agreement and that citizens could depend on certain explicit rights granted and enforced from on high. Without that step, self-governance is an impossibility and writing rules for self-governance (which we call constitutions) is pointless.

Though many additional barons had grievances with King John, only the twenty-five who were elected by their peers to represent them in the negotiations actually signed the document. By their signatures, they also agreed to guarantee the compliance of all the barons with their side of the bargain. Thus they were referred to as the "sureties."

The twenty-five barons regarded as sureties have had their genealogies worked over with great intensity under many a magnifying glass, and updates with new findings are published every few years—because there are people out there, many of them *Americans*, who really want to know if they are legitimate descendants of the Magna Carta barons and there are authorities who are determined to keep out anyone who does not have a claim that can be proven. Only seventeen of the original twenty-five signers have identifiable descendants who have made it from 1215 into the twenty-first century, and I was delighted to learn that—in the person of my eighth great grandmother Olive Welby (b. 1604), daughter of Frances Bulkeley—I am descended from eleven of them. Or rather, after I found I was a descendant of eleven of them, I stopped looking. I may have some connection to the other six as well, but I thought eleven was enough.

Because I can prove descent from at least one of the Magna Carta barons, I am eligible to become a lifetime member of the Magna Carta Society, though I have not yet done so. Well, I must first pay $200 (or $235 if requesting a large insignia rather than small at the time of enrollment). The insignia, I assume, would attest to my status as a bona fide descendant of the Magna Carta barons and would be suitable for framing, so that I could mount it upon my wall and impress or humiliate my friends who might wish they had such august ancestors themselves—and probably do but simply don't know it yet! For an additional $70, I may also purchase Gold Enamel Cuff-links and a Tie-bar bearing the Royal Signet Insignia, and I am entitled to purchase a charm bracelet for my wife with sterling silver charms in the lion rampant, the royal signet, or the charter scroll design. In addition, and most important, if I become a member, I will be referred to as a Magna Carta Baron myself—at least by fellow members of the Society. However, I have my doubts that this is a distinction worth noting, since such Barons must be everywhere.

According to Gary Boyd Roberts, approximately 100 million living Americans have some New England colonial ancestry, and most middle-class Americans with at least some of this Yankee blood will have a half-dozen or more ancestors who were immigrants of royal or noble descent, were the forbears of one or more American presidents, or were passengers on the Mayflower.[1] Most

---

[1] Roughly ten percent of the American population, or 35-million people, are direct descendants of the original Mayflower pilgrims.

of these Americans with New England ancestry can also claim over five hundred notable Americans as 8th to 12th cousins and are probably eligible for membership in the Magna Carta Society.

Whatever you may think of it, how is it that so many of us are descended from royalty and nobility? According to Roberts: "Royal descent occurs, of course, because the younger sons and daughters of kings become or marry nobles; the younger sons and daughters of nobles become or marry landed gentry; the younger sons and daughters of landed gentry become bureaucrats or professionals (clerics, university fellows, lawyers, soldiers, etc.); and the younger sons and daughters of professional elites have become the middle-class citizenry of the Anglo-American and British-derived world, in the U.S., Canada, Australia, India, South Africa, etc. And kings and royal families, of course, were derived from barbarian chieftains who led the tribes that successfully invaded and intermarried with the patriciate of the late Roman Empire." So a number of us must be related to Roman emperors and barbarian chieftains as well!

Carlos Bellamy with Madge Bellamy just after WWI

Madge's star on Hollywood Boulevard

7.

Kissing Cousins

How is it that—as we go back in time—we have more and more ancestors, yet—as we go back in time—there were actually fewer and fewer people alive on earth? At some point, each of us seems to have a greater number of ancestors than there were humans on the earth. Not only that, but not everyone who was alive in 100 A.D., let's say, reproduced or had a line of descendants who made it all the way to today. Our ancestors were unique: *Every one of them* lived long enough to reproduce, and *every one who followed* did the same. Consider the odds against them. They didn't die as infants, though many other infants who were their contemporaries surely did die. They didn't die of disease or war or accidents or mayhem before bearing at least one child or impregnating at least one woman beforehand. What a staggering success rate! But if we subtract all the lines of descent that did not make it to the present, there were even fewer people in the past from whom we may have descended.

The answer to this apparent conundrum, in a word, is cousins! Like many husbands and wives, my parents had no idea they were distant cousins, tenth or eleventh cousins, in their case, through the Bulkeleys. But, in fact, every one of us has numerous cousin marriages in our genealogical trees. Had to have. There would be no other way to explain the simple mathematics of genealogy. The one indisputable fact about cousin marriages is that they allow for early ancestors to fill in more than one limb of each tree, so that some ancestors can be counted more than once. The lines preceding the Bulkeley sisters in my parents' ancestry, for instance, are identical on both sides. So the total number of ancestors in their combined trees is reduced from the mathematical whole, and this sort of duplication and reduction must take place many times in order for the number of ancestors to correspond correctly with the number of people who were actually alive at various points in the past and who managed to reproduce.

In the past, American families tended to cluster together almost like small tribes. Often they were intermarried. Often when some group of young people decided to go off to find new territory, others from some other nearby family in the cluster would accompany them. In Henry County, Virginia, for instance, just after the Revolution and just before the War of 1812, some of the families that surrounded the Bellamys were named Amos, Pace, Pelphrey, Philpott, Rigg, and Hannah. We know that Bellamys married Hannahs and Paces and Amoses and Riggs, but in many instances, records, if they were ever kept, have been lost or obliterated; so we do not know the maiden names of many of the wives of these folks. But we may surmise that, in many cases, the wives were probably from among these same families.

Just after WWI, my Uncle Carlos Bellamy was sent to Denver and given six months to live. He had been gassed in the trenches. Carlos Bellamy met a young woman named Margaret Philpott, who was born in Texas. Neither Carlos nor Madge knew that Bellamys and Philpotts had been families who lived in close proximity in Henry County, Virginia, as recently as 1800, and who lived next door to each other as early as 1638. Surely these families had intermarried before. Neither of them knew that they might be cousins or that their families had ever known one another previously, but they knew they were extremely attracted to one another in spite of circumstances that militated against their relationship. Madge was an aspiring actress who was spending all her time in the local theater. Carlos was trying to establish himself in business and in his life in spite of the fact that he was supposed to die at any moment.

Carlos and Madge were married, and thus Margaret Philpott became Madge Bellamy; and, as Madge Bellamy, she was cast as the dream girl opposite William Gillette in Sir James Barrie's *Dear Brutus* at the Empire Theatre on Broadway, replacing Helen Hayes. Her rise was meteoric. Madge Bellamy suddenly became a movie star, one of the brighter lights of the silent screen. I do not know the exact details of their break up. I imagine it was a case where Madge's success and growing fame took her away from Denver—to New York and Hollywood. And Carlos could not leave Denver, both because of his health and because he was in the construction business. His work was uniquely attached to the spot where it began.

Madge probably asked herself: "Am I going to continue with a man who might not live until next week in this cow town? Or am I going to have the guts to seize the opportunity to become the actress Madge Bellamy?" As it turned out, she chose the latter alternative. She went on to make over fifty films, including *The Iron Horse* (1924), directed by John Ford, and *Under Your Spell* (1936), directed by Otto Preminger. She had tea at the White House with President and Mrs. Harding and had her picture taken on the steps outside with General John J. "Black Jack" Pershing, another of the guests.

In her autobiography, *A Darling of the Twenties*, Madge tells what must have become a familiar lie about where she got her name. She says her agent suggested it! It was a time when divorce was considered a terrible scandal, and perhaps she wanted to preserve the idea of the innocence she projected on the screen. But I have her divorce record. Carlos never talked about any of it, but my mother knew; and that is how I found out. Madge was married at least one other time, but it lasted only four days. Later in life, a millionaire who had proposed to her decided to marry someone else, and Madge shot him to show what she thought of the idea. Some might say she had a chip on her shoulder. Carlos was happily remarried and became the millionaire that Madge might have wished for after her career was over, and he lived to be eighty-eight! The construction company that Carlos founded built the big downtown library in the City of Denver, among many other sizable projects. Would they ever have come together in the first place if they had not been distant cousins? What is a cousin (of the opposite sex), after all, but a composite of all the traits that all of one's previous ancestors and near relatives have found to be most desirable?

Traditionally, Americans have had a phobia against cousin marriages and have confused such unions with incest. In fact, cousin marriages are thought to be such a risk to overall health and well-being that thirty-one states have passed laws prohibiting or limiting marriages between first cousins. We are comfortable enough with the idea that inbreeding can produce marvelous improvements in the traits of domestic livestock, race horses, or show dogs, that we have no qualms about mating canine "cousins," for instance, who embody the desirable characteristics we seek and "breeding them back." But somehow the idea that cousin marriages between human beings might actually improve or consolidate desirable traits, rather than increase only negative possibilities, is alien to us.

This American prejudice seems to have been a legacy of the eugenics movement of the early twentieth century and of early medical discoveries about the dangers of recessive genes associated with diseases like sickle-cell anemia, cystic fibrosis, mental retardation, and a variety of birth defects. Lethal gene combinations do not usually appear and cause damage to offspring unless they are inherited from both parents. So it seems to make sense that when both parents originate from the same genetic background, the odds are much greater that some dangerous and potentially lethal combination will follow.

However, this risk potential is apparently much lower than previously believed. A recent study by Dr. Arno Motulsky and colleagues at the University of Washington that looked at thousands of births has revealed that close cousin marriages show only a minor increase in the potential for birth defects over marriages between unrelated couples—about two percent above average—and this only for first cousins. Medical geneticists have known this for a long time, according to Dr. Motulsky, but the facts have not become generally known, even among some doctors.

Unlike the United States, Europe has no prohibitions against marriage between cousins; and in parts of the Middle East, Asia, and Africa, it is considered far preferable to marry a close cousin than to marry an outsider.

According to Gary Boyd Roberts, before the Industrial Revolution of the 1840s "an estimated 40 percent of all marriages in New England towns, English parishes, many European communities, and the Virginia Tidewater especially, were between first, second, and third cousins. Basically when people lived in villages or on farms associated with parish churches, they often married cousins. Children of first cousins might marry second or third cousins; in the next generation some marriages might occur to outsiders or recent migrants; but in the next generation second or third cousins would intermarry again. Over time this intermarriage produces enormously intricate kinship. And of course if thirty or so founding families produce several thousand descendants in 5-7 generations, and in-migration is only moderate, at some point one can marry *only* cousins, although perhaps more distant than first, second, or third. Thus each section of one's ancestry that is associated with a particular region is likely to contain several or more cousin intermarriages. This pattern is to be expected, and no genetic deficiencies need result."

According to anthropologist Robin Fox, roughly 80 percent of all marriages *in history* have been between second cousins or nearer. If this is even close to the truth, you see what a huge case of duplicate-tree-creation and "collapsing" trees we are dealing with in examining genealogical evidence from the distant past.

You may be sure of this at least: Every person reading this has many cousins in his or her family tree, including several married first cousins who had perfectly healthy children. If there were any truth to the myth that cousin marriages contribute inexorably to birth defects, we would all be victims of many ailments we seem to be entirely free of.

Aside from the issues raised by close cousin marriages and their consequences for genealogy, what about the enormous question of what Nature actually intends for us matrimonially? Are we better off—from a purely biological perspective—marrying outside our own gene pool or fairly close but not too close? Are we programmed to seek potential mates who are like or unlike ourselves? Do we really have any choice in these matters? These are questions I could not help asking after examining my own newly discovered and rapidly expanding ancestral charts and those of my wife and, more recently, of my daughter-in-law.

Without giving any thought to it at all at the time, I married a woman who is, ethnically speaking, very similar to myself. If anyone had suggested to me at the time that I was attracted to her for anything other than purely romantic reasons, I would have been very skeptical. In fact, I would have thought it was a ludicrous idea. I would have said that I simply admired her and thought she was enormously talented, beautiful, and lovable (and I still feel that way, incidentally, decades later). But there is no question that my wife and I are very close to one another, ethnically speaking. She also has Puritans and Mennonites in her background. As we study our ancestors, we continually marvel at the coincidences we discover between and among them—common surnames cropping up, common migration patterns, common histories. We are probably no closer than 8th to 12th cousins, but that is closer than we ever imagined.

Recently, I've discovered that my son Sam has done exactly the same thing I did. He married a woman who is, ethnically speaking, very near to himself. For a while there, I didn't think he was ever going to find the right woman. From my point of view, it took him a very long time. He was in his early thirties when one day he walked into a boardroom at Smith Barney in Winter Park, Florida, and there she was, Kristen Andrews, a blond-haired young woman sitting at the mahogany table with a group of older men in dark suits. She was introduced as the new hire. Sam reached across the table to shake her outstretched hand, and he knew immediately that she was the one.

He did not know, at the time, that Kristen Andrews is a direct descendant of the same Bulkeley family whose ancestry my parents shared! She is a direct descendant of yet another of the Bulkeley daughters, Martha Bulkeley (1572-1639), and therefore also a direct descendant of Edward Plantagenet and of various Magna Carta barons. You couldn't make up such a connection, or, if you did, no one would believe it. But my daughter-in-law is absolutely a descendant of Martha Bulkeley—I've proven it. Overall, my son and daughter-in-law are probably no closer than 8th to 12th cousins, but they had no idea of any such thing in advance of their wedding. They see no significance in it, and, in fact, they would rather not hear about it. I think they are secretly afraid that if someone in authority finds out they are distant cousins, their marriage license will be revoked.

In my father's immediate family, two of his brothers married Asian women who were, ethnically, about as far away from each of the brothers as could be. But my father and two others of his brothers married women who were very close to themselves, though they all traveled a certain distance to find them.

In spite of the rumor about "six degrees of separation," i.e. that no one is more than six steps away from anyone else on earth, the truth, according to anthropologists, is that everyone on earth is no more distant than a 40th to 50th cousin from anyone else. To be a 40th to 50th cousin is to be so distant as hardly to be related at all.

Approximately 100 million living Americans have some New England colonial ancestry, and most of these Americans, according to genealogist Gary Boyd Roberts, can also claim over five hundred notable Americans, including former presidents, as 8th to 12th cousins—and are themselves 8th to 12th cousins of each other. Roberts: "I often say that members of the 'New England Family' are 8th to 12th cousins, and my non-fans think that kinships this distant are meaningless. They are wrong! Such relationships show us the extent of kinship among various classes and nations, and they suggest the century in which common ancestry for very different groups can be traced." Such relationships also show that, in some cases, for whatever reasons, these descendants of the Great Migration continue to constitute a tribe of sorts—by marrying one another long after the regional, religious, and cultural ties that bound them have disappeared.

My father, Orin Ross
"Jim" Bellamy, and me

My mother, Beulah Zutavern Bellamy, and me

8.

Our Year in Bloomville

All our lives together, my father and I waited for the Cincinnati Reds to win the World Series, and they never did—except the year before I was born and the year after he died. Already, as a teenager, when I couldn't sleep from grieving over the errors and failed opportunities that had cost the Reds the game that day, I learned that you don't place your only chance for happiness on factors so utterly beyond your control.

During much of my childhood and adolescence, my father worked as a traveling salesman and he was often absent during the week, but he always came back to us. Perhaps that was the greatest impression he made upon me during those years, that no matter how far away he travelled, no matter what dangers he faced—obscene traffic, Japanese kamikazes during the War, planes veering out of control, vicious businessmen, muggers, murderers, the Mafia—he always came back to us, his face weary, his shoulders tightening under the weight of briefcases and luggage at the door. It began to seem almost magical when I considered the odds against him—his bellicose attitude when behind the wheel of the Oldsmobile, his desire to pass everyone on the road, cursing in a cloud of Camel's smoke, the sheer frequency of his trampings up and down the stairs of furious airliners—that he always beat the odds and returned. I must have worried that he wouldn't survive the dangers I imagined for him, but what I remember is my sense that his survival was somehow magical, that his bond with us was a kind of charm that would always bring him safely home.

Before my father returned from the War in 1945, it had been just my mother and me, and no one could have been more attentive than my mother. But it was wonderful having a father and seeing what it meant to be a man. It was a big responsibility having a father at all, of course, but especially having one who was a war hero! But I was ready for it.

My father was always an expert at articulating the reasons why we should or shouldn't do a thing. When we moved, for instance, which we did quite often, he would sit down with my mother and me and tell us the reasons why he was thinking of leaving his present employment and what it would mean for the family. He always said he couldn't do it without our consent and cooperation. We had to be behind him one hundred percent or else he would stay put, even if he didn't like what he was doing. He always wanted to know our opinions about it, he said, because we were the most important people in his life and he needed to know our true feelings. If we couldn't form an opinion right away, he always said he wanted us to "think about it" and "let him know."

At the beginning of this conversation, I might be dead set against leaving where we were, for a variety of reasons. I often was. It wasn't easy to always be the new kid in school, a stranger to everyone, to finally break the ice with my new classmates; and then to learn, soon after, that we would probably be moving again. But I would always listen to my father's reasons, and no matter what my initial objections, I could feel myself going over to his point of view. His reasons were always better than mine. There would always be many negatives attached to our present location and his present job and amazing positives in the new city that hadn't occurred to us.

Of course, I didn't want him to be unhappy. I wanted to listen as carefully and thoughtfully to his reasons as he was listening to mine and my mother's. I wanted to be as generous with him as he was with us, and once you listened to his reasons and took everything and everybody into account, as he was doing so conscientiously, he was always right. He accomplished this transformation in both my mother and me without bullying of any kind, and by the end of it, we were both committed to his choice and flattered to have been consulted.

Occasionally, when we moved to the new location, if any of us encountered any difficulties or problems or looked back longingly or nostalgically at what we had left behind, he would remind us that we had talked this thing over together and we had all willingly agreed to this move and we would just have to make the best of it. But he was never a bore or a bully about it. He was as hard on himself as he was on us, harder, in fact. Of course, things did not always go as planned—that was life. If your plans didn't work out, then you looked around for something else and you made the best choices you could, at that point, and you moved on.

I was in a different school every year from kindergarten through the eighth grade, except for the fifth grade when I was in two different schools in one year. Then I was in two different high schools, and two different undergraduate colleges; though the latter was entirely my own choosing. The fact was that until I was twenty years old, I had never lived anywhere more than two years in a row, and that had only happened twice. Mostly, it was one and gone. Yet I longed for stability all that time. I longed for a life in one place, and I envied my fellow students who had had the good fortune to know each other since they had been in grade school. I never had the experience of having a friend for that long a time—I was always leaving them behind and missing them.

The only place in my life that remained the same, that I always returned to, was the farm in Bloomville—until Gram died and my mother and her sisters sold it—and the only people in my life who remained the same were my parents, my grandparents, and my aunts and uncles—until they all died. Is it any wonder, after that happened, that a person like me would turn to genealogy as a way to try to put a family back together again and to want to find out all the places they had once lived?

"My father was a traveling salesman and my mother was a

farmer's daughter," I said, "but their marriage was no joke—not to me at least, and certainly not to you."

I pulled off to the side of the road and let the station wagon idle. Across the fields and the marsh, the familiar silver-roofed barns of my grandmother Zutavern's farm reflected the afternoon sunlight as if illuminated by some celestial beacon. I turned around to look at the kids in the backseat. I wanted them to remember this.

"When my father was selling vacuum cleaners door to door in 1938," I said, "if he hadn't driven down *this* road, you wouldn't be here today, and neither would I." The side road I was talking about was paved but narrow and humped in the middle, a simple country road like many others in the area. The odds against his turning down that particular road forty years before seemed staggering.

"Let's go," my daughter said. "I really do have to pee, Papa."

"She was born having to pee," my wife said.

"Where are the cows?" my son said.

We were in north central Ohio, just outside Bloomville in Seneca County, on our way to Cincinnati to visit my father, who had been very ill again, and my mother, who was exhausted by then, taking care of him. I wanted the children to know about his life because I was afraid he was dying.

My father, O.R. "Jim" Bellamy, had arrived outside Bloomville that day in 1938 from the river town of Portsmouth in southern Ohio. While he was trying to sell my grandmother an Airway vacuum cleaner, he saw my mother's picture in a gilt frame on top of the piano and his life was never the same again. "Who is that woman?" he said, and you know the rest. My grandmother listened to his sales pitch and she purchased the vacuum cleaner.

I should add that my father had a knack for selling vacuum cleaners, for selling anything. Selling vacuum cleaners, he had navigated the Depression years, and by 1935, at the age of 27, he was a branch manager, in which role he organized and directed the sales efforts of 118 men. He wore expensive suits and a reddish mustache and drove a succession of sporty automobiles that were never more than a year old. My mother's father got one look at him and wanted to chase him away with his ten-gauge shotgun. In 1938, the year he eloped with my mother, my father's branch of Airway Vacuum Cleaners sold more sweepers in Ohio, Kentucky, and West Virginia than any other regional division in the country and were declared "International Champions."

He was a restless, good-natured, ambitious man who could charm the socks off total strangers but could not explain his talent for selling. "At some point in my sales pitch, there is a critical moment. When I sense it, I hand them a pen and say, 'Sign on this line,' or 'You can't afford not to,' and they look me in the eye and take the pen and I point to the line and, even though they might not want to do it, they sign their names. It's an amazing thing—a gift—almost like hypnosis."

He was of English and Scottish descent—he had the lightest blue eyes and a straight, well-defined, narrow-bridged nose— but his temperament was more characteristically "Irish": affable, pugnacious, talkative, generous, argumentative, spontaneous, and proud.[2] He was the second youngest son in a family of five boys and four girls, and his mother had been the youngest of twenty-six children! I suppose if her father, my great grandfather, had been a reasonable and temperate man and had stopped at twenty-five children, my father would never have been born and I would not be here to tell about it.

Whenever my father took over a project or a business, he expected to turn it around overnight, to show measurable results almost immediately, to push it out of the red ink into the black. He built his entire career around such performances. When the manufacture of electrical appliances was frozen during the War

---

[2] My father lived his whole life thinking he was Irish, and so far I have not found a single Irishman in his background. His tree is almost entirely English, and the ones who are not English are Scots. My father's opinion of British soldiers he met during WW II, incidentally, was that they were the most courageous and professional and admirable of soldiers he encountered among all nations other than the U.S. He held this opinion without knowing or in any way acknowledging that he was primarily of English descent himself. As far as he was concerned, he was an American, and that was the beginning and the end of it.

years, he found a job selling radio time for WSAI in Cincinnati. Maybe he wanted to prove that a man who could sell machines—hard goods designed for the removal of dirt—could also sell air. His sales total in the first year was equal to the output of the three other salesmen combined. He started to learn the radio business.

In 1944, he enlisted in the United States Marine Corps and was sent to officer's training school at Quantico, Virginia. (He had no idea that his Bellamy ancestors were Virginians.) One of my earliest memories is watching a long parade, my nose pressed against an iron fence, my mother holding me up high, while row after row of red, white, and navy blue Marines file past. Somewhere out there, limber and tough, is my father; and we are straining our eyes to pick him out.

He was sent into the Pacific as an Air Support Control officer and was wounded on Okinawa by flying shrapnel and received one-hundred eighty-eight shots of penicillin and the Purple Heart. He was a Captain.

The day he came home in his uniform, he walked right past me, sitting on my tricycle in someone's front yard, without knowing who I was, but I didn't mind. He didn't like to talk about the war, and sometimes he would wake up in the night screaming. One night almost two years after the war was over, he leaped out of bed during some nightmare about the war and broke his toe on the chest of drawers. He went back into radio, selling air time, then later, as an account executive, hitting the road again, selling syndicated radio programs to stations throughout Ohio and Kentucky.

I had a suspicion that my father was (or soon would be) a celebrity. Of course, he was already well-known in the business community, but I mean I felt it was something really big, much bigger than that. This man had charisma and brains and confidence. He *was* obviously somebody important—anybody could see that. Either he was already famous but was keeping it a secret for very good reasons of his own, like Batman, or if he wasn't already a celebrity, he soon would be—right up there with Roy Rogers, my favorite cowboy, and the President and Hopalong Cassidy and Superman, who also had to hide his true identity in order to get along in the real world. Other people might not be aware of how important my father really was, or soon would be, but I had very little doubt. I sensed exactly what a big-shot he already was, and I respected him for it and for his discretion and modesty in keeping it private.

In the late forties, he landed a job in Pittsburgh, Pennsylvania, as General Manager of one of the big, downtown city radio stations; and we moved from a modest buff-brick with a bare, fenced-in backyard in a subdivision in Cincinnati to an English-Tudor-style mansion on a hill in Fox Chapel, Pennsylvania, a glitsy, wooded suburb. That year, Mr. Haan, who lived down the block and who owned a furniture store and was my friend Jimmy's father, brought home the first TV set anyone had ever seen. It had a seven-inch porthole screen, and all the kids in the neighborhood hunched in front of it for hours every day until Jimmy's mother chased us out of the house. Mr. Haan said he thought it was just a gimmick, a passing fancy, but my father maintained that it was the wave of the future and the world would never be the same.

The end of our lives in Pittsburgh was brought on by a terrible automobile accident my father suffered in his brand new robin's-egg-blue Buick Roadmaster convertible, which he totaled on a rainy night by colliding with a steel and cement abutment. Both he and his secretary, who was a passenger in the car, were in critical condition for days but both survived. He crushed the bridge of his nose on the steering wheel and had to have his nose reconstructed by plastic surgery, but except for the scars it didn't look any different.

After that, my father took us back to Cincinnati, where he founded Television Stores Incorporated, which, within two years time, became the largest retail outlet for TV sets in Greater Cincinnati.

In 1951, when he was 43, my father sold Television Stores Incorporated, and our new house and our box seat at Crosley Field, packed up all our furniture, and we moved from Cincinnati to my mother's girlhood home in Bloomville, Ohio, a town of 700 people, to take over the farm for my grandmother Zutavern, who, since the death of my grandfather ten years before, had been victimized by a series of bad tenant farmers who were always "robbing her blind."

Never mind that my father was not and never had been a farmer. The silver-roofed barns of Bloomville had always held a special fascination for him. He considered it a place of destiny. He had discovered my mother there, after all, and was under the impression that as the only male relative with any interest in or capacity for the pastoral life, the farm would eventually be at least partly his to inherit. He felt he had accomplished all he could as a merchandizer of TV sets. Now he could still "be his own boss" but would have the freedom to set his own schedule, get away from the heavy, tedious demands of running his own business, and breathe fresh air every day like a normal healthy human being, a kind of country gentleman. He poured his now substantial fortune into buying farm equipment, seed, fertilizer, and livestock.

We bought three huge International Harvester tractors, plows, rakes, mowing machines, a grain drill, a combine, a hay bailer, a new stainless steel freezer for the dairy barn, twenty-nine head of dairy cattle that had to be milked at dawn and dinnertime every day of the year, a flock of over a hundred sheep, a barnyard full of brood sows, a chicken house full of laying hens; and there were over two hundred acres of tillable land that had to be plowed, grated, fertilized, planted, cultivated, and harvested. My father commuted to Ohio State two days a week to study agriculture under provisions of the GI Bill of Rights.

Almost from the first day, he was embroiled in rabid arguments with my grandmother about how things ought to be done. She must have felt threatened by the sheer extravagance of his commitment and his obvious lack of experience. My grandmother was accustomed to ordering the tenant farmers around and to expressing her most paranoid fears about how they might be cheating her. Her habit was to accuse them of such behavior without a shred of evidence just in case they might be considering trying anything—in the mistaken idea that this would somehow prevent it. She had seen how things ought to be done on a farm for the last sixty years through direct observation, and she saw no reason why they ought to be done any differently now. Suddenly, this new man, her son-in-law whom she had known previously as a vacuum cleaner salesman, was marching up and down the land as if he owned the place, cruising by the front picture window in a great hurry on a brand new $12,000 Farmall, trying to grow oats using some cockeyed formula for fertilizer he had read about in a book, planting all the crops in the wrong fields, and endangering the soil by stuffing it with nitrogen it didn't need.

My father was a man accustomed to giving orders, not taking them, and certainly not taking orders from a woman who was impolite, even if she was his mother-in-law, *especially* if she was his mother-in-law. Here he had changed his whole life, sold a prosperous business, moved his family, invested his life savings, and was, visibly and literally, knocking himself out, probably working himself into an early grave, giving every ounce of his strength to help her, and did she show even the slightest particle of gratitude? No, she didn't. Not only that, she openly implied that he didn't know what he was doing, didn't know what he was talking about, and that he might actually have set out to deceive her, that he might have some secret plan for taking over the farm and sending her to the poorhouse; and, short of that, even if he hadn't intended it, they were all going to end up in the poorhouse anyway because the farm was going downhill so fast at the rate they were going they would both be bankrupt within the year.

In the beginning, I could barely lift a full pail of water, but my chores required the carrying of pail after pail. Within months, I could carry two two-and-a-half-gallon pails of dry corn from the corncrib to the barnyard for the hogs or two full pails of water to the chicken coop or anywhere you wanted to take them, and I began to acquire respectable muscles in my arms for the first time in my life. In the course of a year, I went from a skinny strike-out artist, the last kid picked for softball at the playground at recess, to one of the demon home run hitters in the fifth grade.

Over that same year, my father lost forty pounds and pushed

himself so hard physically that he developed tendonitis in both arms. He weighed 138 pounds, less than in high school, and his elbows hurt so severely that he couldn't pick up a cup of coffee without spilling it. My Uncle Doc came for a visit and advised my father that he would be dead inside another year if he didn't quit and find a more satisfying occupation.

In the meantime, my father's farming methods had produced greater bushels-per-acre yields of corn, wheat, oats, and soya beans than had ever before been measured at the Bloomville mill. Our cows had higher and higher butterfat content in their milk, which brought in record receipts, and half-a-barnful of new calves. On the other hand, one of our sows gave birth to nineteen piglets but was so heavy and awkward she suffocated or bit and killed all but two of them. Chicken thieves broke into the henhouse, and several baby lambs wandered too close to the marsh and got entangled in the mud and undergrowth and eventually drowned or died of exposure.

One day, the brake slipped as my father was preparing to back into the low barn opening where he usually parked the tractor. Suddenly, the tractor started rolling backwards and pinned his shoulders against the barn wall just above the framing. The angle of the small incline was just enough to keep the weight of the tractor locked against him and the steering wheel mashed tightly against his chest and under his chin in such a way as to make it impossible to reach the brake with either leg. He was barely able to get his toe on the clutch pedal in order to disengage the gears before he was crushed, but his purchase was so tenuous that he was reluctant to move for fear his toe would slip and the tractor would kick back into reverse and take his head off. It was exactly the sort of freakish farm accident that one was always reading about in the local paper, just a matter of not ducking his head in time in order to clear the overhang. Pressed this way against the barn, unable to reach the gearshift or to dislodge himself, and feeling like the biggest horse's ass who ever tried to learn how to be a farmer, he called out for my mother and me. He shouted our names over and over again, as loudly as he could until he grew hoarse; but no one came to help. She was out of earshot, especially with the roar of the tractor drowning out his cries, and I was in school.

Finally, after two hours of desperation, during which time my father had imagined the irony of his likely decapitation by means of his own tractor and his own carelessness so often that he was seething, and by which time his left leg was so stiff and numb that it had begun to shake precariously on the clutch pedal, the Farmall ran out of gas and he was able to release the clutch and after some hard squirming, work himself free and stumble toward the house to tell the tale of his harrowing escape.

The author as "Bondie" with Santa in Albany, NY, circa 1952

9.

THE GREATEST PITCHER IN BASEBALL

Ultimately, my father realized that Gram would never accept him there, no matter how well he performed, and that the struggle would always be a bitter one. He reasoned that if he went back into radio then, there would still be some openings. If he waited too much longer, he would be out of circulation too long and no longer "a marketable commodity." At the end of a year and a half, we had an all-day sale and auctioned off every sheep, pig, and cow—each of which I knew by name and considered a close personal friend—every piece of farm equipment my grandmother didn't want to keep—all at a stupendous loss.

Somehow or other he had managed to secure a job as General Manager of a prestigious station in Albany, New York, the state capital. After the tragedy of the sale, my father went almost instantly from frayed cotton flannel and down-at-the-heel clodhoppers, green with manure, to two-martini lunches, silk suits, and $30 neckties[3]. Albany was the pinnacle of his career in radio. His offices and the studio were in the posh Ten Eych Hotel in the middle of downtown Albany and were owned by the Shines, who also owned ten other hotels, including the Ronnie Plaza in Miami Beach, and over one hundred movie theatres and were supposed to be worth around $200 million but were "impossible to deal with," according to some sources my father consulted. But that didn't stop him.

---

[3] For the contemporary equivalent, multiply by a factor of ten.

That year I was a bookish, bespectacled sixth-grader who had a mysterious alternate life as a radio celebrity. For a month before Christmas, every day after school, I would report to the studio and tape a program with Santa Claus (who was impersonated by the Program Director). I was one of Santa Claus's main elves, named Bondie—the program was sponsored by Bond Bread—and I would read letters to Santa and tell stories about what Rudolph had done that day and give weather reports on the generally blustery conditions at the North Pole.

I would make personal appearances with Santa Claus at area schools and Cub Scout meetings, wearing a white apron and a baker's cap and pretending to be a more-or-less supernatural being, which was often the way I was treated. I hung around with other radio personalities at the station but especially our Sports Director, who, during the summer months had another job—as first baseman for the Philadelphia Phillies—and because of his friendship, I once met and actually shook hands with Robin Roberts, who at that time was a young man and the greatest pitcher in baseball, even if he wasn't a Cincinnati Red.

I also have a dim memory of being escorted with great fanfare by my father into a ballroom-size office at the Ten Eyck and shaking hands with Meyer Shine, whom I expected to look like a cross between Al Capone and a fire-breathing dragon but who, in fact, resembled no one so much as one of my kindly uncles. He held a gigantic cigar and smiled sweetly at me while he pumped my hand and seemed genuinely delighted to meet one of his more famous employees, a person—little did he suspect—who had, only the year before, been slopping the pigs, petting the cows, and conferring privately with a flock of chickens in Bloomville, Ohio.

But my father complained that the Shines were "eating him alive," always "on his back," no matter how well he did. Fairly soon, he began to feel that the job was too high-pressure, that there was too much tension. Now he could see why they had driven away every manager they had ever had. If he didn't find something better, he said, he was going to have an ulcer or a heart attack and that would be the end of it. His first year there, sales increased 250%.

We returned to Cincinnati, where he was Spot Sales Manager for a company syndicating TV programs. His territory was the eastern half of the United States. He paid visits to presidents of companies, whipped out his 16mm projector and showed them installments of "Lassie," or "The Cisco Kid," or "The Millionaires," which were still new and exciting for the time, and tried to convince them to spend hundreds of thousands of dollars to sponsor the programs on national or regional television. This time he was using machines to sell air. He was on the road for weeks at a time. When I made the high school basketball team, I remember telling him about it by a long distance call to some lonely motel room in West Virginia.

Before he started Bellamy Realty, he left Cincinnati and went back into radio one last time. I was in college by then in North Carolina. He and my mother moved to Florida and he managed a problematic station in Delray Beach, Florida. After two years under his guidance, the owners sold the station for seven times what they had paid for it three years before, and he was fifty-six years old with a heart condition and out of work and money again and very discouraged—too old for anyone to want to hire him for anything ever again, he said.

Within a year after they returned to Cincinnati and he started Bellamy Realty, he was driving a green Eldorado and opening up new branches all over the city. Every Sunday in the *Cincinnati Enquirer*, the smart little Bellamy Realty insignia were emblazoned all over the real estate pages. "I wish I had started in this business thirty years ago," he said. "If I had, right now I'd be a millionaire several times over and I could retire and play golf and spend some time at the ballpark." He went from selling single family units, to apartment buildings, to skyscrapers. That was before inflation and interest rates went out of sight and knocked the bottom out of the real estate market.

Bulkeley

10.

WE GOT BEEF

Since the evidence indicated that I had Bulkeleys on both sides of my family tree, a double dose of Bulkeley genes, I thought I had better find out, if I could, who these Bulkeleys were. All I knew at that point was that both Frances (my mother's ancestor) and Sarah (my father's) were daughters of the Rev. Edward Bulkeley (b. 1540) and his wife, Olive Irby (b. 1547). They were English, but that was about all I knew. It is one thing to learn the names and nationalities of one's ancestors and quite something else to find out anything useful about the actual lives of people who lived four hundred years ago. My chances of finding anything more seemed remote.

I did a random search on Google, not expecting much, and hit upon an English site called Smartgroups where a passel of other living Bulkeley descendants from Great Britain, the USA, Canada, Australia, New Zealand, and India were busily communicating with one another; and they *were* smart. I introduced myself, and my Bulkeley lines of descent, and joined the group. Most of my U.S. cousins were descendants of Frances and Sarah's brother Peter Bulkeley, who had succeeded his father in the parish of Odell but was silenced for non-conformity because of his Puritan sympathies and thereafter emigrated to the Massachusetts Bay Colony aboard the *Susan & Ellin* in 1635 and founded Concord, Massachusetts. Brother Peter was, apparently, a shining example of Puritan piety and sacrifice for Cotton Mather, who wrote a lengthy appreciation of him in his *Magnalia Christi Americana*, and also well-known to Oliver Cromwell (in fact, a cousin by marriage).

Many, many Bulkeley facts were reported on the site, but my cousins informed me that if I wanted additional information about the family, one of the most preeminent American genealogists, Donald Lines Jacobus, had published a definitive genealogy and history of the Bulkeleys in 1933 called *The Bulkeley Genealogy*—1066 pages worth—which traced the Bulkeleys in several unimpeachable trees back to 1200 A.D! In the meantime, some of my cousins were busily arguing online about filling in the gap between 1200 and 1066. There was good information all the way back to William the Conqueror, who was, quite possibly, a relative.

BULKELEY (Bulkley, Buckley). The name, originally spelled Buclough and Bulculogh, is thought to signify "a large mountain." Other possible meanings of the name: "Clearing or pasture where bullocks graze," a corruption of "Bullock-field" or "Bulluch-ley." One source said that a likely update would be the equivalent of "Bull-gulch," and the Bulkeley coat-of-arms seems to bear out that interpretation: three bulls' heads with their tongues sticking out—in the silver and black of the Oakland Raiders. It seems almost comical to my hopelessly contemporary eye, but I suspect having a lot of meat on the hoof was important to my ancestors. Showing their bulls' heads on their coat-of-arms must have been a way of saying, "We got beef" or, alternately, "You don't want to have a beef with us."

One correspondent stated: "The name is only correctly spelled 'Bulkeley.' That branch of the family that went to New York is the only one which ever altered the spelling [to 'Buckley'], though it is usually pronounced 'Buckley' in Connecticut. It is not misused in Massachusetts." To which another replied: "I have a small suspicion that 'correctly' means 'how the Anglo-Welsh nobility and the College of Arms spell it.' I thought there was a little war back in 1776 when Americans decided to have no more truck with that sort of thing." (The well-known family of Buckleys which includes William F. Buckley is of Irish extraction and not related.)

According to Jacobus, the Bulkeley family is of great antiquity in England, where the family is connected to the town of Bulkeley in Cheshire County. As early as 1200, Bulkeleys were lords of the manor in Bulkeley, Cheshire. "Bulkeley is a sequestered and beautiful township, situated about twelve miles southeast of Chester, in the line between Bunbury and Malpas, shaded on the northwest by the Bickerton Hills."

The Reverand Edward Bulkeley, second son of Thomas Bulkeley of Woore, Shropshire, by his wife Elizabeth, daughter of Randall Grosvenor, was born near 1540. He was not merely a country preacher. He matriculated at St. John's College, Cambridge, in 1555; Scholar, 1555; BA, 1559-60; Fellow, 1560; MA, 1563; BD, 1569; Doctor of Divinity, 1578. In about 1566, Edward married Olive Irby of Lincolnshire, daughter of John and Rose (Overton) Irby, and with Olive eventually had three sons (one of whom founded Concord, Massachusetts) and twelve daughters (two of whom were my distant grandmothers). He obtained the rectorship of Odell in Bedfordshire, probably in 1571. He "compounded" for the living at Odell, 6 March, 1571/72, as is shown by the Bishops' Certificates of the Diocese of Canterbury. According to Jacobus, this means that he then paid to his superior his first year's salary, as was then the custom in the English Church.

In 1580, he was listed as a Burgess of Shrewsbury and Professor of Theology. Somewhere along the line Dr. Bulkeley became a moderate Puritan. He resigned his pastorate in 1609, either because his nonconformist views did not sit well with the English church hierarchy or because of increasing age, and died at Odell early in January 1620/21. His burial on 5 January 1620/21 was entered in the Odell registers by his son Peter, who had succeeded him as Rector and had not yet been silenced.

Another interesting tidbit unearthed by my Bulkeley cousins at Smartgroups: my mother, Beulah Bellamy, b. 1918, who was a great admirer of the actress Katharine Hepburn, b. 1909, was actually rather closely related to her. Katharine Hepburn was also a descendent of Frances Bulkeley and Richard Welby, and the first four generations of Katharine Hepburn's ancestral line from Frances Bulkeley and Richard Welby are identical to my mother's—same mothers, same fathers. Quite remarkable.

Frances Bulkeley + Richard Welby

Olive Welby + Henry Farwell

Olive Farwell + Benjamin Spalding

Edward Spalding + Mary Adams

Ephraim Spalding + Abigail Bullard

Oliver Spalding + Mary Witter

Erastus Spalding + Jennet Mack

Martha Spalding + Leman Garlinghouse

Carline Garlinghouse + Alfred Houghton

Katharine Houghton + Thomas Hepburn

Katharine Hepburn, actress, b. 1909

Frances Bulkeley + Richard Welby

Olive Welby + Henry Farwell

Olive Farwell + Benjamin Spalding

Edward Spalding + Mary Adams

Thomas Spalding + Abigail Brown

William Spalding + Mary Dunham

Thomas Spalding + Elizabeth Ayres

Samuel Spalding + Mary Ann Trail

Alveda Spalding + Paul Zutavern

Rolla Zutavern + Harriet Kagy

Beulah Pearl Zutavern, b. 1918

Oliver Cromwell

11.

THE GREAT MIGRATION

Before she died in 1611, my tenth great grandmother Sarah Bulkeley, who had married Oliver St. John, the son of Oliver St. John, the first earl of Bolingbroke, gave birth to yet another St. John named Oliver. This Oliver eventually became a member of Parliament, Counselor to the King, and Lord Chief Justice of England during the period of the English Civil War.

To complicate matters further for this last Mr. St. John, his first wife was a distant cousin of Oliver Cromwell, the King's bitter enemy; and after that wife died, his second wife was also a cousin and close friend and confidante of Cromwell's. St. John himself was sympathetic to the Puritan cause but was pledged to defend the rights of the King at a time when even members of Parliament sometimes lost their heads if they were found to be on the wrong side of an issue. It may be a tribute to Lord St. John's skill as an attorney that he managed to keep his own head while the King eventually lost his.

My other Bulkeley great grandmother, Frances Bulkeley, married Richard Welby and died in 1610. Like her sister Sarah, Frances never left England, but her daughter, Olive Welby of Moulton (named for Frances's mother) married local Boston (Lincolnshire) resident Henry Farwell in 1629, and the Farwells immigrated to the English colonies in Massachusetts and appeared on their uncle Rev. Peter Bulkeley's doorstep in Concord in 1640. Their daughter, Olive Farwell, was born in Concord in 1647, and she married Benjamin Spalding; and six generations later my great grandmother Alveda Spalding was born in this line. (It may be worth mentioning that the village of Moulton in Lincolnshire is roughly five miles from the village of Spalding; and the town of Boston is about fifteen miles from Spalding. Could Olive's parents have known the Spaldings before they left England? It's possible.)

Since little more could be discovered about my dual great grandmothers, Frances and Sarah Bulkeley, who were, after all, born in the sixteenth century and died before the cataclysm of the English Civil War created martyrs and heroes and the Great Migration, I focused on their younger brother Peter Bulkeley, about whose life quite a bit more is known, thanks partly to the genealogist Jacobus and the fact that Peter Bulkeley did come to America, and thanks largely to Peter Bulkeley's near contemporary, the eminent Puritan divine Cotton Mather, whose biography of Bulkeley is part of Mather's *Magnalia Christi Americana*.

Peter Bulkeley was born at Odell in Bedford County, England, in 1582/83, where his father Edward was rector—and his two older sisters were still unmarried and at home. He was educated in the same college, St. John's College, Cambridge, where his father had received his Bachelors, Masters, and Doctor of Divinity degrees. Mather says: "His education was answerable unto his original; it was learned, it was genteel, and, which was the top of all, it was very *pious*." In Mather's nomenclature, piety was undoubtedly the supreme virtue. Peter Bulkeley became "a thundering preacher, and a judicious divine," according to the historian Daniel Neal.

Mather continues: "When he came abroad in the world, a good benefice befel him, added unto the estate of a gentleman, left him by his father; whom he succeeded in his ministry at the place of his nativity, which one would imagine *temptations* enough to keep him out of a *wilderness*." The wilderness Mather refers to was, of course, the American colony of Massachusetts Bay, where Peter eventually emigrated. The temptations, I assume, were the prospect of continuing in the rather cushy environment of home, where he was well-established, well-connected, and a kind of gentleman of means as well as the Rector of Odell. Many another might have been willing to bend his principles and compromise with authorities of the English Church, which he represented, in order to maintain such a position.

"To too many ministers of Bulkeley's generation, the ministry was merely a convenient and genteel way of obtaining a livelihood," according to Jacobus. But Peter Bulkeley was too devout and committed to the saving of souls to deny his growing attraction to Puritan ideals, which were at first intended merely to reform the practices of the Church. The Puritans believed that the English Church had become too formal and concerned with superficial rituals and self-aggrandizement and that it was not sufficiently involved in the daily lives and concerned with the religious needs of average citizens and parishioners. Puritanism appealed to many devout and sincere clergyman of the time because of its simplicity, earnestness, and definite ideas about reform.

As Peter Bulkeley gradually began to incorporate Puritan ideals into his practice at Odell, he was more and more in opposition to the hierarchy of the English Church. He was known to be a non-conformist, but his immediate superior, the Lord Keeper Williams, formerly his Diocesan and his personal friend, "desired to deal gently with his non-conformity" and essentially ignored it as a matter of no great consequence, as he had Peter's father's similar tendencies for twenty years.

But when Bishop Laud became Primate of England in 1633, trouble came to good Bishop Williams, who was sent to the Tower, and to Bulkeley as well, since Laud was determined to root out this growing scourge of Puritan idealism. The crisis for Bulkeley came in 1634 when he was suspended for failing to attend a ceremony held by Sir Nathaniel Brent, Laud's Vicar-General. Rev. Bulkeley's other infractions were that he did not wear an ecclesiastical gown and he did not make the sign of the cross in baptism, regarding these practices as superstitious hocus-pocus that might create barriers between himself and his flock. Even worse for him, his success at winning converts using his methods was far too enormous to be ignored.

Peter Bulkeley was "silenced" with no hope of reinstatement. In a word, he was fired. He was stripped of his pulpit and his vocation in the prime of his life, and it was the only life he had prepared for and the only life he had ever known.

"It must be confessed that the zeal of the Puritans was not always well regulated," according to the historian Daniel Neal, "nor were their ministers so much on their guard in the pulpit or in conversation as they ought, considering the number of informers that entered all their churches, that insinuated themselves into all public conversation, and, like so many locusts, covered the land. These were so numerous and corrupt that the king was obliged to bring them under certain regulations; for no man was safe in public company, nor even in conversing with his friends and neighbors. Many broke up housekeeping, that they might breathe in a freer air, which the council being informed of, a proclamation was published, forbidding all persons except soldiers, mariners, merchants and their factors, to depart the kingdom without his majesty's license."

As the Archbishop of Canterbury, William Laud resorted to punishments that were hardly ever laudable. Bulkeley's fate was less horrific than some others who were sent to the Tower, who were branded, or who lost their ears. As a result of Laud's "bloody cruelty," many "godly preachers and true Christians...were caused to slip into the deserts of America," Henry Bolton wrote in 1645.

About 65,000 people crossed the Atlantic from England in the 1630s, creating what has been called "the Great Migration," and setting the stage for an American Revolution in the next century, for they were a stubborn, determined, and recalcitrant lot. As I've recently learned—to my astonishment—most of my earliest English ancestors in America were among them—Adams, Allen, Ayers, Bacon, Baxter, Beal, Brown, Bulkeley, Clark, Cooke, Dunham, Farwell, Flagg, Fuller, Haynes, Jones, Lockwood, Lord, Lothrop, Pike, Spencer, Spalding, Stevens, Stone, Treadway, Vassall, Wheeler, and Whipple, just to name a few of the obvious ones. Incidentally, in 1645 when Cromwell and the Puritans gained ascendancy during the English Civil War, Archbishop Laud was one of the first to lose his head.

KNOWN ARRIVAL DATES

Thomas Chapman, Jamestown, Virginia, 1610

Francis Mason, Jamestown, Virginia, 1613

Edward Spalding, Jamestown, Virginia, 1619, Massachusetts Bay, 1640 or earlier

John Adams, Plymouth Colony, Massachusetts, 1621

William Stafford, Jamestown, Virginia, 1622

William Vassall, Massachusetts Bay Colony, 1628

Gregory Baxter, Massachusetts Bay Colony, 1630

Gerard Spencer, Massachusetts Bay Colony, 1630

Deacon John Dunham, Plymouth Colony, 1632

Rev. John Lothrop, Massachusetts Bay Colony, 1634

Rev. Peter Bulkeley, Massachusetts Bay Colony, 1635

John Ayer, Massachusetts Bay Colony, 1635

Nathaniel Treadway, Massachusetts Bay Colony, 1635

Henry Stevens, Massachusetts Bay Colony, 1635

John Pike, Massachusetts Bay Colony, 1635 or earlier

Thomas Lord, Massachusetts Bay Colony & Hartford, CT, 1635

Thomas Flagg, Massachusetts Bay Colony, 1637

Matthew Whipple, Massachusetts Bay Colony, 1638 or earlier

Walter Haynes, Massachusetts Bay Colony, 1638

John Beal, Massachusetts Bay Colony, 1638

Henry and Edith Squire Adams, Massachusetts Bay Colony, 1639

Joseph Clarke, Massachusetts Bay Colony, 1640 or earlier

Lewis Jones, Massachusetts Bay Colony, 1640 or earlier

Michael Bacon, Massachusetts Bay Colony, 1640 or earlier

Thomas Fuller, Massachusetts Bay Colony, 1640

Henry and Olive Welby Farwell, Massachusetts Bay Colony, 1640

Thomas Barnum, Connecticut Colony, 1640

Edmund Sheffield, Massachusetts Bay Colony, 1644 or earlier

Thomas Fairchild, Connecticut Colony, 1646

Gregory Cooke, Massachusetts Bay Colony, 1646

John Marshall, Massachusetts Bay Colony, before 1659

Thomas Wedge, Massachusetts Bay Colony, before 1667

William Brown, Massachusetts Bay Colony, 1685

Archbishop William Laud

12.

Bulkeley's Departure

In 1635, however, Archbishop Laud was still in power, and Peter Bulkeley had a decision to make. If he stayed in Odell and opened his mouth to express his true beliefs, he was in danger of being arrested. He was in danger of being arrested even if he did not open his mouth. He was a widower with a large family to take care of and a comfortable estate. But he wished to continue to practice his religion, which was his whole life. Therefore, he laid plans to emigrate to New England, where he could preach completely from the heart and not be subject to tyrannical administrators and what he considered idiotic prohibitions and small-minded insinuations. To leave England, however, was against the law.

Careful preparation had to be made for his departure and for that of his family. A non-conformist minister, in particular, if recognized, would have been apprehended. Furthermore, the law required those who were leaving the country to present certificates from a minister and Justices of the Peace of their conformity to the orders and discipline of the Church of England, and that they were not subsidy men. The subsidy was a special tax to which certain individuals were liable, and the government did not wish to have its revenue from this source reduced by the departure of men who were liable to the tax. In fact, the government employed spies to prevent the departure of those whose presence in England was desired. However, there were sympathetic ministers who made a specialty of providing non-conformists with certificates of conformity, and there were ways to elude the spies.

First, Bulkeley quietly sold his substantial estate, at an estimated worth of six thousand pounds, or about $30,000, which was a considerable fortune in those times. Then Peter's eldest son, Edward, was dispatched to New England in advance of the rest of the family, perhaps taking with him some of the family property, and with instructions to prepare for the advent of his relatives. Edward was at that time barely twenty-one years old.

Peter Bulkeley's first wife, and the mother of his children, whom he had married in 1613, was Jane Allen, daughter of Thomas Allen of Goldington, Bedfordshire, England. Jane Allen was aunt of the Lord Mayor of London, Sir Thomas Allen, and she was said to have been a most virtuous gentlewoman. Peter and Jane had had seven sons (some historical writings say they had nine or even ten sons) and two daughters. In any case, all but five sons and one daughter died in childhood. After Jane's death (she was buried at Odell, December 8, 1626) Rev. Bulkeley lived eight years a widower. However, on the verge of departing for Massachusetts Bay, he quickly and quietly married Grace Chetwoode, the daughter of Sir Richard Chetwoode and Dorothy Needham Chetwoode. Grace was a woman of thirty-three at the time, nearly twenty years younger than Peter.

Most of the shipping lists from this period have not been found or preserved, but fortunately those for the year 1635 are fairly complete. By a thorough examination of these lists, Jacobus provides a detailed account of just how the Bulkeley family managed to escape detection and flee to the wilds of Massachusetts: "It is interesting to observe that on April 13, 1635, the name 'Jo Backley,' aged 15, was entered in the list of those accepted for sailing on the *Susan & Ellen*. Five days later, 'Ben Buckley,' aged 11, and 'Daniell Buckley,' aged 9, were accepted as passengers to sail on the same ship. These were undoubtedly Mr. Bulkeley's three sons, John, Joseph and Daniel, whose ages correspond very closely with those given. It will be noticed that no care was taken to give the correct spelling of the surname, and that even the Christian name of Joseph was incorrectly entered as Benjamin. It is to be presumed that Puritan friends or acquaintances of Mr. Bulkeley took these boys separately to the shipping office and they gave the impression that they were members of their own household, and they may have been garbed like apprentice boys rather than as sons of a well-to-do clergyman."

"To run no unnecessary risk of discovery, we find that on May 8, 1635, 'Grace Bulkeley,' age 33, was entered as a passenger on the *Elizabeth & Ann*, while on the following day 'Peter Bulkeley,' age 50, was entered as a passenger on the *Susan & Ellen*." As desirous as they may have been to avoid being caught, it is interesting to me that they were unwilling to disguise or misspell their own names! Perhaps their consciences would not allow it. These two ships were expected to sail about the same time, but it is highly unlikely that Rev. Bulkeley's pregnant young bride was ever intended to sail alone on a different ship.

Probably another woman sailing on the other ship, possibly even a member of Peter Bulkeley's own congregation who was not too different in appearance from Grace Bulkeley, was asked to undergo the preliminary examination at the shipping office and to be accepted as a passenger on the *Susan & Ellen*. Grace Bulkeley then took the other woman's place in being entered as a passenger intending to sail on the *Elizabeth & Ann*. There would have been great risk of discovery if Mrs. Bulkeley had presented herself with her husband long before their ships sailed. By adopting this strategy, there was nothing to connect Rev. Bulkeley and his wife in the eyes of the shipping clerks. Then, at the last moment Mrs. Bulkeley embarked with her husband, while the other woman embarked in the other ship as had been her intention all along. By the methods described, Rev. Bulkeley, his wife, and the three boys found themselves together on the same ship.

Since Edward had already crossed to New England, this accounts for all the surviving Bulkeley sons except Thomas, who was then about eighteen years old. Jacobus speculates that unless Thomas travelled with his brother Edward, it is probable that he came on the same ship with his father and stepmother; but if he did, his name was so disguised that it could not be recognized on the shipping list. However, a later researcher found evidence that Thomas made the journey on yet another ship, the *Plaine Joanne*, in May, 1635.

The voyage to New England was traumatic in the extreme for Peter Bulkeley, because following upon the anxiety of their secretive departure, his lovely new bride Grace grew pale and ill and then suddenly died on shipboard near the end of the voyage. Rev. Bulkeley, who supposed land was near and who was unwilling to consign his beloved's body to a watery grave, urgently insisted to the Captain that the body should be kept one more day, in hopes that they might be able to bury her on dry land, and the Captain consented. When land had not been spotted by the next day, Peter again refused to let his beloved Grace be tossed overboard. He blocked the entrance of two sailors sent by the Captain to prepare her body for internment, and he was forced into an angry confrontation with the Captain over it; but as no signs of decay appeared, the Captain finally relented.

Peter prayed without ceasing. He prayed for Grace's soul as it rose toward Heaven. He prayed for the ship's swift passage that she might be buried on dry land. He prayed that he might be forgiven for his angry outburst with the Captain and for the prideful yearning he felt in his bereavement that he might be simply granted the opportunity to visit her gravesite—because at least then he would still possess her. It did not even occur to him to pray that she might come back to life—he had already prayed for that before she died—but that is what happened. On the third day, to the amazement of everyone, symptoms of vitality returned and Grace Bulkeley opened her eyes and blinked, and before land was reached, the color returned to her face. Although she had to be carried from the ship, Grace recovered completely and lived to old age. Thus the Bulkeleys landed at Boston in midsummer, 1635. All those people who are descended from Peter and Grace Bulkeley in North America can thank the stubbornness and devotion of Peter Bulkeley for their existence.

Rev. Peter Bulkeley

13.

The Man of Big Prayer

The Bulkeley family proceeded immediately to Cambridge, then called New Towne, where Edward had rented a house for them. Peter Bulkeley was welcomed as a valuable addition to the new colony, not least of all for his wealth and powerful connections in England, but also for his piety, intellect, and commitment to Puritan principles. Peter became acquainted with many of the colony's settlers and ministers in the Boston area. He and the well-known minister John Cotton, of Boston's First Church, were both Cambridge graduates and residents of the same diocese in England.

When Grace's first child was born about four months later, the name of Gershom was bestowed upon him. This was not a family name on either side, but was chosen from the Bible to commemorate the fact that the child was born far from home. Though they were exiles, the Bulkeleys still regarded England as home. (Exodus 2:22: "Moses' wife Zipporah bore him a son, and he called his name Gershom; for he said I have been a stranger in a strange land.") Eventually, Peter and Grace would have three more children, two sons and a daughter.

The leadership in Boston, including Governor John Winthrop and Rev. John Cotton, agreed that Bulkeley and a man named Simon Willard should lead an expedition of about one hundred families some fifteen to twenty miles west through the wilderness and establish a new church and village in the Musketaquid area, later to become Concord, Massachusetts. Willard was a thirty-year-old Kentish soldier, trader, and surveyor.

The hardships that this journey entailed have been described by Scudder:

"They make their way through unknown woods, through watery swamps, through thickets their hands must tear open that their bodies may pass. They come to scorching plains where their feet and legs are torn by ragged bushes, until the blood trickles down at every step. After such toilsome days, they rest on the rocks when night takes them, having no repast but a pittance of bread. Finally they reach the desired haven, and here they burrow in the earth and under the hillside and build some sort of temporary shelter for their wives and little ones."

The first order of business was to execute a treaty with the Indians, which took place at Jethro's Oak. Simon Willard led the negotiations with the squaw sachem for the purchase of six square miles of land. In payment the settlers offered: "one parcel of wampum, several knives and hatchets, some hoes to replace their cultivating sticks and clamshells, some cotton clothes and shirts.... To the medicine man, the squaw sachem's husband, a suit of cotton cloth, a high-crowned hat of heavy English felt, shoes, stockings, and a greatcoat."

It is worthy of note that Peter Bulkeley was among the first to instruct the Indians in the knowledge of the Gospel, and the singular immunity from Indian attacks that Concord enjoyed over the early years of the settlement, was largely credited, by tradition, to his friendship and influence with the Indians. The Indians named him "the man of big prayer."

The land purchased at Musketaquid was at the confluence of two small rivers and was, in many ways, like Odell, where Peter had grown up and lived his whole life except for his years in Cambridge. Reynolds writes of the similarity: "The same green meadows, the same upland plains, the same tranquil stream, meet the gaze in the one case as in the other." Scudder describes the site as having, "seven natural ponds, more than nine miles of beaver-haunted fish-abounding river, bordered by meadows of lush grass…excellent for cattle; any number of lesser streams on which to build mills, several small cornfields already under Indian cultivation, and plenty of rich bottom land for clearing…."

Bulkeley contributed disproportionately to the development of the town by furnishing capital and supplies for a number of his parishioners, servants, and employees. Bulkeley still had his 6000 pounds, or what was left of it, which made him one of the richest men in the area, and he had brought with him a number of servants, including Thomas Dane, a skilled carpenter who later built Peter's home in Concord, as well as Peter's corn mill and his saw mill on Mill Brook in Concord. As Mather described it: "Here [in Concord] he *buried* a great estate, while he *raised* one still for almost every person whom he employed in the affairs of his husbandry. He had many and godly servants, whom, after they had lived with him a fit number of years, he still dismissed with bestowing *farms* upon them."

Still, the hardships involved in hewing a civilized community out of a wilderness site were immense. The development of Concord required sacrifice, patience, and dedicated physical effort from every family. The winters were much more severe than the English were accustomed to, and it took them several years to adapt their farming methods to the late frosts, spring flooding, and scorching summers. As Paul D. Kilburn describes it: "Fish were abundant but wolves often dug up the fish placed around corn hillocks to fertilize the new corn. Flooding by the river often destroyed crops planted in the fertile soil of the flood plain. The meadow grass proved too rich for the cattle and many became sick. Hogs escaped from Hogpen Walk and were killed and eaten by lynx. In these harsh conditions many children died." But the settlers persevered, adjusted their expectations and their farming methods, and gradually their circumstances improved.

Peter Bulkeley became an important leader of the town of Concord and of the colony. He often fulfilled tasks for the leadership in Boston, such as investigating high prices and assembling and publishing the laws of the colony. Bulkeley lost one significant battle in the town, however. He could not persuade enough of the Concord families to support the hiring of a schoolmaster, which was a requirement for all towns in the Massachusetts Bay Colony with fifty or more householders. Concord voted, instead, to pay the five-pound fine levied each year by the General Court because citizens felt that their children needed to work at home to help support their families rather than take the time away from the fields to attend school. As a consequence, many of Concord's first crop of children, as adults, were so illiterate they could not sign their names on land deeds.

On another matter concerning education, Rev. Bulkeley was successful, however. He persuaded some forty-two residents of Concord to pledge five pounds per year for seven years in order to help launch the fledging new college in New Towne called Harvard. Later Harvard President Charles Chauncy, who was Peter's son Gershom's father-in-law, said the Rev. Bulkeley of Concord was "esteemed in his day as one of the greatest men in this part of the world."

An anecdote concerning Rev. Bulkeley's influence has survived as well:

"A church in the neighbourhood had fallen into unhappy divisions and contentions, which they were unable to adjust among themselves. They deputed one of their numbers to ask the venerable Bulkeley for his advice, with the request that he would send it to them in writing. It so happened that Mr. Bulkeley had a farm in the extreme end of the town, upon which he had placed a tenant. In addressing the two letters, the one for the church was, by mistake, directed to the tenant, and the one for the tenant, to the church. The church was convened in order to hear the advice, which was to settle all their disputes. The moderator read as follows: 'You will see to the repair of the fences that they be built high and strong, and you will take special care of the old black bull.'

"This mystical advice puzzled the church very much at first, but an interpreter among the more discerning ones was soon found who said: 'Brethren, this is the very advice we most need; the direction to repair the fences is to admonish us to take good heed in the admission and government of our members; we must guard the church by our Master's laws, and keep out strange cattle from the fold. And we must in a particular manner set a watchful guard over the devil, the old black bull, who has done so much harm of late.' All perceived the wisdom and fitness of Mr. Bulkeley's advice, and resolved to be governed by it. The consequence was that all the animosities subsided and harmony was restored to the afflicted church. What the subject matter of the letter received by the tenant was we are not informed, and what good effect it had on him the story does not tell."

The Gospel Covenant, or the Covenant of Grace Opened is a book of Rev. Bulkeley's sermons, published first in 1642 at the request of his parishioners. Two printings were made of the book in the colonies. It was among the first books written in New England and one of the first books published in North America. It also went through several editions in England. Granted that the religious concept of grace was of overwhelming importance to the Puritans, still one wonders if the fact that Grace was the name of his wife might have influenced Bulkeley's choice of title. Was it intentional, a pre-Freudian slip, or merely coincidence that Bulkeley included the name of his wife in the title? Cotton Mather's review of the *The Gospel Covenant* was as follows: "He was a most excellent scholar, a very well-read person, and one who, in his advice to young students, gave demonstrations that he knew what would go to make a scholar.... It is remarked, that a man's *whole religion* is according to his acquaintance with the *new covenant*. If then, any person would know what Mr. Bulkly was, let him read his judicious and savoury treatise of the *gospel covenant*; which has passed through several editions, with much acceptance from the people of God."

The Gospel Covenant was dedicated to his nephew, Lord Chief Justice of England, Oliver St. John, whose mother, you may recall, was Peter's sister, Sarah Bulkeley. It is perhaps worth exploring some of St. John's family connections in order to understand the next chapter in Peter Bulkeley's life. Lord Oliver St. John's first wife was Johanna Altham, whose grandmother Joan Cromwell (daughter of Sir Henry Cromwell of Hinchingbroke) was aunt both of Oliver Cromwell, the Protector, and of John Hampden, an important member of Parliament during the period of the English Civil War. Oliver St. John's second wife was Elizabeth Cromwell, daughter of Henry Cromwell of Upwood, the Protector's uncle, and this cousin Elizabeth was also a close friend, correspondent, and confidante of Oliver Cromwell.

Given these family connections and his strong Puritan affiliations, it does not seem quite so surprising that in the year 1650, after he was well-established in New England, Peter Bulkeley received an invitation from Oliver Cromwell, the Lord Protector, which was sent to "six prominent men of Massachusetts," though Rev. Peter Bulkeley's name was at the top of the list and second was Rev. Samuel Whiting, son of the mayor of Boston (in Lincolnshire), John Whiting and his wife Elizabeth St. John, Lord Oliver's sister (and Sarah Bulkeley's daughter and Peter Bulkeley's niece)—i.e. both men—Bulkeley and Whiting—with close family connections to Cromwell.

Cromwell was concerned about the Irish situation and invited Bulkeley and the others to consider leaving Massachusetts Bay to lead the effort Cromwell wished to undertake in the founding of a Puritan stronghold in Ireland. Cromwell implied that all necessary resources would be made available. It must have been a very flattering opportunity, coming as it did from one of the most powerful men in the known world at the height of Puritan ascendancy in England, especially after all Rev. Bulkeley had suffered to uphold the spirit of Puritanism.

But Peter Bulkeley was already sixty-eight years old. He had been building a life for himself and his family in the hamlet of Concord for fifteen years, a life he had scraped out of the virgin wilderness. He was probably tired. He was probably not especially eager to pull up stakes, move everyone back across the Atlantic, and start up another enclave in Ireland, which was then regarded as a most ravaged and primitive place. But, apparently, Bulkeley and the others did give Cromwell's offer serious consideration, as indicated by the answer they gave to Cromwell that has survived for over 350 years (see Appendix).

The conditions which these ministers and godly persons proposed previous to setting out for Ireland are entered upon another page. They were as follows:

"*That in matter of Religion we may have like liberty established by favor of the State of England for the exercise and the worship and government of Christ as here we enjoy in New England.

*That such a proportion of outward encouragements in houses and lands as the State shall thinke fit in favor to bestow upon such as principally and personally engage in this worke may be set forth by the Parliament or Counsel of State, and after divisions to be made by us with some appointed by the Parliament to our Assocyates.

*That some quantity of land may be granted for the advancing of learning, by a Free-Scoole and College.

*That we may have free choyce of the cheife military governors to be over the Garrison where we shall sit downe, and such a one as may be of our owne company, if we have any fit person amongst us, or if not, that we may have liberty to nominate some other godly man which the State of England may approve of.

*That in regard we come from a pure Ayre, we may have a place in the most healthfull part of the country.

*That of regard to the meanness and inability of sundry godly persons (which doe or may desire to joyne with us) to transport themselves and families, the State would be pleased to think of some way of lending them some helpe.

*That we and our company may be for some yeares freed from publique chayes.

*That noe Irish may inhabit amongst us, but such as we shall like of.

*That we and our company may have convenyent tyme allowed us for our transportion into Ireland.

*Lastly intimate our sufferings under the tyranny of Episcopacy which forced us into exile (to our great hazard and losse) for noe other offence but professing that truth which (through mercy) is now acknowledged."

Apparently, nothing came of these deliberations; and it is not clear exactly why. Perhaps Cromwell was offended that these fellows in New England should set forth such elaborate conditions for their participation in this venture, or perhaps he thought the conditions too expensive. The New Englanders were asking for a great deal of land, money, authority, and autonomy, in addition to freedom from taxation and recompense for their earlier losses, which had been substantial; plus the involvement of Parliament they requested seems unnecessarily problematic. After all of that, they wished to have the freedom to avoid associating with the Irish altogether! Perhaps Bulkeley and the others deliberately set conditions they knew Cromwell would reject because they did not actually wish to go to Ireland. At the same time, they certainly did not want to offend the Lord Protector, so rather than simply saying "no," perhaps they intentionally framed an answer that would flatter him but not encourage him to follow through on his original offer to them.

Peter Bulkeley carried on as he had in Concord for the best part of another decade and died in the same year as Cromwell, 1659, though Peter was seventy-seven at the time of his death and Cromwell was only fifty-nine.

Peter Bulkeley's will is the first I have ever seen that actually leaves books to his loved ones, and the books are listed by title and the books are mentioned first, before money or property. He must have had a great many books because, according to Cotton Mather, he gave the bulk of them to help start the Harvard library. He was also a writer of verse in Latin, and his book *The Gospel Covenant*, as mentioned earlier, was one of the first books published in North America. Is there a gene, I wonder, for wanting to own books, read books, and write and publish books? If so, I may have inherited that gene from my great Uncle Peter Bulkeley, which had to skip over several generations to find me.

Peter Bulkeley's granddaughter Elizabeth Bulkeley became the wife of the Rev. Joseph Emerson, and her great grandson, Rev. William Emerson, was the grandfather of the great Transcendentalist Ralph Waldo Emerson. Members of the Waldo family married into my Spalding lines at various times as well, so I am also related to Ralph Waldo Emerson a second way through the Spaldings.

I cannot say whether it is a genetic affinity, of course, but I have always been keenly (and therefore warily) susceptible to the writings of Ralph Waldo Emerson, since I began reading him as a teenager. I often think of his line "pray without ceasing." I believe Emerson's line is perhaps the best advice ever given about writing—in the sense that writing, like prayer, involves deep meditation, yearning, and a desire to make order out of the Universe.

As I was reading in Emerson's journals recently, I noticed an interesting connection that seems to exist between the reasons given for Peter Bulkeley's (and the Puritans') displeasure with the English Church and Emerson's journal entries about his own disillusionment with the Church in his time. They both complained of too much focus on formal elements and rituals and "pomp" and not enough attention to the personal needs and individual caring about members. (This is exactly my own complaint about the academic world.) Has anyone ever traced a connection between Puritanism and Transcendentalism? Could be, in this case, it's genetic.

Finding my Mother's Ancestors

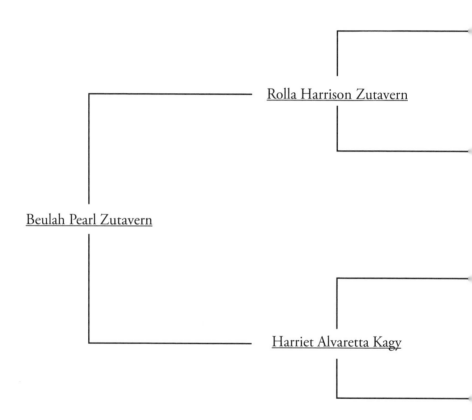

Rolla Harrison Zutavern

Beulah Pearl Zutavern

Harriet Alvaretta Kagy

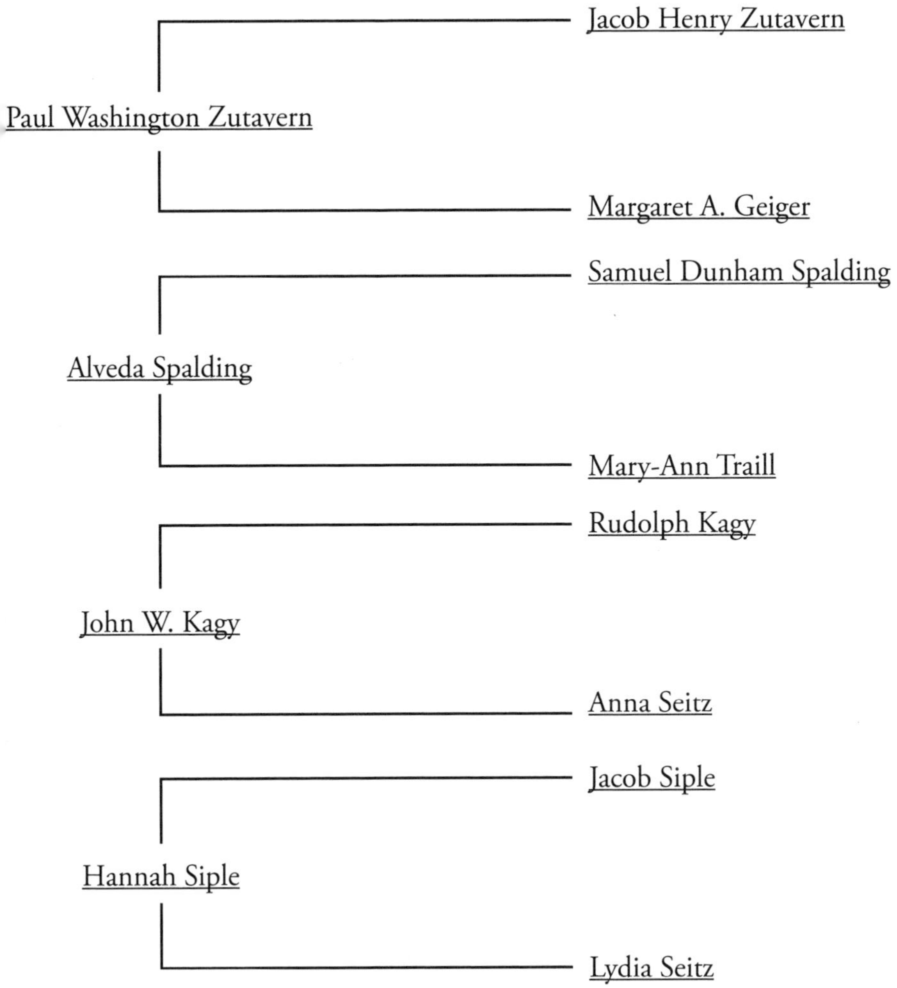

Paul Washington Zutavern
- Jacob Henry Zutavern
- Margaret A. Geiger

Alveda Spalding
- Samuel Dunham Spalding
- Mary-Ann Traill

John W. Kagy
- Rudolph Kagy
- Anna Seitz

Hannah Siple
- Jacob Siple
- Lydia Seitz

The old mill near Freeland, Maryland

14.

MARTYRS MIRROR OF THE DEFENSELESS MENNONITES

In 1966, with my wife and new daughter, I lived for a brief season in a primitive old mill near Freeland, Maryland, just across the border from Pennsylvania. I had quit my job as an Assistant College Editor in order to write the great American novel, and I had chanced upon a "back to the land" group that had purchased the mill in hopes of making it their national headquarters. They hired me for $100/month plus free lodging and "all the food we could grow" to oversee the place and to help supervise improvements with the eventual plan of starting several homesteads on the surrounding acreage. I imagined that we might do the same—retire from civilization, start a homestead, grow our own food, and write—it sounded like heaven to me. We were young and poor and, even in 1966, $100/month was slave labor wages. My first impulse was to turn them down in spite of my hopefulness about the opportunity, but I visited the mill, and there was something about the place that persuaded me to take the leap. It did not resemble Bloomville, Ohio, but it was beautiful country nevertheless, beautiful land.

The mill was located in a deep valley, and the only way to get there was by winding on down a narrow humped-back country road that followed a broad creek as it meandered through the valley between steep hillsides engulfed with thick forest. The loudest sounds were the soughing of the trees and the splashing of the creek water as it cascaded over the rocky creek bed.

Down the valley maybe three miles, the land opened up and several fields could be seen above the road to the right and across the creek on the other side, where the road curved back on itself and a large red barn was nestled. Then, immediately on the right, you could see the white-washed walls of the old mill coming into view, an immense three-story structure of masonry and logs with twelve-pane windows and elaborate chimneys.

I could easily imagine myself on a spring day out in one of the nearby fields with a rake in my hand. My shirt was thrown over the rail of a distant fence, and I had a dark tan and was getting back in shape again. My muscles were alive in my arms. My hands were strong as they gripped the rake-handle. The leaves of a row of maple and oak trees at the edge of the field riffled in the wind, and the water from the nearby stream burbled in my ear. The sun shone hard across my shoulder blades, but it was a feeling that I relished.

The mill was very old, something out of the eighteenth century; and even though it was no longer used as a mill and the mill-wheel, which had been repaired, was merely decorative, all the old enormous structure of gears, beams, belts, and pulleys was still intact inside the building, like a colossal roughhewn engine left by an ancient race, waiting for the work to resume. Though the mill had probably not been used for anything other than storage for decades, until my back-to-the-land group took it over, it had originally been built to last and the basic shell was solid. It made an imposing appearance, suitable for a national headquarters, though, once inside, one could see it was, after all, mainly just a big drafty barn with a large high-ceilinged space suitable for a meeting room and, at the other end, a honeycomb of small rooms and alcoves and a half-finished living quarters.

I do not believe in reincarnation or predestination, and I am, in fact, unusually skeptical even about "coincidence." I do not believe in "mysterious forces" of fate or in "God's intention." I certainly do not believe that "everything has a purpose" or that "everything will always turn out for the best." But for whatever reason it occurred—whatever powerful impulse drew me to that spot on the earth—what I know now, but did not know then, is that the old mill in Maryland is *less than five miles* from where my Swiss-American ancestors lived and built a village 250 years earlier!

Several of my ancestors are buried near there too. How can that be explained exactly?—ancestral memory, genetic predisposition, pure chance? Some of them might have brought wagonloads of wheat, barley, or oats to the mill to be ground into flour! Some of them might have helped to haul lumber or stones to build the mill! One of them might have sat by the edge of the creek and dipped a tin cup into the water and tilted his head back to take a deep drink on a hot day in July. And for them, this place was an earthly paradise, half-a-world from the madness and viciousness that had hounded them into leaving, a place where they could practice what they believed, a place blessed with both freedom and love.

That is what we were hoping for too, but for us, it was not blessed at all. We lasted about four months in the middle of the winter and almost froze to death, crouching by the fireplace and near our one wood stove. With the first taste of spring, after we planted our garden, I resigned, and we packed our meager belongings into our VW bus and headed for Iowa City and graduate school at the University of Iowa. We never did eat "all the food we could grow" or even the food that grew after we left. But maybe someone did.

What I know now, but did not know then, is that I am a direct descendant of the Swiss Mennonites who founded the Pequea Settlement in Conestoga, Pennsylvania in 1710, and who spread out from there to other small nearby villages such as Millersville and Seitzland, Pennsylvania. These were people who fled Europe because they were on the receiving end of the brutality of the Reformation.

There was a holocaust before the Holocaust! It happened in some of the same places, and it was horrific. Hundreds of thousands of innocent people were tortured and died. But, now, it has been largely forgotten—even by those who are descendants of the victims.

The early Mennonites were moral exemplars in many ways. Thousands of them were tortured and burned as heretics in Europe, or had their tongues cut out, for their stubborn adherence to beliefs that may seem, now, like minor departures or differences from accepted church practices in the sixteenth century. They believed it was pointless, for example, to baptize infants who could not possibly know the significance attached to such a rite; they preferred to wait to baptize until the devout chose to join the church of their own volition, as adults, knowing what it meant to do so. To me this seems an entirely sensible idea, but for this idea alone, they were labeled as Anabaptists and persecuted unmercifully.

Like other Anabaptist leaders, Menno Simons, founder of the Mennonites, differed from reformers such as Martin Luther on a central theological point. Where Luther emphasized faith alone for salvation, Menno contended that faith must be demonstrated through *good works.* Oh, yes, and my Swiss ancestors were *pacifists*, declining to take up the sword to defend themselves or the state, preferring to practice Christ's admonition *to turn the other cheek.* (What a power trip it must have been for the maniacal authorities to torture people whose most cherished beliefs involved the daily practice of simple benevolence towards others and a refusal to defend themselves. I sometimes wonder if there isn't some connection between the ouster of such groups—people of conscience—from Austria, Germany, and Switzerland during and after the Reformation and the eventual rise of the Nazis.)

These gentle Mennonite people were much less rigid, isolationist, and authoritarian than the Old Order Amish or some more restrictive modern Mennonite sects. In many ways, they were gut-level liberals. Once transplanted to American soil, they carried on a fruitful trading enterprise with the distant cosmopolitan city of Philadelphia via the Conestoga wagon, which they invented; and they practiced a "live and let live" attitude, in general, unlike those who had persecuted them so viciously. This pervasive sense of tolerance was one factor that allowed them to prosper in the virgin wilderness of Pennsylvania surrounded by Indians. The Mennonites and the Conestoga Indians not only tolerated each other's presence, they lived in peace and harmony together on perfect terms of friendship. They helped one another to wrest a living from the wilderness, and their children played side by side. The Indians often supplied them with fish or venison, which they gave in exchange for bread.

These bearded Switzers with their tall blond wives and their many, many children were clever, industrious farmers who helped turn Lancaster County, Pennsylvania, into one of the garden spots of the earth. Some of them—many in my line, in fact—were ministers as well as farmers, still concerned, centuries later, about moral and celestial issues that had gotten their ancestors scalded, drowned, and beheaded in Zurich and Bern, in Augsburg and Schleitheim. One of them in my line, Rev. Lewis Seitz, moved his church and his entire congregation to Ohio from Virginia in 1801 in order to make a statement against slavery.

But, early on, they prospered in rural Pennsylvania and married within their own group for generations. Eventually, after they had immigrated to Ohio, one of the charming daughters met and fell in love with a man of English descent named Bellamy, and the long chain was broken and by then the bitter history of martyrdom and struggle followed by two centuries of splendid pastoral solitude and the blossoming of the land in that place under their care was forgotten.

But is it possible that some dimly perceived remnant of it still exists somewhere inside me?—unrealized aptitudes, unsatisfied yearnings, fragments of ethnic memory or the collective imagination? Can the past be forgotten so easily once it is imprinted in one's genes and nerve endings?

In researching Anabaptist history, I came upon a remarkable work entitled *The Bloody Theater or Martyrs Mirror of the Defenseless Christians*, written and compiled in 1659 by Thieleman J. van Braght. This book attempts to list every Anabaptist martyr who died between the first century A.D. and 1660 and, if possible, to describe the manner of his or her death and the culprits responsible for it. It is still regarded as a holy book by the Mennonites.

Here follows a few excerpts, using just surnames that I find within by own family tree:

"In 1567, Bro. Nicholas Geyer, a miller, and deacon, was apprehended for the faith, at Innsbruck, in the earldom of Tyrol. There the Jesuits and others assailed him in many and various ways, and, in the examination, dealt with him in a cruel and satanical manner. But he did not suffer himself to be moved from the faith, but steadfastly persevered as a Christian hero, and having evinced great constancy, he was condemned to death by the children of Caiaphas and Pilate. The priests...were determined to have his head, which they also obtained, for he was executed with the sword, and then burnt, thus valiantly gaining the victory in Christ, in the noble fight of faith...whom no tribulation, torture or vexation could cause to despair. No water could quench his love, no sword separate it, no fire consume it...."

—*Martyrs Mirror of the Defenseless Christians*, p. 703

"In the year 1569, the 25th of June, there was put to death for the testimony of the truth, in Briel...Maerten Pieters of Maesland, a village near Delft...and with him Grietgen Jans, wife of Adrian Heynsen, a weaver of Swartewael. Maerten Pieters was beheaded with the sword, and Grietgen Jans was burnt at the stake, in the town, whereupon their dead bodies were taken down and conveyed out of the town, to the place of execution.... Here Maerten Pieters was laid upon a wheel, and his head upon a stake. And Grietgen Jans was again tied to a stake, and thus given for food to the fowls of the heavens. And all this they suffered for the testimony of the truth, were in no manner charged with any evil works, but accused simply on account of having united with those called Mennists, and having, according to the doctrine of Christ, been baptized upon their faith, seeking thus to please their Creator, according to all their ability.

—,*Martyrs Mirror of the Defenseless Christians*, p. 740

Barbara Neeft, A. D. 1643

"This woman was very near her confinement, when she was driven hither and thither through the persecution. After she was delivered and had lain in three days, she was betrayed and apprehended. She was forthwith, in the bitter cold of winter, taken to prison, a distance of four hours' walk, in which, on account of the intolerable cold, her health became irrevocably ruined, so that she . . . died soon after, and is now resting with her soul under the altar of God."

—*Martyrs Mirror of the Defenseless Christians*, p. 1121.

Martin Schrag in his book, *The European History of the Swiss Mennonites*, explains this about my ancestors: "The Mennonites were, for the most part, peasant farmers, separated from the world. They wanted, above all else, to be true to their God.... They were a tolerated, peculiar people, viewed from outside the community. They tried to be self-reliant in material things, and thus by example of labor and industry, hoped to gain respect and consideration from their neighbors." In his book on the Mennonites of Conestoga, Steve Friesen makes the point that unlike the English settlers who built their houses on the edges of their property, facing out, with easy access to the roads and the outside world, the Swiss and Germans built their houses in the middle of their 500-acre plots and they were mainly concerned with their lives within that small estate. Thus, it was the English who organized village, town, and city government, and the Mennonites who excelled at farming.

Both these descriptions appeal to me because they describe my own relation to the community, to any community I've ever been a part of; and it suggests some of the reasons why I have sometimes been misunderstood. Though I am English too, I seem to have inherited the Mennonite way of thinking in relation to social interactions. Given a choice, I would prefer to build my house in the middle of my land, not on the edge of it. Given a choice, I would prefer to focus my attention on my family and on my immediate tasks and not at all on my neighbors. Given a choice, I would prefer to avoid thinking about village or local government, in particular, though I realize that such an attitude invites exploitation. Given a choice, I would rather follow the ass of a horse around and around a field all day long, breathing in the good air and the rich scent of loam, than sit inside in a meeting with a jury of my peers for more than an hour.

My grandmother, Harriet Kagy Zutavern, and me

15.

THE VON GEMMINGEN CONNECTION

My grandmother had Mennonite Seitzes on both sides of her family, so naturally I followed those Seitz lines back as far as I could go until I ran into the Seitz immigrant progenitor of both lines, who was supposedly a man named Johannes Seitz, who arrived on these shores from Germany in 1764. Then I met cousin Caral Mechling Bennett on the internet, who had been searching for the details of Johannes Seitz's life for a lot longer than I had been.

The family story of Johannes Seitz's European origin that Caral had tracked down was that Johannes Seitz came from "Augen-haven, Ammer Valley, Bavaria" and that he was educated at the Ettal Monastery. Caral wrote to the monastery and received the same reply that other researchers had: there was no record of a Johannes Seitz having attended there.

Caral sifted through several old letters she had inherited on this subject from an earlier generation of Seitzes trying to locate their roots. In a letter in 1921 from Dr. William Clinton Seitz, Caral found this: "My ancestor is supposed to have come from a town called Otten Hoffen…." A patient of Dr. Seitz's apparently told him that "Otten Hoffen" was actually Aughenhaun, Bavaria, which seems to be the source of the name of the mysterious village of "Augenhaven."

In another letter, Caral found this: "Records in York Co, Penn-sylvania, say he [Johannes Seitz] came from 'Ottle Hoffel' (possibly

Prussia). Now I can find no Ottle Hoffel in all the German gazetteers…. However, a Dr. W. C. Seitz, of Glen Rock, Pennsylvania, has found an Outten Hoffen in Baden."

Caral was perplexed, full of curiosity, and determined to find the truth in this mystery. Where did her ancestor, Johannes Seitz, come from? There seemed to be no solution except to travel to Germany herself, so finally Caral made the journey.

This is what she found: In the 1987 "700th Anniversary" book of Adelshofen in Baden was a history of the village, originally called the "Hof des Otolf" (farm of Otolf). Alternate spellings for the name were listed as Ottelshoven, Odelshoven, Adelshoven, and Adelshofen. The nearby monasteries of Lorsch and Herrenalb, which had been there since at least the twelfth century, could well have provided an education for Johannes Seitz, since the Seitz family Caral found conclusive evidence of in Adelshofen had some status as town officials.

Johannes Seitz had definitely been a resident of this place. However, Caral could find no record that Johannes Seitz had fathered a son in Adelshofen, and she knew that his son Lewis was a babe in arms when Johannes and his wife arrived in Philadelphia. How could that be explained?

Then in the birth records section of the Adelshofen Evangelical Church book, Caral found this: "Dorothea Welck, the single daughter of citizen Johan Michael Welck, dairymaster"—whose family lived and worked at the Dammhof near Adelshofen, a large tract of land and a farm controlled by the aristocratic landlords, the von Gemmingen family—"gave birth to a son, 'Ludwig,' 05 January 1763." The father of her child is listed as: "Very Honorable Johann Philipp von Gemmingen zu Babstatt, also single." This Philipp von Gemmingen was none other than the young son of the Lord of the Manor, Baron Friedrich von Gemmingen-Hornberg and his equally aristocratic wife, Wilhelmine Leopoldine Ruedt von Collenberg.

Several other crucial details from the record began to clarify the story for Caral. Caral found that Johannes Seitz, the twenty-four-year-old immigrant and the presumed progenitor for this line of

Seitzes in America, was married 08 May 1764 to one Anna Catharine Ripp, and eight days later the newyweds left for America, arriving at Philadephia 20 October 1764 aboard the ship *Richmond*. With them was a baby named "Lewis" who was one year and ten months old—the exact age of Ludwig, the illegitimate son of Johann Philipp von Gemmingen and his dairymaid lover Dorothea Welck.

In fact, in his will twenty-nine years later, Johannes Seitz refers to Lewis as "my son Ludwig." Aside from the birth of Lewis/Ludwig's sister Catherine in January, 1765, no other birth records exist for Johannes and Anna Catherine Seitz in Germany in a location where impartial and meticulous records were recorded for every human action, so this child Lewis/Ludwig whom the Seitzes had brought with them to America, was, in all probability, not their own.

The critical link that Caral discovered in Germany is that dairymaster Johan Michael Welck, the father of the unwed mother, was the brother of Anna Welck, who had married into the Seitz family. Anna Welck Seitz was the mother of Johannes (John) Seitz, the immigrant! To make the best of a potentially difficult and embarrassing situation—to help save face for all concerned—the father of the unwed mother and his sister (with the consent of the von Gemmingens?) undoubtedly arranged for her son and his wife to adopt the child and take him to America. Quite possibly, the von Gemmingens even provided funds for the journey.

The church records also reveal these details: Johann Philipp von Gemmingen, the new father, was indeed the Baron's son, but the Baron himself, Friedrich von Gemmingen-Hornberg, had died in 1738, in Hornberg, of consumption. Also, the Baron had had, in succession, two wives and one son with each wife, so Johann Philipp had an older half-brother. Also, Johann Philipp's mother was gravely ill and near death at the time of the illegitimate Ludwig's birth, and the disgrace of his birth could not have come at a worse time.

Perhaps in an effort to set things right, less than two years later, Johann Philipp was properly married to Dorothea Regina Eleanora von Stein zum Rechtenstein, and a year after that another (legitimate) son named Ludwig was born in Germany. However, the new father himself died just two months after the birth of this second Ludwig, and by that time, the first Ludwig, my 4th great grandfather, was already in America, growing up as the son of John and Catherine Seitz.

If the von Gemmingens had known that Johann Philipp would die so young—he was only 36 years old—perhaps they would not have sent young baby Lewis/Ludwig away. But perhaps it was unavoidable—to spare the child as well as his unfortunate parents.

Further thoughts: at the time of Lewis/Ludwig's birth, Johann Philipp's father, as I say, was already long dead and his mother was either near death or already dead also (she died in 1763). Perhaps it was his half-brother Wilhelm who was running the show at that point and who knew the right thing to be done and helped to arrange or enforce the departure. If Johann Philipp had not made love to the comely milkmaid Dorothea Welck and impregnated her, then he would have halved his genetic contribution to the human race (and I would not be here).

But what became of my 4th great grandmother Dorothea, the spurned darling of the dairy barn? Did she cry when they took her baby son away? Was she the object of scorn by members of the community? Did she ever see Philipp again—other than from a distance? Did she mope when she learned that he was to marry the lady Dorothea Regina Eleanora von Stein zum Rechtenstein? Did she mourn his death when her lover passed away such a short time later? Did she ever marry and live a normal life and give birth to other children she could be a mother to? How long did she live? Dorothea Welck, however they wronged you, whatever your failings, we remember you here with appreciation and respect.

Lewis/Ludwig Seitz Memorial

16.

Lewis/Ludwig "Seitz"'s Life in America

He is half the son of a German nobleman (named Von Gemmingen) and half the son of the dairymaster's daughter (named Welck) but most likely thinks he is the natural child of Johannes and Catharine Seitz, who are humble immigrants. He arrives at Philadelphia in 1764 as an infant in the company of his adoptive parents and becomes a part of the very religious German community near York, Pennsylvania, where the Mennonites had been building a settlement since about 1710.

A momentous event, which the Seitzes could not have anticipated but which would soon overtake them all, was the Revolutionary War. Lewis/Ludwig was too young to have been a legitimate soldier, but the record shows that Johannes Seitz, in spite of the fact that he lived in a community containing many pacifist Mennonites, was listed as a member of Capt. J. Erman's Company (7th Battalion, 5th company) from York, Pennsylvania, in 1777-78.[4] Johannes and family survived the War, and Johannes purchased land in Shrewsbury Township in 1786 near the present village of Seitzland.

Circa 1788, Lewis/Ludwig married one Anna Beery, daughter

---

[4] Every grade school child is taught that the Hessians were formidable allies of the British during the Revolution. But little is said about the German immigrants to the colonies who fought on our side. In a very real sense, in this war, it was their Germans versus our Germans as much as it was the English from Britain versus the English from the colonies.

of John Beery and Catherina Hunsaker Beery. (John Beery's father Nicholas Beery/Bieri had emigrated from Switzerland.) Shortly after his marriage to Anna, circa 1790, he and Anna moved to the Shenandoah Valley of Virginia, a garden spot with rich soil and mild climate that led many Germans to settle there. Among his neighbors were the Beery, Hite, Spitler, Bretz, Bibler, and Schwartz families.

There Lewis/Ludwig-Welck-von-Gemmingen and Anna Beery Seitz raised a large family, and Lewis became a pastor for the Whitehouse Church. Although his adoptive father Johannes had been a soldier during the Revolution, and perhaps because of this, it appears that Lewis/Ludwig must have been attracted to the pacifist inclinations of his Mennonite neighbors. The Primitive Baptist Church formed at Whitehouse was strongly influenced by Martin Kaufman and those of Mennonite ancestry who believed that it was wrong to take up arms. They were also strongly opposed to slavery and legal oaths of any kind.

It is of some considerable interest in this regard that the "Lords and Landowners" near Adelshofen, where his own von Gemmingen family reigned, and where Lewis/Ludwig was born, had a history of religious tolerance and open-mindedness. In fact, in a world of oppression and merciless persecution of religious minorities and free-thinkers during the Reformation, the von Gemmingens were notorious for aiding the persecuted and for helping them to escape through a kind of von Gemmingen Underground Railroad at Castle Hornberg and Castle Guttenberg. This pattern was established as early as 1518 when Dietrich, Wolf, and Philipp von Gemmingen received their father's rich inheritance. Dietrich inherited Castle Guttenberg and its estate, Wolf inherited the homestead at Gemmingen, and Philipp inherited the newly acquired Furfield estate. (Castle Hornberg was not acquired until 1612.)

The brothers could have engaged successfully in regional politics, and could have founded a small principality. However, they turned passionately toward the spiritual streams of the time. Perhaps they even listened to Luther's debates in 1518 at Heidelberg with many young humanists and theologians, many of whom would later speak up in behalf of the Reformation in southern Germany. At any rate, the ideas proposed there thoroughly impressed them and gave their lives a new goal. Dietrich and Wolf were among the first in the region to introduce and support the Reformation. Already by Christmas, 1521, the sermons at Castle Guttenburg were held in a Protestant manner, which was courageous indeed. Dietrich employed young reformers as preachers, many of whom had been expelled from other regions and found refuge at the castle. At times, there were as many as twenty of them in residence at Guttenberg.

In 1525, on the so-called Guttenberg Day, representatives of Zwingli and Luther met to debate the interpretation of the Holy Communion. The emperor, Charles V, disliked it so much, in fact, that he personally went to Heilbronn in order to persuade the Gemmingen brothers back to the old faith. However, they supposedly answered him: "We are utterly sorry to distress or act against the will of His Imperial Majesty—the supreme power below God. Yet, we would rather do that than distress God himself and abolish his true doctrine!"

The emperor did not forget this answer. Later during the Schmalkaldic War of 1545, he threatened the brothers with imperial banishment because they supported the Protestant Union with vast amounts of financial assistance. At the time it was also possible to avert the impending legal action of imperial banishment by ransoming oneself, since the emperor was constantly in financial distress. Hence, the brothers ransomed themselves by paying 3000 florins and continued their support of the Protestant cause.

Lewis/Ludwig's adoptive father, the American Revolutionary War veteran Johannes Seitz of Adelshofen, Baden, Germany, died in April, 1793, and was buried at the St. Peters Reformed Church Cemetery near Glen Rock, Pennsylvania.

In 1801, Lewis/Ludwig's impatience with the institution of slavery reached a crisis point in Virginia, and he set in motion a long immigration of families from Virginia to the Ohio Territory. First, Lewis traveled himself to an area in what eventually became Fairfield County, Ohio, and selected land for a home. (This land is located on the east of where the Mt. Tabor Evangelical Church now stands.) In 1802, he returned to Virginia, sold many of his household effects, then placed the rest in wagons, and with his wife and all his children who had been born in Virginia (ten children, the oldest being only about twelve years old), started out on the long, perilous journey to Ohio.

Lewis/Ludwig must have been a charismatic fellow because he was accompanied and followed by nearly his entire congregation and many of the German families from the Shenandoah Valley. In Ohio in 1806, Lewis founded and was the first minister of the Pleasant Run Baptist Church, where he preached in both English and German. The area is now known as Baptist Corner and is located eight miles east of Lancaster, Ohio.

In 1804, Lewis/Ludwig served as judge of an election in Rush Creek Township, Fairfield County, Ohio, extending his influence to civic matters. In 1806, he performed the marriage ceremony for Isaac Beery, first cousin to Anna, his wife.

In 1822, Lewis/Ludwig took a trip on horseback to Rockingham County, Virginia, and to York County, Pennsylvania, preaching at the different Baptist churches en route and visiting his old home and relatives. Rev. Edward Seitz Shumaker wrote: "With these sweet memories to cheer him, Lewis started on his homeward journey, still preaching as he went, but God had other plans for his servant, for in Washington, Pennsylvania, Lewis sickened, and in the land of strangers, perhaps alone with God—God took him to be with Him. We do not know the date of his death, neither do we know of his burial place, and it is quite probable that his grave is unmarked, as he slumbers in that strange land, awaiting the resurrection of the just."

The firstborn son of Lewis/Ludwig Welck von Gemmingen Seitz, the illegitimate son of a milkmaid and a German nobleman who became a Primitive Baptist preacher, and his Swiss Mennonite wife Anna Beery Seitz was John Seitz (1790-1874), and their eleventh child was their sixth son, Lewis Seitz (1802-1890). I am descended from both of these sons, so, it may be said, that I have a double dose of Von Gemmingen/Beery genes—from Gram, my maternal grandmother.

Lewis Seitz, the sixth son of Lewis Seitz and Anna Beery, who followed in his father's footsteps as a minister, married a Kagy, and that Lewis Seitz's granddaughter also married a Kagy. The firstborn son of Lewis Seitz and Anna Beery, John Seitz, did not marry a Kagy, but his daughter did; and that daughter's son, John W. Kagy, married Elder Lewis Seitz and Barbara Kagy's granddaughter, Hannah Siple. So, I fear that in the person of my grandmother, Harriet Kagy Zutavern, the von Gemmingen genes, not to mention the Kagy genes, were concentrated through complex intermarriages. The Siple family also shows up on both sides of these lines—so add a double dose of Siple genes into the mix. The fact of the matter is that these families lived in close proximity for a couple of centuries in Pennsylvania, Virginia, and Ohio, and many of them had probably lived in close proximity in Germany and Switzerland before arriving in this country.

What were the consequences of this much intermarriage between and among cousins? I can honestly say I don't know of any negative consequences at all—no more madness, drunkenness, stupidity, or deformity than other families. In fact, I would guess, quite a bit less, on average. These people were strong, capable, and hard-working; and they produced strong, capable, and hard-working children.

My grandmother, whose personality was the end point or epitome of the accumulated genes of so many of these folks, was a person of huge talent and ego. She could have ruled in any von Gemmingen castle, no doubt. Lesser mortals (all mortals) usually found some convenient orbit around her, for she always filled the center; and she was indominable. She was not always right, but she was always a force to reckon with, as my father found out, to his everlasting regret. Because I was a boy—my grandmother had had three girls herself and all of her male siblings had died in infancy or boyhood—and because I was the firstborn brown-eyed grandchild of the firstborn brown-eyed daughter (in a family of blue-eyed people except for herself), I lived a charmed existence, as far as she was concerned. I called her Gram, and she called me Joey; and she was as affectionate and sweet and attentive to me as she was cruel and merciless to my father. She took me on walks around the farm, baked me pies, and insisted, on visits when I was a child, that I sleep with her in her bed, which was an innocent excuse to cuddle with me all night long. Her husband, my grandfather, had died just before I was born. So, probably, she was lonely. But she made an excellent bed partner—I had no objections whatsoever. Growing up, I loved her without reservation—probably more than anyone else in the world except my mother and father.

Rev. John Seitz, the firstborn son of Lewis/Ludwig, came to Fairfield County, Ohio, with his parents in 1801, before Ohio was officially a state. In 1811, he married Miss Magdalena Spitler, a daughter of the Spitler family from the Shenandoah Valley of Virginia, whose family had followed Lewis Seitz, Sr., to Ohio. In 1822, John Seitz ventured in a northwesterly direction from Fairfield County into the Ohio wilderness, and when he found a suitable spot, he bought land, built a house, and named the township Bloom Township—not for the flowers, trees, and plants growing there, or the crops that might eventually bloom there, as is sometimes supposed—but in honor of the German hero Bloom. The following year he located his family permanently in Bloom Township, Seneca County. John Seitz was serving as County Commissioner when the first courthouse was built in Tiffin in 1834 and also filled the office of Justice of the Peace for about fifteen years. He died September 27, 1874, his wife having preceded him in 1862. The *History of Seneca County* says of them: "They were upright pioneers and helped develop the resources of Seneca County, and their names will long be revered by the citizens of Bloom Township."

My other Seitz forbearer, Elder Lewis Seitz, the eleventh child of Lewis/Ludwig and Anna Beery, was born October 21, 1802, in Fairfield Co., Ohio, and died in 1890. Lewis married Barbara Kagy and had fourteen children with her before she died September 27, 1848. Elder Lewis Seitz was baptized as an "Old School" or "Primitive Baptist" and became pastor of the Honey Creek Baptist Church in Bloom township around 1830 and was still in that office over fifty years later.

He began preaching at twenty-five years of age, and, according to *The History of Seneca County*, "has labored in the Lord's vineyard almost continuously ever since, and, though now in his 83rd year, yet preaches one hour or more at a stretch. He has traveled many miles through the dangers of a new country, and asked for no compensation for his time…. He moved to Bloom Township, this county, October 17, 1825, and here began life in the wilderness. The Indians, who were quite numerous here at that time, always found in him a warm friend."

Lewis also served as a trustee of the village of Bloomville for several years during the 1830s. In fact, from the 1830s through the 1880s, there was seldom a year during which at least one of my ancestral grandfathers or cousins—a Kagy, a Seitz, a Spitler, or a Geiger—was not elected to serve the village government.

Lewis Seitz' daughter Lydia was my great great grandmother.

Lewis Seitz' son John surely must have inherited some of the von Gemmingen genes because he became a prominent Ohio politician who served in the state legislature and was three times a candidate for Governor of Ohio. All three times he was defeated, although he received more votes each time he ran.

During the year 2000, my adventuresome daughter Lael Bellamy was planning a trip to Germany with her husband. When she heard about my work on the von Gemmingens, she searched the internet and found the ancestral castle near Neckarzimmern—Castle Hornberg—had been turned into a hotel. Lael booked it on her trip and spent several nights there, thus completing a cycle that began when a branch of those same von Gemmingens left Hornberg three centuries earlier.

The website has this to say about Castle Hornberg: "Castle Hornberg, an 11ᵗʰ-century knight's castle, stands proudly amid the vineyards high above the romantic valley of the River Neckar. For many centuries it was a fief of the Bishop of Speyer. In 1517, Hornberg was purchased by Goetz von Berlichingen and became his only residence. (Goetz von Berlichingen was later the subject of a play by Goethe.) He spent forty-five years of his eventful life here and died in 1562. His grandson sold the castle in 1612 to the Barons of Gemmingen, of whom the twelfth generation still owns it today. In 1953, a hotel and restaurant were opened in the former stables, maintaining all the authentic, unmistakable charm of Castle Hornberg and its romantic setting. This attractive contrast between past and present will not fail to delight you."

1. Johann Philipp von Gemmingen (1729–1766) + Dorothea Welck

2. Rev. Lewis Seitz, Sr. (1763–1822) + Anna Beery (1768–1831)

3. Elder Lewis Seitz (1802–1890) + Barbara Kagy (1807–1848)

4. Lydia Seitz (1826–1903) + Jacob Siple (1822–1881)

5. Hannah Siple (1850 –1913) + John W. Kaga (1841–1896)

6. Harriet Alvaretta Kaga (1892–1981) + Rolla Harrison Zutavern (1888–1941)

7. Beulah Pearl Zutavern (1918–1998) + Orin Ross Bellamy (1908–1974)

8. Joe David Bellamy (1941–)

1. Johann Philipp von Gemmingen (1729 –1766) + Dorothea Welck

2. Rev. Lewis Seitz, Sr. (1763–1822) + Anna Beery (1768–1831)

3. Rev. John Seitz (1790–1874) + Magdalena Spitler (1786–1862)

4. Anna Seitz (1818–1868) + Rudolph Kaga (1818–1866)

5. John W. Kaga (1841–1896) + Hannah Siple (1850–1913)

6. Harriet Alvaretta Kaga (1892–1981) + Rolla Harrison Zutavern (1888 –1941)

7. Beulah Pearl Zutavern (1918–1998) + Orin Ross Bellamy (1908–1974)

8. Joe David Bellamy (1941–)

John W. Kagy   Hannah Siple

17.

HANNAH SIPLE

My mother's mother's mother was named Hannah Siple, and of my grandmother's three daughters, my mother most resembled Hannah. After searching for years on the internet, I was finally able to locate a photograph of Hannah Siple as a young woman and also a photograph of John W. Kagy, whom she married in 1874 in Bloomville, Ohio. The photographs are probably wedding pictures, and they show a fine-featured, hopeful young woman with large eyes, wearing a lace collar and with a scarf knotted loosely around her neck, and a stalwart-looking young man with a red beard who, except for his high Victorian collar, resembles John Lennon. For reasons I can't adequately explain, Hannah is a woman whom I immediately want to hug. I suppose it's because she so closely resembles my mother, and because I know her terrible story.

Also while searching on the internet I was able to find a photograph of a handsome old gristmill in Bucks County, Pennsylvania, built in the 1700s by Hannah's immigrant ancestor, her great, great grandfather, George Heinrich Siple[5] (1711-1784). It is three stories high and, except for the updated roof treatment, constructed entirely of the original stone. The windows are boarded up, and the surrounding land is overgrown with scrub trees and underbrush, but this mill was built to last. A couple of hundred thousand dollars and some granite counter tops would put it in move-in condition.

---

[5] Variants of Siple are Seiple, Seibel, and Sebald, among others.

Hannah's ancestors immigrated from Hassloch, Germany, some time between 1736 and 1745. Hannah was the eldest daughter of Jacob Siple and Lydia Seitz Siple, and of the eleven children born in this Ohio family between 1850 and the end of

George Heinrich Siple's grist mill in Bucks County, Pennsylvania

the century, seven were still living in 1899: Hannah and her five sisters, Matilda, Jennie, May, Minerva, and Harriet, and her one brother, George (see photo). The one ancient relative I was able to find who had known these Siples said they were "a wonderful family, very musical and strong." Strong was not the first adjective that came to my mind when I thought of Hannah's story, but of course she *must* have been strong.

Hannah's husband John W. Kagy taught school up to the time of his marriage to Hannah, then engaged full-time in farming in Bloomville, Ohio. Though his ancestors had been Swiss Mennonites fleeing Germany in the 1700s for the paradise of Lancaster County, Pennsylvania, five generations later John is listed in the Keagey genealogy as being a Democrat in politics but making no profession of religion. Hannah was a member of the Primitive Baptist Society, probably the same church where her grandfather, Elder Lewis Seitz, was pastor. (By this period these descendants of the early Mennonite immigrants to Pennsylvania and Virginia transplanted to Seneca County who had any religious affiliation

Hannah is in the back row, second from the left.
May is immediately to Hannah's left.

seem to have become mostly "Primitive Baptists," which was perhaps another form of being a Mennonite.)

John and Hannah had ten children, and by the year 1895, they had lost only two of the ten, one at age 9, one at age 10—difficult, I'm sure, more difficult in some ways than losing children as infants, but probably not that unusual for the times. But in one terrible year, 1895-96, when Hannah was 44, she suddenly lost (1) her baby daughter Laura, (2) her 5-year-old daughter Bessie, (3) her 14-year-old son Budd, (4) her 19-year-old son Claude, and (5) her husband John. The genealogist Franklin Keagey comments: "In one year this dear mother buried her husband, two sons, and two daughters. She was obliged to sell a beautiful home to meet the expenses of the physicians' and undertakers' bills." The simple description of Hannah's grief that has been passed down to those of us in the family is this: "Hannah cried until she couldn't cry anymore." Yet her suffering was not over, for in 1899 she also lost her 11-year-old daughter Georgia.

Hannah, herself, lived for fourteen more years after that—until 1913, when she was 63 years old—and for all of those remaining years she lived in extremely humble circumstances in the village of

Bloomville and took in washing to make ends meet. Her younger sister, May, had married David Dellinger, a successful local dealer in livestock; and one day in the early twentieth century, May Dellinger, who was rich (see photo), was entertaining visitors from the East, whom she was showing around town. They happened to stroll down the street where Hannah lived, where Hannah happened to be out in the yard hanging up her laundry in the pale afternoon sunshine. May and her guests walked on past Hannah, who had paused for a moment to look at them, and May pretended she did not have the slightest idea who her sister Hannah was. Need I add that this was an offense my grandmother was still fuming about eighty years later.

Hannah's three remaining daughters—Maude, Belle, and my grandmother Harriet, the youngest—all lived to adulthood and into old age. These girls did not die until they were 81, 86, and 89, respectively. My grandmother Harriet (Gram) outlived them all. (The Franklin Keagey genealogy unaccountably lists my grandmother as having died at nine days old, perhaps confusing her with her sister Laura. But she certainly did not die at nine days old. She lived to be 89!)

May Siple Dellinger

My grandmother once took me to the cemetery where her parents and her many brothers and sisters are buried, Pleasant View Cemetery in Bloomville, Ohio. It is a quiet rural spot, very green, and it was somewhat overgrown that day, the tall grass nearly overlapping some of the markers. Most of the Siple stones were plain and faced the sky. I was quite surprised to learn that my grandmother had had so many brothers and sisters and so many who had died young. "What in the world did they all die from?" I asked.

"Most of them died of 'inflammation of the bowel,'" she said, "which they had no cure for in those days." Inflammation of the bowel is better known today as appendicitis. Most of them died of appendicitis![6]

Since my grandmother Harriet was the youngest—only three in 1895 when her father and four siblings died—she could scarcely remember them. She grew up in a family of women, a mother and three sisters, one of whom died when Gram was seven. After that, a mother and just two sisters, living in poverty and bereavement, probably wondering who would die next. Yet Hannah hung on valiantly until all her remaining daughters were grown. Her mother died when Gram was 21, and Gram married the prosperous young farmer Rolla Harrison Zutavern less than two years later.

I happen to have an 1892 copy of the "Rules and Regulations of the Pleasant View Cemetery Association," where Gram's Siple siblings and her mother and father are buried. It shows that John Seitz, former unsuccessful candidate for Governor of Ohio, was President of the Association, and a Patterson and two Spitlers were officers. Among the trustees were a Seitz, two Spitlers, and a Kagy, and the stock-holders included two Seitzes, nine Spitlers, a Kagy, a Patterson, and two Siples—all undoubtedly related to me. The "Rules and Regulations for the Government of the Members, Officers, and Lot Owners" are nearly sufficient for the running of a small country. Rules included the following: "Heavily laden teams with monuments must not enter the grounds in wet weather, and under no circumstances will vehicles be allowed to drive on or across a lot. . . . Horses and teams must not be left without being tied, or some suitable person in charge, and must not be fastened to any thing except the posts provided for that purpose . . . Discharging of firearms is strictly prohibited in the grounds. . . . No admission fee shall be charged, at any time, at the gate."

---

[6] Other diseases that might have been described as inflammation of the bowel are typhoid and salmonella poisoning, which seem somewhat more plausible.

Farmers

My father used to say that when he was a boy 90 percent of the people were farmers because it took that many farmers to feed everyone. But later on, when he became a man, only about 10 percent of U. S. citizens had to be farmers in order to feed themselves and the other 90 percent—because farming methods had improved so much during the twentieth century. I'm not certain how closely my father's statistics might agree with those of the U. S. Department of Agriculture, but he did have the gist of it right. Most Americans of the nineteenth century were, indeed, at least part-time farmers, even if they held other occupations; and the majority of them were full-time farmers. Go back two or three generations and the ancestors of most Americans were farmers, and, of course, all of the generations before that since the time before the discovery of agriculture when humans were primarily hunter-gatherers, a space of roughly 10,000 years.

One fact we can be sure about is that most of our ancestors from the most recent ten millennia were nothing but farmers. It would have been quite unusual if they had been anything but farmers. We *evolved* as farmers. That is, those traits that helped us succeed as farmers tended to predominate: our almost universal admiration, for example, for fields of waving grain and of any pregnant length of sod.

Golf and baseball developed into such obsessions in the twentieth century, I believe, partly because they speak to our nostalgia for farming, to our ancient desire to be out in a very green space swinging an implement all day long. My son Sam, who is a devoted golfer, thinks this is a ludicrous idea, but I think I am right about this. He grew up in a time and place where farmers were viewed as members of a backward class, and where golfers were presidents, sports heroes, and millionaires. So it is harder for him to see the connection. But Sam's deep ancestors were farmers too, as were some of his recent ones, and I believe it is his "farming genes" that attract him to the nearest golf course—like a bee to a flower.

BLUE EYES AND BROWN EYES

In my family, growing up, I was one of the few brown-eyed persons in an extended family of blue-eyed people. All the Bellamys were blue-eyed, and there were a lot of them. On my mother's side, she was brown-eyed and Gram was brown-eyed, but my mother's sisters were both blue-eyed, and there were no Zutavern men still living—so I did not know what color their eyes might have been. As it turns out, their eyes were blue too. I married a blue-eyed wife, and we had two blue-eyed children. At this moment, I am the only brown-eyed person in the family still living except for my dog.[7]

When you represent a minority of this sort, you can't help wondering about it from time to time. But I did not actually think about it very much until I began my genealogical obsession. *Where did these brown eyes come from?* Where did Gram get her brown eyes? From the few photographs I have, there is no doubt that Hannah Siple was brown-eyed, and most of her family members, in fact, also had brown eyes. Hannah's mother, Lydia Seitz (Welck/Von Gemmingen) also had brown eyes. (The trait seems to follow my maternal line all the way back.) In the photo of Hannah's husband, John Kagy, it's hard to tell. Whoever the brown eyes came from, they came from the Swiss/German side, a Siple, a Seitz, possibly a Kagy—or all three. But aren't Germans supposed to be blue-eyed?

Puzzled by this conundrum, I once asked a colleague, a German professor, who was also a native-born German—and very blue-eyed—how it could be that I might have inherited brown eyes from my German ancestors. She gave me a certain look and said: "You have to remember that the Romans occupied southern Germany for *five hundred years*. A lot of Germans are brown-eyed!"

---

[7] I wrote this before my brown-eyed daughter-in-law joined the family and before her two beautiful brown-eyed daughters were born.

"You mean I could have gotten brown eyes from the Romans?"

"Of course."

Aside from the uncomfortable realization that this meant that at least one of my ancestors might have slept with "the enemy" (maybe she didn't have any choice!), the conversation reminded me of a scene from the Sopranos where mob boss Tony Soprano is shaking down a Jewish motel manager who hasn't been making his required payments. Tony has the manager by the throat and is just about to hit him, and the guy says, "People like you have been beating up on the Jews since the time of the Romans, and look where the Jews are today! And where are the Romans?"

"You're lookin' at 'em!" says Tony. *You're lookin' at 'em!* Then he hits him.

So now when I look at myself in the mirror and ask where these brown eyes came from and wonder if these are Roman eyes looking back at me, I can sometimes hear Tony Soprano's immortal words in my head.

"Where are the Romans now?"

"You're lookin' at 'em!"

On the other hand, according to my mtDNA test, my mother is a descendant of Tara, one of the "Seven Daughters of Eve" who lived in Tuscany 17,000 years ago in the depths of the last Ice Age. If that is true, I could have gotten my brown eyes a lot further back than the Johnny-come-lately Romans.

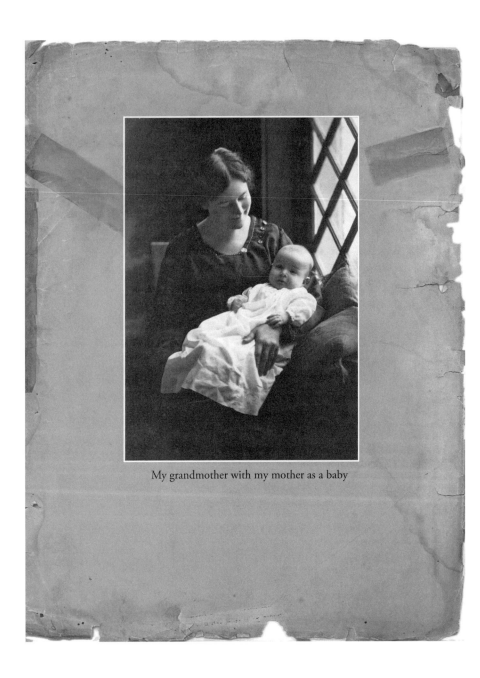

My grandmother with my mother as a baby

18.

THE HARD-LUCK KAGYS

My dear great grandmother Hannah Siple had the worst luck, but Gram's American Kagy line—and the families they married—seemed plagued by very bad luck almost as soon as they arrived on these shores in the early 1700s. At least two of Gram's ancestors settled in that part of Pennsylvania, just north of the Maryland line, in an area that became part of the disputed territory between the two states that led to Cresap's War (1729-1737), an ongoing border crisis that was not entirely settled until the drawing of the Mason-Dixon line in 1760. For several years Thomas Cresap and a group of vigilantes harassed Swiss and German settlers living along the Susquehanna—settlers who lived there under Pennsylvania land permits.

The first known Kagy in the New World, Hans Rudolph, arrived in 1715 and owned land in the Conestoga Settlement, which was in southeastern Pennsylvania just south of Lancaster. His wife, Rebecca Patterson Kagy, was the third daughter of James Patterson, my 7th great grandfather, a man who was extensively engaged in the Indian trade on the Potomac and had what is now called a ranch at the entrance to Conojohela Valley on the Susquehanna, which was smack dab in the middle of the disputed territory claimed by the authorities of both Pennsylvania and Maryland.

One day, entirely without warning or provocation, this madman Thomas Cresap appeared out of the Maryland wilderness and with several of his energetic followers built a blockhouse in the middle of one of James Patterson's pastures and claimed the land was Maryland territory and they were going to defend it to the death. They shot some of Patterson's horses and drove away the rest and further claimed all of Patterson's ranch in the name of Lord Baltimore. Cresap demanded that Patterson show a Maryland warrant or patent for the land, threatening an appeal to the King in his own behalf and that of Maryland. Patterson's defiant answer was, "Penn is our King!" And that was the beginning of Cresap's War.

The dispute waxed hot and heavy and led to bloodshed and years of skirmishes on Patterson's ranch and elsewhere along the disputed border. The father of Rebecca Patterson Kagy continued to be a partisan of the claims of the Penns—John, Thomas, and Richard—in this boundary dispute, as was Thomas Cresap of the claims of Lord Baltimore. The most intense fighting lasted from 1732 until 1736, when Cresap was seized and the Maryland intruders were overcome. Cresap was incorrigible to the last. When he was paraded through the streets of Philadelphia, one of his captors apparently asked him what he thought of this city, which he had never seen before. Cresap reportedly said he thought Philadelphia was the most beautiful city he had ever seen in Maryland.

When the established boundary line between the states was made July 4, 1760, by Charles Mason and Jeremiah Dixon, two English astronomers who were appointed to run the lines by the Penns and Lord Baltimore, the settlement gave not only Patterson's ranch and the nearby disputed territory, but considerably more land to Pennsylvania. However, James Patterson did not live to see the resolution of the conflict that probably hastened his end, for he dropped dead from a heart attack in 1735.

My 6th great grandfather, Nicholas Beery, was also involved as a victim of Cresap's War. Nicholas was arrested in 1736/37 and taken to Annapolis by Maryland authorities who accused him of illegal ownership of his own property. Pennsylvania colonial records reveal the details of hearings held in 1747/48 concerning this "Nicholas Pieri" and the unsuccessful attempt by a Capt. Higginbotham to evict Nicholas Beery on the basis of a Maryland land grant.

Nicholas Bieri (Beery) was a Swiss Mennonite who had arrived on the ship *Friendship* in Philadelphia on October 16, 1727, with a large group of Mennonites. He settled in York County shortly after his arrival and was granted a patent for 200 acres on October 11, 1736, on Codorus Creek. He patented more land in York County in 1742 and 1755.

This was a man who had escaped religious persecution as a boy in Switzerland by hiding in a cheese barrel. Nicholas and his parents were among those who were driven out of Berne during the period of severe persecution prior to 1711 and found refuge in the Palatinate in Germany, near Ibersheim.

When Nicholas immigrated to Pennsylvania, the *Friendship* was the last of five ships to arrive that year from Rotterdam, carrying 150 Swiss Mennonite families, who had, in the spring of that year, made the long journey down the Rhine to Holland. After leaving Holland, the *Friendship* met with adverse winds and required four months to make the voyage across the Atlantic. The hardships for those on board were so great that a fifth of the passengers died at sea. But Nicholas and his family survived the voyage.

Like virtually all of the Swiss Mennonites, Nicholas had become a farmer like his father and possessed the extraordinary industry and skill in agriculture for which the Swiss Mennonites were noted. Apparently undaunted by the legal difficulties of trying to establish ownership of his land, he persisted with his farming and he gave his wife many, many children.

Nicholas died intestate in York County, Pennsylvania, in October, 1762. It may be assumed that he had been a still vigorous man and died unexpectedly, because he had not made a will and he had been an unusually prosperous farmer. The inventory of his estate was appraised on November 2, 1762, at around 1300 pounds at a time when an estate of as little as 150 pounds has been called by historians a "splendid monument to the industry and economy" of pioneer Germans and an "eloquent witness to their superior skill." Magdalena (Bieri) Hunziker's bible states "27th Jul 1788, Barbara (a born Miller) [and Nicholas's widow] mother of Magdalena Hunsaker died in the 81st year and left 120 children, grandchildren, and great grandchildren."

The next stage of the hardships and bad luck of Gram's Kagy line occurred to another Rudolph Kagy. This Rudolph Kagy (1725-1793) settled in Pennsylvania and remained there until after the close of the Revolution.[8]

Though Kagy is a Swiss name and though Rudolph was said by at least one source to have come directly from Switzerland, a letter from Rudolph's grandson (John Kagy of Tiffin, Ohio, to his son, Dr. Isaac Kagy) indicated that both his grandparents arrived from Germany—which is evidence that they had been forced out of Switzerland, like so many others.

According to John Kagy's letter: They both arrived "from Germany and settled in Pennsylvania, where they had a good property, which grandfather sold and took the avails of it all in Continental money. He intended to move from Pennsylvania to Virginia to buy property at the latter place, but he delayed so long doing so that the money he had received for his Pennsylvania property became worthless, and so he became poor and dependent on manual labor to make a living. He however moved to Virginia and raised quite a large family. They lived in Shenandoah County on a small stream called Holeman's creek, where he undertook to raise a sawmill."

One day Rudolph and another man went out into the woods to prepare some timber for the mill. The man who was with Rudolph cut down a tree which fell against another tree and then bounced back and crashed down where Rudolph was standing, struck him in the head, and knocked him down. He was not instantly killed

---

[8] There is still an argument going on between and among Kagy researchers as to whether he is in the direct line from the Hans Rudoph whose wife's father was a victim of Cresap's War or whether he was a nephew or cousin. At any rate, this Rudolph was either already in Pennsylvania, the son of Hans Rudolph; or he was the Rudolph who arrived on October 27, 1764, aboard the ship *Hero*, from Rotterdam (Ralph Forster, captain) with 500 passengers aboard—194 of whom were adults, the remainder under 16 years of age.

but never regained consciousness, dying at midnight of the same day. Rudolph's granddaughter recalls that her mother remembered how her father looked when brought to his home. The sight of his mutilated, bleeding body was indelibly impressed upon her memory. He was buried in a nearby graveyard. At this time, they lived in a place called Boiling Spring, about three miles northwest of New Market, Shenandoah County, Virginia. The exact locality of his gravesite is not now known. His youngest daughter and child was born in 1793, three months after the death of her father.

Though Franklin Keagy says that in religious faith, both Rudolph Kagy and his wife were "Mennists," a letter from a son of Barbara Kagy Zirkle (one of Rudolph's daughters) to Franklin Keagy in 1890 states: "I recollect hearing my mother say that her father told her that he came from Switzerland; he was a Mennonite and brought his church letter with him. My mother always said, in speaking of the Shenandoah County Kageys, that they were cousins in Switzerland." In regard to the Continental money that Rudolph Kagy received for his property sold in Pennsylvania, Mr. Zirkle said: "My mother told me that they left Pennsylvania in the fall of the year and by spring the money became worthless. A handkerchief full of it was used to light the fire in cooking."

Of the four sons of Rudolph Kagy, one was accidentally shot and killed by his brother in a hunting accident. Of the remaining three sons of old Rudy—Christian, Rudolph, and Jacob—all left Virginia about the year 1818 or 1819 and settled in Ohio and, according to Franklin Keagy, "became pioneers in the upbuilding of that great State, and from whence their descendants have gone out into every State and Territory, and by their industry have added to the wealth of the country and have shaped and administered its laws, with honor to themselves and to the satisfaction of their fellow-citizens. In every walk and avocation of life is found some one of this worthy people, adorning their calling with credit and ability, exhibiting all the virtues that ennoble manhood and womanhood."

This third Rudolph, one of the three surviving sons of the

Rudolph killed by the falling tree, was the father of a fourth Rudolph who was Gram's grandfather on her father's side and her great grandfather on her mother's side.

Now it is probably worth trying to describe some of the tangled genealogy of Gram's tree. Gram's parents were John Washington Kagy and Hannah Siple, okay. Both of their mothers were Seitzes (i.e., Welck/von Gemmingens, that is). John Kagy's paternal grandmother was a Siple (in fact, a *Hannah* Siple). His wife Hannah Siple's maternal grandmother was a Kagy.

John's paternal grandparents were the *same people* as Hannah's maternal great grandparents. Two of Hannah's paternal great grandparents were the *same people* as two of John's paternal great grandparents. Two of John's maternal great grandparents were the same people as two of Hannah's *other* maternal great grandparents.

According to my FamilyTreeMaker software, John W. Kagy was his wife Hannah Siple's first cousin once removed, also her second cousin, as well as her husband; and my relationship to Hannah is as follows: I am her great grandson. I am also her second cousin twice removed, her second cousin three times removed, her second cousin four times removed, and also her husband's (my great grandfather's) first cousin four times removed, and her husband's (my great grandfather's) second cousin three times removed. No wonder I feel like hugging her!

1. John "Hanse" Rudolph Kagy (1690–) + Rebecca Patterson (1703–)

2. Rudolph Kagy (1740–1793 + Veronica Bachmann

3. Rudolph Kagy (1773–1829) + Hannah Siple (1780–1871)

4. Barbara Kagy (1807–1848) + Elder Lewis Seitz (1802–1890)

5. Lydia Seitz (1826 – 1903) + Jacob Siple (1822–1881)

6. Hannah Siple (1850–1913) + John W. Kagy (1841–1896)

7. Harriet Kagy (1892–1981) + Rolla Harrison Zutavern (1888–1941)

8. Beulah Pearl Zutavern (1918–1998) + Orin Ross Bellamy (1908–1974)

9. Joe David Bellamy (1941–)

❧ ❧

1. John "Hanse" Rudolph Kagy (1690–) + Rebecca Patterson (1703–)

2. Rudolph Kagy (1740–1793) + Veronica Bachmann

3. Rudolph Kagy (1773–1829) + Hannah Siple (1780–1871)

4. Rudolph Kagy (1818–1866) + Anna Seitz (1818–1868)

5. John W. Kagy (1841–1896) + Hannah Siple (1850–1913)

6. Harriet Kagy (1892–1981) + Rolla Harrison Zutavern (1888–1941)

7. Beulah Pearl Zutavern (1918–1998) + Orin Ross Bellamy (1908–1974)

8. Joe David Bellamy (1941–)

An early photograph of the farm in Bloomville. Paul Zutavern, far right,
Alveda Spalding Zutavern, far left.

19.

THE END OF THE FARM

It was 1967. I was twenty-five and knew I wanted to be a writer. I was just about to end up at the Iowa Writers Workshop and then climb up onto the treadmill of a teaching career that would last for over thirty years, but I didn't know that yet. I had a bright idea, an idea that seemed perfect to me.

On the farm, Gram had an apartment that was separated from the main part of the house, and no one was living there then. It was just one bedroom, a kitchen, a bath, and a living area. But you entered it through the old summer kitchen, and from those steps you could look out over the barns and the deep green lawn and the row of poplars and the wood house and the fields in all directions—fields thick with wheat and waving fronds of corn—and in all directions—as far as the eye could see—the land was ours. My idea was that I might live there in that little apartment with my young wife and baby and write my book. It would be an inexpensive place to live, as inexpensive as any we could find anywhere, and I knew I could do it. I was willing to bet on it.

My wife Connie was not enamored of the idea. To her it seemed unnecessary deprivation in an alien and uncivilized rural backwater. But we talked it over, and she was willing to go along with it if it meant that I could write my damned book there and get it over with.

So we planned a trip to Bloomville, one of many we made there; and my plan was to wait for just the right moment and then explain my radical idea to my grandmother and seek her permission. Actually, I thought she would love the idea. She loved babies, and we had a baby. She had always loved *me*. I thought she would like the idea of having a man on the farm, a man who was part of the family and had her interests in mind. I might be able to help her in ways that no one else could, and I was more than willing. I could only write so many hours a day, after all, and then I would be free to do anything; and there was a part of me that had always wanted to be on the farm—on *that* farm.

We made the trip, and the moment of truth arrived. We sat down in front of the big picture window, my grandmother and I, and I explained it all to her in some excruciating detail. The only way that you become a writer, I said, is that you write your book, and then, with luck, your book is good enough, and someone publishes it. "Oh, I see," she said. But she lacked all enthusiasm from the start. She did not say, "What if it's *not* good enough?" But I could tell she was thinking that. She did not know anything at all about writers, but she was thinking this was the most hare-brained idea she had ever heard. Maybe she was thinking that I was trying to retreat from the world and therefore needed a swift kick in the rear. Maybe it seemed part of the paranoid nightmare she had always entertained—that someone was going to wrest the farm from her grasp and she would be out on the street like her mother and sisters had been. Maybe my imperious wife frightened her.

"This is my chance," I said. "I need to do this now. It would mean everything to me. I would be eternally grateful."

It would not have cost her anything. The apartment was not being used, and she did not need the income. All she had to do was put up with us—but at a distance. Surely the grandmother I remembered would not turn me down when I came to her for help, even if I was no longer her little Joey but was now a grown man with a family of my own. But she did. She said no, and I thought her reasons were screwy: (1) She thought there might not be enough water from the well if more people were using it, so

"What will I do about my hair?" and (2) People in town would not know what to make of *my beard*!

This was in the late sixties when beards were a sign of the counter culture and were severely threatening to certain citizens. But the idea that my grandmother would reject me because of what *others might think* was very disillusioning. Ironically, with my well-clipped red beard, if I resembled anyone in the family it was her own father, John W. Kagy, who also had a red beard; and I imagine that every Kagy male in the last ten thousand years had had a red beard just like mine, only a lot bushier, though since Gram's father had died when she was only three-years-old, maybe she didn't remember it. Probably some of the Bellamys and Browns and Clarks and Whipples had had red beards too.

I'm sure there was a time when insulting a man's beard could get you killed, or at least, invited to take part in a duel. But I accepted her decision to cast me out. What else could I do? She had driven away every male who could have saved the farm, and now she was driving me away too, and I was the last chance. It seemed extremely selfish and short-sighted to me on her part, but it was her call. I don't know if I would have become a farmer, or a farmer who also wrote books. But I think I might have. I do know that I felt a powerful instinctive urge to stay there. The land spoke to me. It was in my blood. It had been in my blood for longer than it had been in hers.

The farm had been some part of my family for a hundred and fifty years. She had married into it. It was the only home place I had ever known. I had fond memories of slopping the pigs and milking the cows from when I was in the fourth and fifth grades, helping my father, and I had fond memories of gathering the eggs from when I could barely walk and carrying them to my grandmother who acted as if I had just performed a small miracle. I had fond memories of being a kind of celebrity guest, one who got to sleep with the madam of the house who cuddled with me all night long. It is a sad thing to admit—maybe it was my grandfather Rolla's genes within me, those genes that had fought to preserve the farm—but I had a hard time forgiving her. I did forgive her eventually—of course I did.

By the next time we visited the farm, I had long since forgiven her. We had a new son and a station wagon; and I was an assistant professor of English. I must have been under the spell of the first ripples of interest in family history too because I remember I brought along a tape recorder with the explicit intention of coaxing Gram into telling some of her stories for the record. I remember thinking: *She's always been a marvelous story-teller, and she isn't getting any younger.*

When the moment seemed right, I sat down with Gram in front of the big picture window again—which had a nice view of the corn fields beyond the yard—and said a few words in hopes of eliciting some reminiscences. My wife Connie sat down with us too, and Gram started in. I did not want to bring in the tape recorder at the beginning because I was afraid it might spook her or make her self-conscious, but as she started to talk I could see she was in fine form and not likely to have any problem at all. I wished then that I had the tape recorder, but I was so intent on listening to what she was saying—and so certain I would remember every word of it—that the need for the tape recorder seemed less important.

I did have the presence of mind to ask Connie if she would be willing to go out to the car to retrieve the tape recorder, but she was so intent on Gram's current story too that she didn't want to leave—for fear of missing a single word. The upshot of it was that, like the Ancient Mariner, Gram entertained us for the better part of an hour with stories that were so riveting that Connie and I both seemed locked in some sort of helpless catatonic embrace, and I missed an opportunity to record Gram's important recollections in her inimitable style and voice. In spite of my surety that I could not possibly forget it, I cannot remember a single word. What a loss! What an idiot I was!

If Gram had recognized it, she would have seen that the young man in front of her resembled her long dead husband and her long dead father. Perhaps she did not remember her father, and she probably remembered her husband Rolla as an older, clean-shaven man. But maybe she did recognize me, recognize with a certain despair that I had taken after the two most important men in her life, that I was her grandchild through and through and yet would be denied the inheritance intended for me. Maybe she saw her mistake and wondered what would become of me, but probably not. Probably, she was only thinking about the stories she was telling.

My Grandfather Rolla knew a thing or two about Harriet's irrational flights of fancy, and also the emotional injuries her poverty-stricken upbringing had caused her. At the same time, I think he considered himself the custodian of his family's legacy, and that legacy was primarily the land they had worked for 120 years at the time he made his will, for four generations. He knew the land (the farm) would always provide for those who took care of it. And so, in his will, Harriet was given a "life-lease" on the farm (after which it would pass on to his daughters), and I think he must have hoped that at least one of his daughters would find a man who wished to be a farmer or who was herself a farmer and who, therefore, would find a way to keep the land within the family. The point of the life-lease was that Harriet could not sell the farm. It was not hers to sell.

I have no doubt that he was right to have done this, though I think Gram was rankled by it. I have no doubt that Harriet would have sold the farm at the earliest opportunity, moved to Florida, bought a big house and a Cadillac, and squandered the human capital from four generations of hard-working Spaldings and Zutaverns without giving it a second thought.

Of course, my father could have been the man my Grandfather Rolla hoped would come along, and if Rolla had not died so young and had been present to help make the transition stick, I doubt my grandmother could have prevented it. Even I *could* have been the man my grandfather Rolla hoped would come along. He is *in* me, after all. He is me, in a sense, and I am him. I could have done it—I know that. Rolla would have been proud of what I might have accomplished.

But it didn't work out that way—my grandmother drove my father and me away. My mother's next youngest sister moved to Florida and never married, and the youngest married an engineer and moved to Pittsburgh. By the time of my grandmother's death, there was no one left to take over. So Rolla's daughters did what he feared Gram might do. They sold it all.

If I had wanted to be a farmer so badly, why didn't I step in at that point and buy the farm myself, you might ask. But it was too late by then. I was fifteen years into an academic career. I had young children to raise, and I couldn't have afforded it anyway. I argued against selling it—I thought it was an abominable idea. I flipped out completely and hung up on my mother and almost broke the telephone when she told me what they were going to do. I see now that part of my anger had to do with the fact that, for me, the farm was the only permanent home I had ever known; and the thought of losing everything I associated with that place was devastating.

The final irony (and a good thing, in this case) is that my mother and my aunts ended up selling the farm to a Kagy—of all people—not *because* he was a Kagy or a distant cousin but because he had the money to buy it. He was a young Kagy with young children, some of whom might eventually grow up to be farmers themselves. And the mother of this Kagy was the same girl I had had a secret crush on in the fifth grade and the one I am quite certain I would have married if I had remained in Bloomville after the fifth grade and had grown up there, as I so much wanted to do.

Just think of it—that lovely girl married a Kagy! She was a daughter of one of the local ministers. She seemed more serious and sensitive to me than the rest, and she was kind. That a Kagy ended up with the farm would have pleased my grandmother in spite of herself. Maybe, at last, the luck of these resilient, persistent Kagys, which had been so bad for so long, has turned for the better. If so, after three centuries of misery and hard work, they certainly deserve a break.

Samuel Dunham Spalding, Alveda's father, my gg grandfather

20.

The Plymouth Colony and Charlemagne

My 6th great grandmother in the Spalding line, Mercy Mary Adams, was comparatively easy to find, but when I got to my 5th, Abigail Brown, I was stumped. No one had walked this ground before me, or if they had, they had come up empty. Abigail must have been all the rage as a name for daughters during the middle eighteenth century in New England because, especially considering the sparse population of the time, there were Abigails everywhere; and of course there were Browns everywhere. There were Abigail Browns everywhere!

My branch of the Spaldings had left Massachusetts by the time of Thomas Spalding's marriage to Abigail Brown in 1742. They were living in Windham County, Connecticut, in a sparsely populated area near Canterbury they shared with some of the overflowing population from the Plymouth Colony to the northeast, who had been attracted to the region by the fur trade and other commerce in the fertile river valleys in eastern Connecticut.

I identified four couples in Canterbury, Windham County, Connecticut, or with connections to Windham County, that seemed likely prospects. Each husband was named Brown, and this man and his wife were the right ages to have been Abigail's parents. I wanted to know definitively: Which Abigail Brown married my Thomas Spalding in 1742? I'll number them here in the order of likelihood:

There was Abigail Brown, the daughter of Deacon Deliverance Brown and his wife Abigail Waldo. This Abigail Brown was born April 11, 1720, just about right for marrying Thomas Spalding in 1742. Also, this Deliverance Brown was the son of Eleazer Brown of Concord and Dinah Spalding, who was my Thomas Spalding's great aunt. Eleazer had come to Canterbury with Deliverance and the rest of the family early on, and Eleazer was the first Deacon of the Congregational Church in Canterbury; and these Browns had already married into the Spalding family! A hot prospect! Unfortunately for me, the records showed that this Abigail married Hezekiah Pellett.

There was Abigail Brown, the daughter of Eleazer Brown and Abigail Chandler. This Abigail Brown was born in 1717, also a good age for my purposes of identification. This Eleazer was also the son of the earlier Deacon Eleazer and the older brother of Deacon Deliverance plus he had a wife named Abigail, but unfortunately these folks stayed in the Concord area and never moved to Canterbury. Nevertheless, they did have obvious connections to Canterbury, and surely they visited their parents and siblings there; and surely the Browns of Canterbury visited their old haunts in Concord. So, clearly, a daughter of Eleazer Brown and Abigail Chandler who might have lived in Concord could easily have met a Brown who lived in Connecticut and eventually married him, and these Concord Browns did indeed have a daughter named Abigail! Upon further investigation, no record of a husband for this Abigail turned up, but a birth record did, which indicated that she was actually born Feb. 5, 1705, and she was *christened* in 1717. Would young Thomas Spalding have married a 37-year-old woman who continued to have children for the next twenty years? Not likely.

Then there was a Thomas Brown with a wife named Rachel Leavens. This Thomas Brown was also a son of Deacon Eleazer and a brother of both (1) and (2) above. He was a likely prospect for all the same reasons given earlier and he did live in Canterbury. The trouble with this couple was they seemed to have no daughter named Abigail, but they were so much in the right place at the right time with the correct surname that they couldn't be discounted. Could a daughter named Abigail have been born without a record establishing her existence, perhaps in the middle of a hard winter when the trek to the "courthouse" was five miles through an impassable wilderness of snowdrifts? Or perhaps this Abigail had been born just before these Browns reached Canterbury, CT. Her birth record was somewhere in Massachusetts but had been lost or she had actually been born in transit—so there was no particular place to register her birth. Or perhaps one of the comely daughters of Thomas and Rachel who was on the record in Canterbury had a middle name of Abigail. She was listed as Bridget or Rachel, but she had decided, by the time of her marriage to Thomas Spalding, to use her middle name of Abigail instead, thus confusing genealogists for all time.

Finally, there was Abigail Brown, the daughter of John Brown and Abigail Adams, who were married in Canterbury in 1721. Where this John Brown came from is anybody's guess. He and Abigail Adams had three children, Jabez, b. 1722, John, b. 1723 (died young), and Abigail, b. 1726, and then John Brown, the father, died. Since this Abigail Brown was born so late—she would have been only sixteen if she had been the one to marry Thomas Spalding in 1742—that fact made her seem a somewhat less likely candidate, all things considered. Unfortunately for me, the record showed that even this Abigail Brown was not the one. According to the Canterbury Historical Society, this Abigail married Stephen Backus in 1750, and my Abigail Brown Spalding, who started having Spalding children in 1743 was still having Spalding children as late as 1763; so she could not have married a Backus in 1750!

If none of these panned out, I was in deep trouble because it meant leaving Canterbury and trying to find an Abigail Brown in some other vicinity, and that meant encountering about twenty other known Abigail Browns in an area from Ipswich, Massachusetts, to Stonington, Connecticut, to Providence, Rhode Island, who were all about the right age.

At some point I started corresponding with a friendly, smart, and helpful woman named Isabel Weigold who was the town historian in Willington, Connecticut, but who seemed to know a great deal about the Windham County area and who lived near there. Isabel was supplementing her social security income by providing research services for avid amateur genealogists like me, and she made trips for me both to the Connecticut State Library and to the town halls and courthouses in Windham. From long practice, Isabel could actually read the ancient faded script from courthouse order books and translate it into modern English. So when she provided me with documents, I would regularly receive both a Xerox of the original, which usually resembled an unreadable passage from some Egyptian tomb, plus Isabel's neatly typed transcription, for which I was very grateful.

Isabel was also personally acquainted with the other town historians in Connecticut, so she was able to elicit a civil response from them when she sent inquiries. Elizabeth Fairbrother, the town historian for the Canterbury Historical Society (where my Browns had lived), for instance, whom I was certain was sitting on valuable research, readily and promptly answered Isabel's questions but would not correspond with me. (Perhaps there is some status hierarchy I am unaware of in Connecticut. Historians only correspond with other historians, not with the genealogical rabble, especially when they are from out of state—never mind that their ancestors founded the village where the historian or archivist is currently a resident and an employee.)

Isabel had the additional quality that she seemed to be as deeply excited about finding answers to the mysteries I described to her as I was. Isabel was the Patricia Cornwell of town historians and a wonderful person, but she did make one small mistake. On one of the many documents she translated for me, a document from the Canterbury land records, she mislabeled the contents. She typed: "Transcription of Deed—Jabez Brown sold to Thomas Spaulding and Abigail (his wife), vol. 5, pg. 8, dated February

24, 1743." Like all the documents that Isabel prepared for me, I had skimmed this one over several times without seeing anything worthy of further thought—and without realizing the mistake in its description.

Then one day, with great weariness, after literally a couple of years of bludgeoning this problem to death, I got out all the documents and notes and started plodding through them slowly one more time. The mislabeled document in question was indeed the record of a land transaction, but it wasn't between Jabez Brown and the Spaldings. It was a transaction wherein Thomas Spalding and his wife Abigail *together with* Jabez Brown sold land to two other people. For 308 pounds, they were selling 120 acres of land in Canterbury, all that land *"**formerly belonging to John Brown of Canterbury, deceased!"***

Suddenly I had to ask myself: why would Thomas Spalding, who was not on record as having purchased any land up to that time, be involved in such a transaction at all unless he were the husband of the Abigail Brown who was the daughter of the departed John Brown together with her brother Jabez who had just turned 21? Abigail was still underage in 1743 (still only 17), and so her husband Thomas, who was of age, acted in her behalf for her portion of the land. There was no other explanation for such a record. Bingo! I found her, and I found proof that she was the wife of Thomas Spalding!

Abigail Brown (#4), the daughter of John Brown of Canterbury, did not marry Stephen Backus in 1750—the Canterbury Historical Society had it completely wrong. She married Thomas Spalding in 1742. Yes, she was young. But, after all, she was fatherless. She was my 5th great grandmother. Which Abigail Brown did marry Stephen Backus in 1750? I have no idea, but I do know there is a super-abundance of candidates. I wish Backus researchers a lot of luck.

I would not wish to suggest that any Backus researcher would leap to a false conclusion for dubious reasons, especially since I have Backuses in my family as well (on my father's side). For all

I know, I could be related to this Stephen Backus myself,[9] even if my Abigail Brown was not. But it could be that some earlier Backus researcher was tempted to claim my Abigail Brown for other reasons than the obvious.

Abigail Brown's mother, Abigail Adams, I was to learn, has a pedigree that some people would kill for. She is a direct descendant of John Adams of the Plymouth Colony, who some say was a brother to Henry Adams of Braintree. This John Adams did not arrive on the *Mayflower*, but he arrived in 1621 on the *Fortune*. He was a pilgrim, a very early pilgrim, if not quite a *Mayflower* pilgrim; and there are people, I've discovered, who very much wish to be descended from a pilgrim, any kind of Plymouth Rock pilgrim. Why this is so, I'm not exactly sure. But I think it's because they want to be able to say: "My family goes all the way back to the Pilgrims!" But everybody's family goes back to some pilgrim or other, whether Plymouth Rock or some other kind, and everyone who is alive today has ancestors who go back much farther than the Pilgrims, who go back all the way to the beginning. Everyone!

According to one LDS source,[10] John Adams' wife's mother was Mary Magdalene Winslow, sister of Edward Winslow, Governor of the Massachusetts Bay Colony, and this Winslow line hits a vein at the LDS site that taxes their server and my printer. The line goes back so far, through so many Magna Carta barons, princes and countesses, De Berkeleys and De Harcourts, De Percys and De Nevilles and Plantaganents, all the way to Fergusa, Queen of Scotland (b. 755 A.D.), and, of course, Charlemagne, Emperor of

---

[9] Sure enough—Stephen Backus' grandmother was the sister of my 9th great grandmother, Marah Spencer. Therefore, he is my second cousin, nine times removed.

[10] The most authoritative sources seem to disagree on the lineage of this Ellen Newton. She remains something of a mystery woman, though we do know she was John Adams' wife, and later, after Adams died, the wife of Kenelm Winslow, who was a brother of Edward Winslow, and possibly a cousin of Ellen Newton's.

the Holy Roman Empire—that I stopped printing in exhaustion. I enjoy hitting these LDS bonanzas, but when the dates show up earlier than 1066, I start to feel I am reading an elaborate fiction. Can't help myself.

Just as it is quite common to be descended from English royalty (and who would *want* to be?), apparently it is quite common to be a descendant of Charlemagne, Emperor of the Holy Roman Empire—nothing to get excited about. This is partly due to the fact that Charlemagne lived so long ago that his descendants have had a chance to expand exponentially. But I think it's pretty obvious that one of the problems with the human race may be that so many of us are descended from Charlemagne.

Just about everybody seems to think he *ought to be* Emperor of the Holy Roman Empire (or its equivalent), and if he isn't, somebody's going to hear about it or somebody's going to pay or somebody's hatched a conspiracy to prevent it. Why not just accept the fact that most of us are also descended from rascals and paupers and renegades and the well-meaning and the wrong-headed. We are all just about equal in that regard as well. Why not just calm down and try to go about our business in a more humble manner.

Sturgis Library - home of the Rev. John Lothrop in 1644.

Hon. William Sturgis was born in this house.

Constructed in 1644 for the Reverend John Lothrop, founder of Barnstable, this house forms the original part of the Sturgis Library in Barnstable, Massachusetts, the oldest Library building in the United States.

21.

THE SPANISH ARMADA AND
REV. JOHN LOTHROP

Then there is John Adams' son James, who was married to a woman named Frances Vassall, my 8th great grandmother, and the Vassalls were French! Or had been. If a Frenchman and his descendants in England marry English women for 500 years, are his descendants English or French? English with a French name, I think. John Vassall, the earliest member of this family for whom we have any definite information, was an alderman of London, and in 1588 fitted out at his own expense and commanded two warships—*The Samuel* and *The Little Toby*, named for his sons—with which he joined the royal navy to oppose the Spanish Armada.

For this assistance, he was awarded a Grant of Arms by Queen Elizabeth, which have been used by his family to the present time instead of those of his French ancestors. He was the descendant of an ancient French family, traced back to the eleventh century, of the house of Du Vassall, Barons de Guerden, in Querci, Perigord. He was sent by his father from Rinant by Cany (Caen) in Normandy into England on account of the dissensions then prevailing in Normandy. He was of Ratcliffe, Stepney, and East-wood, County Essex, and was a vestryman of Stepney. He was also a member of the Virginia Company, which made the settlement at Jamestown in 1607. The records of the parish church of St. Dunstan's state he died "of the plague." He had two sons, Samuel and William.

Samuel Vassall, whose name had been engraved on the hull
of his father's ship in 1588, was one of the largest ship owners
of his day and one of the original patentees of lands in Massachusetts in 1628 and an officer in the company. He was builder
and owner of a ship called *The Mayflower*. He was an alderman
of London, and M.P. in 1639-40; took the covenant in 1643; in
1646 was appointed Commissioner for the kingdom of England
for the conservation of peace with Scotland. His monument
in King's Chapel, Boston, New England, erected by Florentius
Vassall in 1766, sets forth that he was "a steady and undaunted
asserter of the liberties of England in 1628; he was the first who
boldly refused to submit to the tax of tonnage and poundage,
an unconstitutional claim of the crown arbitrarily imposed, for
which (to the ruin of his family) his goods were seized and his
person imprisoned by the star chamber court."

William Vassall, my 9th great grandfather, was the first of his
name who came to the colonies, as Assistant in the Massachusetts
Bay Company, and one of the original patentees of New England
lands. At a formal meeting of the Governor and company held
Oct. 15, 1629, he was one of the group appointed "to go over,"
and in the next year he arrived in the New World with John
Winthrop. Having found the place to his liking, he returned to
England and, in 1635 on board the *Blessing*, returned to New
England with his wife, Anna King Vassall, and their six children
(which included my 8th great grandmother Frances Vassall).

William was a man of considerable fortune and of some importance both in England and in the Massachusetts Bay Colony.
A beautiful tract of land on the river in Scituate, in Plymouth
County, was granted to him, by far the largest tract allotted to any
one settler. It contained more than 150 acres, and Vassall began
at once to build his plantation, which he called "West Newland."
The house he began in 1635 was built upon the beautiful slope of
uplands, commanding a spectacular view of the rising sun across
fern meadows, and it was named "Belle House."

A strange coincidence was that William Vassall, my mother's
8th great grandfather, then became a member of a church, whose

minister, Rev. John Lothrop, was my father's 8th great grandfather! In addition, my mother was a descendant of Deacon John Dunham of the Plymouth Colony, and Rev. Lothrop left a diary of his activities which included this notation: "Buryed at Barnstable. Patience, wife of Henry Cobb buryed Mary 4, 1648, the first that was buryed at our new burying place by the meeting house."

The daughter of Henry and Patience Hurst Cobb married Jonathan Dunham in my mother's line. So Rev. Lothrop actually was responsible for burying another of my mother's eighth great grandmothers, Patience Hurst Cobb. Amazed at this coincidence, I did a Google search for Rev. John Lothrop and discovered a cemetery that showed the names and digital photos of some of the grave markers in what is now called Lothrop's Hill Cemetery in Barnstable, Massachusetts.

The Rev. John Lothrop, my father's ancestor, was buried there himself in 1653, and his grave marker is adjacent to that of Henry Cobb, my mother's direct ancestor and Patience Hurst's husband! To think that my parents' ancestors not only knew one another 350 years ago but helped bury one another and are themselves buried next to one another frankly makes my hair stand on end.

The Rev. John Lothrop, my 9th great grandfather, had a life not unlike that of Rev. Peter Bulkeley except that, following receipt of his bachelor's and master's degrees from Queens College, Cambridge, and a successful pastorate in Kent and later London, he was imprisoned by Archbishop Laud's orders.

Perhaps because of his greater proximity to authorities in London, he had to spend two years in Newgate prison for crimes no more serious than Bulkeley's and any number of other Puritan ministers. While he was in prison, his wife died and left his seven children without any parent at home. Some members of Lothrop's congregation dressed the children in their Sunday best and marched them in front of Archbishop Laud and demanded to know who was to take care of them.

Finally Lothrop's petition for freedom was granted provided he agreed to go into foreign exile and gave bond and his word that he would not be present at any private gatherings in England. Laud did not want him to stir up the faithful. Rev. Lothrop sailed in 1634 and after five years in the Plymouth Colony at Scituate, he left there with a number of his followers and founded Barnstable, Massachusetts, in 1639. His grave marker in Barnstable states: "He was a gentle, kindly man and beloved by all who knew him." They might have added: "…except Archbishop Laud."

By all accounts, my 9th great grandfather Vassall, my mother's ancestor, and my 9th great grandfather Lothrop, my father's ancestor, began and remained on friendly terms as minister and parishioner. But when the Rev. Charles Chauncey was settled as Rev. Lothrop's successor in 1641 (following the point when Lothrop left to found Barnstable) Vassall soon found himself in great disfavor with his new pastor who would endure no opposition to views that he felt his talents and learning should make acceptable to all members of his new flock without too much questioning on their part.

Vassall's powers of persuasive argument may have been quite as much in his disfavor as the ideas that he entertained, for Vassall was not in sympathy with the rigid attitudes of the Massachusetts Bay and Plymouth governments towards persons who differed from the received opinions in politics and religion. In particular, Vassall argued for greater charity toward the Quakers. Also, he was quite the equal of his new pastor in religious argument and drew to his opinions many other church members as well as a number of new settlers who were taking up lands upon the river. In consequence of these religious differences within the church, the "Second Church of Christ" in Scituate was formed in Vassall's house on February 2, 1642.[11]

Also in 1642 Vassall was chosen one of a Council of War, in order to counter aggressions threatened by the Narragansetts, and in 1643 his name appears in the militia roll. William Vassall had much to do with public affairs in Scituate. The earliest records

---

[11] Another source says this was 1644-45.

are in his beautiful handwriting in the days before a town clerk was appointed. He held no office in the colonial government, however, perhaps by his disinclination, but more likely because his opinions, both religious and social, differed so greatly from those of the reigning elite. In this regard, Deane, the Scituate historian, says, "It is worthy of remark that most of the principles held by such men as Cudworth, Hatherly, Vassall, and Roger Williams, for which they suffered the persecutions of the early Colonial Governments, were such principles of civil and religious liberty as are now recognized to be the truest and best." Winthrop said of him: "Mr. Vassall [was] a man never at rest, but when he was in the fire of contention." Hutchinson said he was a man of pleasant and affable manners, but always in opposition to government, both in Massachusetts and Plymouth.

Vassall's argumentative disposition kept him in trouble for the next few years. He espoused the cause of the people of Hingham in their protest against a decision of the court relative to their choice of a captain of the town militia, and in 1646 he was chosen as an emissary to England in aid of a petition for the redress of wrongs within the government. He met with no success in this mission, and finding himself out of sympathy with colonial leaders, he joined his brother Samuel in Barbados in 1648, where the Vassalls eventually made large fortunes. He died in the parish of St. Michael's, Barbados, in 1655, leaving a will in which his son, Capt. John Vassall, was named executor.

In the will he mentions his daughter Frances, the wife of James Adams, who had presumably stayed behind in Massachusetts along with other members of his extended family. James Adams and Frances Vassall had at least six children, and their son Richard Adams was the father of the Abigail Adams who married my John Brown and the grandfather of my elusive 5th great grandmother Abigail Brown. Yes, he was.

1. John Vassall (1544–1625) + Anne Russell (1556–1593)

2. William Vassall (1592–1655) + Anna King (1594–1670)

3. Frances Vassall (1623–1670) + James Adams (1630–1652/53)

4. Richard Adams (1651–1728) + Rebecca Davis (1661–)

5. Abigail Adams (1700–)+ John Brown (1700–)

6. Abigail Brown (1717–) + Thomas Spalding (1719–)

7. William Spalding (1754–1829) + Mary Dunham (1759–1836)

8. Thomas Spalding (1783–1850) + Elizabeth Ayers (1789–1852)

9. Samuel Dunham Spalding (1814–1881) + Mary-Ann Traill(1823–1864)

10. Alveda Spalding (1864–1932) + Paul Washington Zutavern (1859–1929)

11. Rolla Harrison Zutavern (1888–1941)
+ Harriet Alvaretta Kaga (1892–1981)

12. Beulah Pearl Zutavern (1918–1998) + Orin Ross Bellamy (1908–1974)

13. Joe David Bellamy (1941–)

1. John Adams (1600–1633) + Ellen Newton (–1681)

2. James Adams (1630–1652/53) + Frances Vassell (1623–1670)

3. Richard Adams (1651–1728) + Rebecca Davis 1661 -

4. Abigail Adams (1700–) + John Brown (1700–)

5. Abigail Brown (1717–) + Thomas Spalding (1719–)

6. William Spalding (1754–1829) + Mary Dunham (1759–1836)

7. Thomas Spalding (1783–1850) + Elizabeth Ayers (1789–1852)

8. Samuel-Dunham Spalding (1814–1881) + Mary-Ann Traill (1823–1864)

9. Alveda Spalding (1864–1932) + Paul Washington Zutavern (1859–1929)

10. Rolla Harrison Zutavern (1888–1941) +
Harriet Alvaretta Kaga (1892–1981)

11. Beulah Pearl Zutavern (1918–1998) + Orin Ross Bellamy (1908–1974)

12. Joe David Bellamy (1941–)

Finding my Father's Ancestors

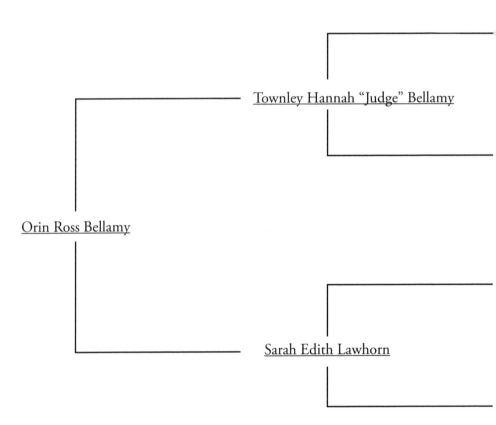

Orin Ross Bellamy

Townley Hannah "Judge" Bellamy

Sarah Edith Lawhorn

Berry Stone Bellamy

Townley Hannah "Tom" Bellamy

Sally Jane Miller

Elizabeth Jarvis

John Jarvis

Elizabeth Baldridge

Rev. John Brown Lawhorn

?

Sarah Lawhorn

Alice Whipple Clark

Benjamin Whipple Clark

Marietta Broadhurst

Rev. John Brown Lawhorn

22.

Be Fruitful and Multiply

My father's mother's father, John Brown Lawhorn, was a fire and brimstone preacher in Eastern Kentucky. It was said that on a Sunday morning his powerful voice could be heard beseeching his followers from a mile away. He was quite an old man when my father's mother was born, and she was his youngest child; so even though he lived to be 89, Rev. John Lawhorn died well before my father was born. Like me, my father never met his maternal grandfather, a loss I'm sure he felt—because, in the 1960s, he made a pilgrimage to Olive Hill, Kentucky, to look for evidence of his lost grandfather. What he found was the church his grandfather had founded, the Bethel Christian Church, and the unmarked grave of his grandfather in the church cemetery. My father left a check with the cousin who showed him the grave, and they agreed that she would use the money to buy a gravestone for John B. However, the check was never cashed, and later descendants have searched for the gravesite there without finding it. Apparently no one is still alive who remembers exactly where the gravesite is located.

Inside the church my father also found an item of considerable interest. It was a painting of the Rev. John Brown Lawhorn himself, still hanging there. My father, who had never seen a likeness of his grandfather before, carried the painting out into the sunshine and took a snapshot of it, and then he carried it back inside the church and hung it carefully on the wall. It showed a tall, well-dressed man with a high forehead, a stern expression, and a fiery look in his eyes. He is clutching a Bible with both hands. One of my cousins-on-the-internet reports that this painting has recently been stolen from the church, but I do still have my father's snapshot of it, for which I am grateful. Otherwise, I would have no idea of what my great grandfather looked like.

When I started to search for the ancestry of John Brown Lawhorn, I ran into trouble. No one seemed to have been down that road before, though several of my internet cousins were then on the case. One of them had settled upon a George W. Lawhorn as John B's father. George seemed the only candidate, and my cousin was certain of it. However, this George W. Lawhorn had been born in 1793, and I knew from family Bible records that John B. Lawhorn had been born in 1803. Even in 1803, ten-year-old boys were not often fathers. However, the cousin in question stubbornly resisted accepting this fact. Another peculiarity from the record was that John B. Lawhorn's mother's maiden name was also Lawhorn!

Then someone sent me some records from Floyd County, Kentucky. Sally Lawhorn, John's mother, married a man named John Iliff in August, 1811. The next record stated: "Lawhorn, John: August, 1813, base born child bound out to Thomas C. Brown, carpenter." John Brown Lawhorn was illegitimate, and this was the real reason my internet cousin was so determined to prove that John B. had a father named George Lawhorn!

So the truth is that my great grandfather, the Rev. John Brown Lawhorn, was born out of wedlock—more of a disgrace in those days than it would be now perhaps—and yet Rev. Lawhorn himself seems to have been a man of surpassing spiritual and worldly accomplishments. He founded a church, which is still in business; built it with his own hands by sawing the logs with the help of his eldest son, the story goes. His painted likeness was still hanging on a wall there over a hundred years after the church's founding until taken recently by thieves, though the old log church has been replaced by a more modern frame structure. Though his parents, Sarah Lawhorn and his unknown father, were unwed when he was born, John Lawhorn spent his long life marrying other people. The records of counties in northeastern Kentucky reveal hundreds of records of the couples he united.

Having perhaps inherited his father's wayward sexual energies, John found a way to channel them, and believing quite literally the Biblical counsel to "be fruitful and mutiply," he produced an enormous family—twenty-six children who lived to adulthood, nine others who died in infancy or childhood—thirty-five in all. With his first wife, he had nine children; and then she died. With his second wife, he had eleven children; and then she died. With his third wife, he had six children and several others who died; and this wife, who was much, much younger than he was, outlived him, but not by much. His very last child of his very last wife, was my paternal grandmother. She was number twenty-six. If the Reverend John Brown Lawhorn had been a less determined man and had been satisfied with only twenty-five children, my grandmother would never have been born, and I would not be here to tell about it. For reasons unknown, Sarah Lawhorn had no other children than John B. Therefore, she ended up with one son and twenty-six grandchildren—which must be one of the greatest returns on an accidental investment ever made.

I do not think we can blame John for an error his father made. I do not blame him, though I would dearly love to know who his father was, the man who impregnated the seventeen-year-old Sarah Lawhorn and then skipped town, an itinerant preacher perhaps, raving about fire and brimstone and the certainty of Judgment Day and then seducing the lovely Sarah after the faithful had departed for their homes; or, whoever he was, perhaps because he was already a man of prominence married to someone else, he simply did not own up to his transgression; and maybe the innocent Sarah, who was in love, protected him by her silence.

At the time of her romance with John's mysterious father, Sarah Lawhorn lived in Virginia on a farm that was, literally, next door to that of Thomas Jefferson, and in 1803, the year of John's birth, Thomas Jefferson was President of the United States. Could John Lawhorn have been an illegitimate son of Thomas Jefferson? It is possible. If so, he would not have been the only one.

Another candidate was the Mr. Brown who took over the apprenticeship of the young John Lawhorn when John was "bound out" at the age of nine or ten. In those days, this is sometimes the way it was done when an illegitimacy was discovered, and this Brown lived next door to Sarah and John Iliff, the man she eventually married, in a town in Floyd County, Kentucky. This Brown was Mr. Thomas C. Brown, who was a carpenter and a Justice of the Peace and the owner of a ferryboat business on the Ohio River. Under his tutelage, John trained to be a carpenter…, and probably watched attentively as Mr. Brown performed the civil ceremony of matrimony, over and over. Whether or not Thomas Brown was John's actual father, at the very least, John must have felt a certain gratitude and filial affection for Mr. Brown because, somehow or other, Brown became his middle name.

And the Rev. Lawhorn was not above changing his name. Late in life, married to his third wife, Alice Whipple Clark, he changed his name from Lawhorn to Lawhun. Was this an effort to keep track of all his different children by giving the new batch a slightly different name? Or perhaps the idea of "horn" in his name had been disparaged by someone as a sign of the devil or a sign of always wanting to "horn in." He would prefer to be seen as a "hun" rather than someone bearing a horn? Or perhaps it was simply a late effort to conceal his illegitimacy. Who knows? But my elderly aunt did inform me in no uncertain terms that her mother's maiden name was "Lawhun" not "Lawhorn," as if she had gotten these instructions from a very authoritative source, probably the old reverend himself.

Some researchers believe that the ancient name for Lawhorn is from the city of Laugharne, Carmarthenshire, south Wales, where the ruins of Laugharne Castle may be seen. The first known reference to this Norman castle is in 1189 when, after the death of King Henry II, it was seized by the Lord Rhys, prince of Deheubarth. But this connection is speculation at best, speculation and a desire for some picturesque ruins, I think; and these ruins are very ancient and ghostly.

The earliest Lawhorns arrived in North America in the late 1600s and early 1700s and made their way steadily across the virgin wilderness of what is now Virginia, and they seem to have been near neighbors of the Bellamys for at least a century before the two families came together in Kentucky. The early Lawhorn records from Goochland and Fluvanna counties in Virginia reveal the names of Woodson, Napier, Cary, Mayo, and Jefferson, names that are also part of the Bellamy record. Whether the Lawhorns knew the Bellamys in Virginia in the very earliest days is impossible to ascertain, but it seems likely they at least knew *of* them; and they may have intermarried sooner than we know, since so many of the maiden names of women from these early Virginia marriages are lost to us.

When the Reverend John Brown Lawhorn married Alice Whipple Clark in Clarksburg, Lewis County, Kentucky, in December of 1863, he was sixty and she was seventeen. (John lied about his age and said he was only fifty-four!) I have thought about this union for a long time: Why a 60-year-old man would marry a 17-year-old woman, and why she would marry him. Perhaps the former is somewhat easier to understand than the latter. John was a very much older man, a widower with twenty children who was old enough to be her grandfather, but he was also a landowner, a charismatic minister with his own church, and a respected member of the community. Perhaps she admired his eloquence in and out of the pulpit, his certainty about divine matters, his social standing. I know this much about John B. Lawhorn. He loved and cared for women more than most other men, he was probably looking for a wife, and he was one of the great breeders.

My great grandmother Alice was the daughter of Benjamin Whipple Clark and Marietta Broadhurst. Her father Benjamin was a steamboat engineer on the Ohio River, and at the time of the Clark family migration to Lewis County, where they were to meet John B. Lawhorn, they seem to have been in transit between Athens County, Ohio, where Alice was born in 1846 (according to her marriage record), and on their way to a homesteading life in Kansas, where Benjamin and Marietta would spend the rest of their days, living at least part of that time in a sod house. It was the middle of the Civil War, and there was a cholera epidemic raging along the river. Perhaps the Clarks were in a hurry to escape the war and the sickness and relished the idea of wide open spaces and waving fields of grain, but perhaps Alice was not so ready to stake her young life on an unknown future in the desolate West— especially not after she met the tall and dignified Rev. Lawhorn, who made her feel safe and grown up and who listened to her so attentively and made her feel womanly at the same time. Once Alice married and her parents left on their journey westward, it is unlikely that she ever saw them again.

I do not mean to imply for an instant that Alice was a gold-digger or an opportunist, though that thought did pass through my mind as a possibility before I learned of her ancestry. It turns out that this brave little 17-year-old girl is one of the bright gems of my gene pool, one of the prime movers, so I must treat her with all the respect she deserves. Alice is the one, I believe, who transformed the Lawhorns and Bellamys into a very different sort of family, just as John Lawhorn's unknown father may have helped to do as well.

The result was the first generation of Bellamys in the New World who were now at least part-time tobacco farmers! That was my father's generation, and it produced among my father's brothers: a Julliard-educated opera singer, a young man gassed in the trenches during WWI and given six months to live who became a millionaire and built the Denver Library, and a surgeon who passed up the opportunity of a posh practice to open an emergency hospital in Cincinnati's Black ghetto and whose son Richard Bellamy became a legendary art dealer in New York and is often credited with changing the course of twentieth century American painting.

Mary Olive Clark, the closest likeness I could find to Alice

23.

NEW ENGLAND ANCESTORS OF LOVELY ALICE CLARK

For a long time I did not even bother to search for Alice Whipple Clark's ancestors. It seemed obvious that with a name like Clark such a quest would be a waste of time. Clark must be one of the most common English names in the United States, only slightly less plentiful than Smith, Jones, or Brown, I reasoned. How could I ever expect to find the right Clarks? What I did not know at the time was that the Clarks, and the Whipples as well, came from New England, and New England genealogy is entirely different from Virginia genealogy.

In Virginia, the records are well-preserved but sporadic. The British burned courthouses in Virginia during the Revolutionary War, and the Union Army burned courthouses in Virginia during the Civil War. So there are some counties—known as "burned counties"—that simply have no records at all prior to the Civil War. If your ancestors happened to live in a burned county before 1865, lots of luck. You're going to need it.

In New England, on the other hand, not only do the records go back a long, long way, but a great many more of them are preserved. Not only that, but it seems that battalions of very keen genealogists have already been at work in New England, laboring earnestly to protect records and to construct and substantiate the ancestral trees of the founders.

The New England Historic and Genealogical Society in Boston has databases and records and resources that Virginians would die for. It is certainly one of the preeminent genealogical organizations in the United States. At present they are in the midst of an heroic effort to compile, evaluate, and publish a definitive history of every surname of every known colonist to New England from 1634 and 1635, called *The Great Migration* project—having already completed such an effort for the years 1620-1633, a series called *The Great Migration Begins*. These books are indispensable resources, monuments of painstaking research and reliable information.

And there is so much information, especially on the internet, that is not at all reliable—well-meaning folks manning websites and publishing trees as fast as they can throw them together or make them up from every source they can find, mostly on the internet, from other people like themselves—without worrying enough (or at all) about the credibility of the information. There are people who believe, for example, that every nugget they find at the LDS site is certified truth, when, in fact, much of it is simply suppositions and guesstimates from other amateur genealogists, many of them Mormons trying to find and "save" their ancestors, but prone to the same defects in research technique as other inexperienced detectives.

As it turned out—because of the New England connection—the Clark family information arrived as a gift. I posted queries on Genforum.com. One of my queries went: "Looking for information about—and possibly a photograph of—Alice Whipple Clark, b. in Cincinnati, OH,[12] April 1, 1846, d. in 1899. Married Rev. John Lawhorn and lived in Lewis and Carter counties in KY." I posted another query regarding Alice's parents on the Broadhurst Genforum site: "Seeking information on Marietta Broadhurst, b. August 10, 1820, in Bedford, NY. She married Benjamin Whipple Clark, Sept. 22, 1839, in Marietta, OH."

---

[12] I had not yet found her marriage record and assumed from other sources that she had been born in Cincinnati.

Within a few weeks I had a reply from Mr. O. W. Smith of Fremont, Nebraska, who offered to give me the whole Clark line going back to Joseph Clark, who immigrated from Banham, Norfolk, England in 1640, and who was one of the first settlers of Dedham and Medfield, Massachusetts. The Clarks were a thriving Puritan family whose members were often involved in town and colonial government.

My distant cousin, O. W. Smith, whom I would ordinarily never have met except for our mutual interest in family history and our Clark connection, turned out to be the Vice President of the International Softball Confederation, and while we were in the midst of corresponding about the Clark family, O.W. had to fly to Winnipeg, Canada, to help preside at the 1999 Pan American Games. His job as head of the Technical Committee and as International Representative for Drug Testing kept him on the fields from 9 a.m. until 10:30 p.m. daily for two weeks, and at the end of the Games he had the honor of presenting the silver medal to the USA Men's Team.

But when he returned to Nebraska, O. W. and I went right back to the Clarks. The first Joseph Clark was made a Freeman in 1652 and served as a Selectman in Medfield in 1660. His grandson, Solomon Clark (1678-1748) was a Selectman, was one of the trustees of the State loan in 1721, and Representative to the General Court of the Massachusetts Bay Colony in 1725. Solomon's grandson, John Clark, married Ruth Baxter, whose ancestor Abigail, I later discovered on my own, had married Joseph Adams, progenitor of the great Adams line that included both President John Adams and revolutionary and Massachusetts Governor Samuel Adams.

Not only did O. W. have the Clarks figured out back to Joe Clark, he had most of their wives. I happen to think wives are the best to find, because with each wife's surname, you discover a whole new family you are related to, and a whole new line to worry about. Also, paternal lines always contain a caveat—was a particular husband really the father? There is no way to know for certain except through DNA testing. What do you really know about your great, great grandfather? He is either *really* your great, great grandfather, or he is merely the legal husband of your great, great grandmother—still a figure of some historical importance but maybe not any relevant genetic importance. With the Clarks, thank heavens, the chances of a non-paternity event were remote. They were Puritans! Still, maternal lines—well-proven and documented—are a lock. This is not astrology.

The Clark wives were named: Micklewoode, Canne, Fenn, Allen, White, Cook, Baxter, Barnum, Whipple, and, of course, Broadhurst. (At least one in that long line was in error—which was not O. W.'s fault—but that is another story—the story of Experience Cook.) But with O.W.'s input, I had a terrific boost. Before very long I had unearthed an authoritative essay published in the *New England Historical and Genealogical Register* entitled, "The English Ancestry of Joseph Clark (1613-1683) of Dedham and Medfield, Massachusetts," which took Joe Clark's line back four more generations in England, corrected some of the wives, and stated that the disproportionate number of Cambridge graduates among the Clarks and several allied families suggested an association that transcended the communities surrounding Banham. In other words, some of them probably met at Cambridge. This seemed to me a stunning distance from white slaves sweating in the tobacco fields of Virginia, as the first three generations of Bellamys had done.

Then I found a family history entitled *Byram-Crawford and Allied Families Genealogy* that corroborated much of the information already received on my Clarks and Whipples and soon after that a Whipple family history and a Whipple website. I had the Clarks and the Whipples nailed down and enough hard data to proceed merrily on my own. The John Clark who married Ruth Baxter had a son in my line who married Relief Barnum. Relief Barnum was also an ancestor of P. T. Barnum, the showman and member of Congress from Connecticut who cast the deciding vote following the Civil War in favor of the abolition of slavery.

The son of John Clark and Relief Barnum had a son named Barnum Clark, who married Lucy Whipple. During the Revolutionary War, Lucy Whipple's mother, Lucy Brown Whipple, holding her baby Lucy in her arms, swam her horse across the Bay from Massachusetts to Rhode Island to deliver an important message to the officer in command of the Continental Army, and safely returned the same way.

My cousin Revolutionary War General William Whipple was a lifelong close friend of my cousin President John Adams. My cousin John Adams Whipple created a famous daguerreotype of my cousin Ralph Waldo Emerson and was an interesting fellow not often mentioned in historical accounts.

According to information at the Whipple site, through these wonderful Whipples, I am related to so many famous people I am too embarrassed to mention them. But if this is true, I owe it all to my great grandmother Alice Whipple Clark, the seventeen-year-old girl who married the Rev. John Brown Lawhorn, and to the Rev. John Brown Lawhorn too, who had the good sense to marry her. In this case and in many others, the maternal lines in my tree are the most impressive, no doubt about it. Whatever one may say about the males in my ancestral tree—most of whom seem to have been decent, hard-working, and full of good intentions— whatever inadequacies they may have had—most of them had an uncanny talent for choosing remarkable women to be their wives. The evidence would seem to indicate that with that talent alone, a man hardly needs any other.

Direct Descendants of Matthew Whipple

1. Matthew Whipple (1560–1618/19) + Joan (1562–1612)

2. Matthew Whipple (Deacon) (1590–1647) + Ann Hawkins (1605–1643)

3. Joseph Whipple (1640–1709) + Sarah Fairchild (1642–1713)

4. John Whipple (1690–) + Mary Fairfield

5. Joseph Whipple (1711–1771) +Mary Whipple (1716/17–1807)

6. Samuel Whipple (1749–1782) +Lucy Brown (1747–1814)

7. Lucy Whipple (1777–1863) +Barnum Clark (1774–1837)

8. Benjamin Whipple Clark (1812–1880) +Marietta Broadhurst (1820–1890)

9. Alice Whipple Clark (1846–1899) +John Brown Lawhorn (1803–1892)

10. Sarah Edith Lawhorn (1876–1934) +
Townley Hannah Bellamy (1873–1959)

11. Orin Ross Bellamy (1908–1974) +Beulah Pearl Zutavern (1918–1998)

12. Joe David Bellamy (1941–)

Back Row, left to right – Charles Edwin Clark; Lula Mae Clark (Tutin); William Tecumseh
Clark; Rosella Clark (Mitchell); Walter A. Clark
Front row, left to right – Mary Olive Clark (Venness); Benjamin Whipple Clark; Maggie Myrtle
Clark (?? Jacobson); Mary Olive (Jarvis) Clark

This Benjamin Whipple Clark (front row) is the grandson of my Benjamin, but
this is the closest likeness I could find.

24.

The Search for Experience Cook

One of the families in my Clark line was that of Jonathan and Experience Clark. Jonathan was born in 1700 to Solomon Clark and Mary White in Medfield, Massachusetts. Long before my cousin O. W. Smith of softball fame had entered the picture, a now anonymous researcher who was the first to discover and describe the Clark line, had listed the maiden name of Jonathan's wife Experience Clark as Cook or Cooke. This was probably because the researcher had found a Cook family in nearby Mendon with a daughter named Experience and then reasoned that since Experience was such a rare name, this must be the family. This information about Experience Cook had been repeated everywhere, in nearly every reference source, including the LDS. So naturally, when I came to that generation in the Clark line, I went looking for the family of Experience Cook—in hopes of expanding that line.

I did a Google search for Experience Cook and got mostly hits on want-ads soliciting experienced people to work in kitchens. I searched for Experience Cook at the LDS site, at Rootsweb, at Ancestry.com, and left messages at Genforum. I researched Cook families all over Massachusetts, and there were some interesting ones I wouldn't mind being associated with.

There was Francis Cooke of the Mayflower who brought his son John with him in 1620. All the Mayflower descendants have been worked over endlessly, so eventually I concluded that *if* Experience Cook was a descendant of Francis Cooke of the Mayflower, someone in Salt Lake City would have figured it out by now. (But if they hadn't, maybe I would.)

There was Elijah Cook who was a firebrand leader during the Revolutionary War, and he had a daughter named Experience, b. 1751, much too young to have been my Experience, but maybe my Experience was related to his family.

There was Walter Cooke who came to Weymouth in 1643, moved to Mendon in 1663 and became a large landowner, and who did indeed have a daughter named Experience, b. in 1662— too old to be my Experience. However, perhaps she had a grand-niece named Experience who would have been the correct age. Walter was mentioned as Sir Walter Cooke in some reports (was this a pretense by some early genealogist or based on fact?) and as a member of "the landed gentry." Two of Walter's brothers, Gregory Cooke and Stephen Cooke, also appear in Mendon, and one report stated authoritatively: "The Mendon Cookes had their names to every town transaction or service, and are to be found on every page of the town records, which suggests that their ancestors in England were alike in prominence, power, and position there, and they in their adopted country acted out that which was theirs by birthright."

Gregory Cooke was a Selectman of Mendon in 1669 and was named constable of Mendon in 1670 (having previously been constable in Cambridge), and in that year Gregory, Walter, and Stephen Cooke signed an agreement regarding the first settle-ment of Minister Joseph Emerson, in Mendon. (This Joseph Emerson was married to Elizabeth Bulkeley, granddaughter of Peter Bulkeley, and Joseph was the 3rd great grandfather of Ralph Waldo Emerson.) This Cooke family, already linked with some other relatives of mine, certainly seemed as if it had to be the family of my Experience if I could only find out which brother's line had produced the daughter in question one or two genera-tions down the road. But there were many, many children in each line and various crucial unresolved details.

In 1675-76 the Cookes and everyone else were driven out of Mendon by the Indians during King Philip's War. Gregory Cooke never returned but moved to a farm he had previously purchased, which was in Cambridge and Newton, Massachusetts, but Walter and his family did return to Mendon. January 3, 1680, at the first Town Meeting since the abandonment of the town on account of the Indians, Deacon Stephen Cooke was chosen a Selectman and Walter's son, John Cooke, was made constable.

Walter's son Peter married a woman named Experience. Did they have any children? I couldn't find any.

Walter's son Walter married Experience Holbrook. Did they have a daughter named Experience? No such daughter was listed anywhere.

Walter's son Samuel with his wife Lydia White had a daughter named Experience born in 1682—and these parents were often listed as the parents of my Experience but in my opinion she was still too old to be the correct Experience. One of the LDS records had her marriage to Jonathan Clark taking place conveniently in 1700, which would have been ideal except for the fact that Jonathan wasn't *born* until 1700! I did not think my ancestor Jonathan would have married a woman eighteen years older than himself and then persisted in having children with her until he was forty and she was fifty-eight.

Samuel Cooke's son Ebenezer had a daughter named Experience, b. in 1734, but she was obviously too young. Experience was not that rare as a name in the 1600s and 1700s. There were Experiences everywhere I looked.

After I had exhausted the possibilities of Experience Cooke as the daughter, granddaughter, or great granddaughter of Walter Cooke or one of his brothers, I started to examine more exotic possibilities. A Seth Cooke, b. in 1699, was a grandson of Walter Cooke; and Seth Cooke had married a woman named Experience Butterworth. I reasoned that if Seth Cooke had died circa 1720-1724, his widow, who would have been named Experience Cooke, might have married Jonathan Clark, even though she was, in fact, a Butterworth. I got excited about the name Butterworth and researched the Butterworths at some length, hoping to prove I was a Butterworth. The Swansea, Massachusetts, records stated: "Experience the daughter of Benjamin Butterworth and Huldah his wife was borne the 23 day of May in the yeare 1701." She was exactly the right age. Was she the one? For a while, I hoped that she was.

Experience Cook became one of my "brick walls," and I beat my head against the mystery of Experience Cook over and over again. The fact was that a woman named Experience who was my 6th great grandmother married my 6th great grandfather Jonathan Clark somewhere in Massachusetts about 1720, and now she was lost and I was determined to find her. If I didn't, she might be lost forever, lost to history, lost in oblivion. Her life made my life possible, after all. She was not just a statistic or a line in a book. I owed her something—the chance to be known, the chance to have her life counted in the grand scheme of things, the chance to become better acquainted with her great, great, great, great, great, great grandson. Sometimes I almost felt as if the ghost of Experience Cook was looking over my shoulder just beyond my eye's periphery, hoping to be found. "Are you going to find me today, Joe Bellamy? Are you ever going to find me?" Or "No one else is searching. Please don't forget me." I understood ancestor worship and the Mormons' obsession with locating ancestors at a much more personal level than ever before, and it made perfect sense to me.

I ordered Tilden's *History of Medfield* and pored over it. I bought a complete set of the "Early Vital Records of the Commonwealth of Massachusetts," containing over 300 Volumes of Massachusetts Records, over 116,000 images, on 9 CDs, and started looking in every town in Massachusetts for a marriage record for Jonathan Clark. I found nothing in Mendon, Medway, Franklin, Wrentham, Medfield, Bellingham, Needham, Weymouth, Braintree, Dedham, Uxbridge, Norton, or Swansea. I kept looking.

Then one day I finally reached Attleborough, Massachusetts, a town about fifteen miles directly south of Medfield, and discovered this: "Jonathan Clark & Experience Weddge, Oct. 29, 1724." Of course, that was it! It wasn't even that hard. Jonathan Clark never did marry Experience Cook or any other Cooke! He married Experience Weddge (or, in more modern spelling, "Wedge"). What had been essentially a guess by an earlier genealogist had thrown me and everyone else off the trail. Goodbye, Experience Cooke, b. circa 1700—you were never real—though your name appears in every Clark reference in print in the English language. Hello, Experience Wedge, my true 6th great grandmother!

Experience Wedge was the granddaughter of Thomas Wedge and Deborah Stevens, and Deborah Stevens was the granddaughter of Nicholas Stevens, who was an officer in Cromwell's Army. Cromwell's Army!

Direct Descendants of Rowland Clarke

1. Rowland Clarke (1530–1579/80) + Margaret Micklewoode (–1593/94)

2. Thomas Clarke (1567–1638) + Mary Canne (1580–1641/42)

3. Joseph Clarke (1613–1683/84) + Alicia Fenn (1619–1710/11)

4. Joseph Clark (1642–1702) + Mary Allen (1641–)

5. Solomon Clark (1678–1748) + Mary White

6. Jonathan Clark (1700–1748) + **Experience Wedge** (1702–)

7. John Clark (1725–) + Ruth Baxter

8. John Clark (1753–) + Relief Barnum (1753–1837)

9. Barnum Clark (1774–1837) + Lucy Whipple (1777–1863)

10. Benjamin Whipple Clark (1812–1880) + Marietta Broadhurst (1820–1890)

11. Alice Whipple Clark (1846–1899) + John Brown Lawhorn (1803–1892)

12. Sarah Edith Lawhorn (1876–1934) + Townley Hannah Bellamy (1873–1959)

13. Orin Ross Bellamy (1908–1974) + Beulah Pearl Zutavern (1918–1998)

14. Joe David Bellamy (1941–)

You might think that all the work I had done on the Cooke family of Mendon was a waste of time, but think again. They are my ancestors too by an entirely different route. Lucy Whipple's mother was named Lucy Brown. You may recall, Lucy Brown Whipple was the one who swam her horse across the Bay from Massachusetts to Rhode Island to deliver an important message to the Continental Army. Lucy Brown's mother was Mary Elizabeth Jones. Mary Elizabeth Jones' mother was Mary Cooke, and Mary Cooke was the granddaughter of Gregory Cooke of Cambridge and Newton, one of the three original Cooke brothers of Mendon—my Cookes after all—and so even those Experience Cookes (b. in 1662 and 1682, respectively) who were not my great grandmothers are, in fact, my cousins.

It was in Gregory Cooke's house, on ground belonging from the earliest settlement to the Cooke family and occupied by John Cooke during the Revolution, that Paul Revere engraved his plates, and, assisted by John Cooke, struck off the Colony notes, by order of the Provincial Congress. Patriot Benjamin Edes first stopped at this house when he escaped from Boston, and the first number of his subversive newspaper *Boston Gazette and Country Journal* was issued from there, the official organ of the Massachusetts Bay Colonists before and during the Revolution. It was in the home of Benjamin Edes that Paul Revere and the Sons of Liberty changed into their Indian costumes for the Boston Tea Party.

Direct Descendants of Gregory Cooke

1. Gregory Cooke (1621–1690/91) + Mary White (1623–1681)

2. Stephen Cook Cooke (1647–1738) + Rebecca Flagg (1660–)

3. Mary Cooke (1681–) + Captain Nathaniel Jones (1674–1745)

4. Mary Elizabeth Jones (1718–1809) + Captain John Brown (1703–1791)

5. Lucy Brown (1747–1814) + Samuel Whipple (1749–1782)

6. Lucy Whipple (1777–1863) + Barnum Clark (1774–1837)

7. Benjamin Whipple Clark (1812–1880) + Marietta Broadhurst (1820–1890)

8. Alice Whipple Clark (1846–1899) + John Brown Lawhorn (1803–1892)

9. Sarah Edith Lawhorn (1876–1934) + Townley Hannah Bellamy (1873–1959)

10. Orin Ross Bellamy (1908–1974) + Beulah Pearl Zutavern (1918–1998)

11. Joe David Bellamy (1941–)

Remains of Gorhambury, the Herefordshire estate of Sir Nicholas Bacon

25.

We've Got Bacon as well as Beef,
Or Do We?

I went looking for Mary Bacon in the New York Public Library. Mary was my 7th great grandmother on my father's side. Her daughter, Mary Fuller, married into my Whipple line and came to me, courtesy of my genetically brilliant great grandmother, Alice Whipple Clark, the precocious seventeen-year-old who became the third wife of the sixty-year-old firebrand preacher, John Brown Lawhorn, in the backwoods of Kentucky in 1863 and gave him six children who lived to adulthood, the youngest of whom was my paternal grandmother.

The Bacon materials available at the New York Public Library seemed promising, especially a volume entitled *Bacon Genealogy: Michael Bacon of Dedham, 1640, and His Descendants*, plus there was some sort of brochure or pamphlet from a church in England involving the tomb of Francis Bacon, which I ordered up just out of curiosity because I had read a book when I was sixteen that claimed that Francis Bacon was really Shakespeare. When the materials arrived, I found that the important first sixty pages of the *Bacon Genealogy* had been unceremoniously ripped out of the book by a previous user (no cousin of mine, I hope), and the pages after that were too late in the trees offered to be of any use to me.

The brochure regarding the tomb of the Bacons, however, was staggeringly beautiful, four-color printing on lovely card stock.

It showed the tombs of both Sir Francis Bacon and of his father Sir Nicholas Bacon, and they were opulent and exotic and still a tourist attraction, apparently. The bodies of Sir Nicholas and his spouse looked as if they had been coated with the purest molten silver. They glowed. Or perhaps it was only the lid of the crypt that was silver with outlines of their bodies beneath carved upon it, but it was spectacular. Sir Francis Bacon had been not only a seminal writer, whose work is still read and taught and admired in English classes, he had been Lord Chancellor of England. Some scholars still argue that Bacon *was* Shakespeare. Maybe he had been Shakespeare! It never occurred to me that Mary Bacon might be related to Sir Francis Bacon, but what if she was? Wow!

There in the New York Public Library, I must confess, I had one of those genealogical moments that reputable genealogists struggle to avoid—because they do not want anything to destroy their utter neutrality and objectivity and unseat their reason. I didn't care a fig if I was related to King Edward, but *Wouldn't it be something*, I thought, if I was related to Francis Bacon! *Fat chance of that*, I thought, *but wouldn't it be something*! Nothing would make me skew the information in order to make it *seem* that I was related to Francis Bacon, you understand, but I have to admit that I definitely wanted to be related to Francis Bacon, and I was going to try to find out if I was.

I made haste to locate an intact version of Baldwin's *Bacon Genealogy: Michael Bacon of Dedham, 1640, and His Descendants* published in Cambridge, Massachusetts, in 1915. My Mary Bacon was the daughter of a Michael Bacon and Sarah Richardson, and the book showed conclusively that Mary Bacon's father, Michael Bacon, was the grandson of the immigrant Michael Bacon of Dedham, Massachusetts, 1640. The book was entirely about my Bacons and it took them back to the Norman Conquest.

Opinions seem to differ upon the origin of the name Bacon, but it is either based on the Saxon word "baccen," meaning "a beech tree," or the word, "bacon," which in both Latin and English means "swine's flesh" of the kind that most Americans are familiar with. Apparently feeding beech trees to pigs is an ancient formula for producing the best bacon, so maybe the Bacon name was a combination of both meanings and intended to convey, in a manner similar to the Bulkeleys, not "We Got Beef," but "We Got Bacon." *Burke's Peerage* says that "Various conjectures have been hazarded as to the origin of the surname of Bacon, but to little purpose. It matters not, however; the antiquity of the family is beyond dispute; and there are few houses in the kingdom more distinguished for the production of great and eminent men." (*Antiquity* seems an important principle with *Burke's Peerage*, but it seems to me that all families are equally ancient—whatever their names may be and however many times their names may change.)

Among the earliest eminent Bacons was Roger Bacon, sometimes called Roger of the Black Art. He was born in 1214 and wrote many books, both scientific and philosophical, and in 1278 his works were condemned and he was imprisoned for fourteen years—frequently a sign of one who may have been in advance of his time.

Bacon Genealogy goes on to mention Sir Nicholas and his son, that during the reign of Queen Elizabeth, Sir Nicholas Bacon was Lord Keeper of the Great Seal, as was his son, Sir Francis Bacon, who was appointed Lord Keeper of the Great Seal in 1617. The Great Seal was not a mammal, you may be quite certain, and the office was apparently a high honor and responsibility. In 1618 Francis was made Lord High Chancellor of England and the same year was created Baron Verulam and Viscount of St. Albans. If Sir Francis was also Shakespeare, he was a very busy man.

The genealogical tree in *Bacon Genealogy*, which includes eighteen generations of Bacons, including the Col. Nathaniel Bacon who, in a later generation, was Governor of Virginia and another Nathaniel Bacon who was responsible for Bacon's Rebellion, revealed that the father of Sir Nicholas Bacon and the great grandfather of Michael Bacon of Dedham were brothers. Michael Bacon of Dedham (b. 1579) was my 10th great grandfather. Therefore, my relation to Sir Nicholas Bacon is that he is my first cousin, fourteen times removed. My relation to Sir Francis Bacon is that he is my second cousin thirteen times removed. My first reaction to this news was a wave of guilt. I thought, "Think what I might have accomplished! I should have worked harder. I should never have questioned my abilities. I should have *applied* myself."

But wait a minute. According to Alfred Dodd in a book entitled *Francis Bacon's Personal Life Story*, Francis Bacon *was* Shakespeare but he was also the secret offspring of Queen Elizabeth, the "Virgin" Queen, and the Duke of Leicester and not the natural son of Sir Nicholas and Lady Bacon at all. According to Dodd, Francis was not illegitimate in the usual sense, but he was born only four months after the secret marriage of his real parents; and therefore knowledge of his birth would have presented a thorny problem for the Queen who had other problems to worry about. So Lord and Lady Bacon, who were close to the Queen and who lived next door to the palace at York House, assumed responsibility for the child and claimed he was their own. As implausible as this may sound, Dodd marshals reams of convincing evidence from Francis Bacon's life to support this scenario, and Dodd spent a lifetime studying every aspect of Renaissance life in England and Bacon's life in particular. Who am I to dispute it?

If Francis Bacon was the natural son of Sir Nicholas Bacon, as most of his contemporaries supposed, Francis Bacon is my second cousin. If Francis Bacon was the secret offspring of Queen Elizabeth, he is a much more distant relation to me.[13] But I am still a first cousin of Sir Nicholas! Alfred Dodd claims that Sir Nicholas was a mere commoner, though he was also an eminently successful barrister, a close confidante of the Queen, a most positive influence during his formative years on the life of the genius Francis Bacon; and his house in sixteenth-century England resembled in grandeur the one occupied by Colin Firth as Lord Darcy in the movie of *Pride and Prejudice*.

---

[12] Queen Elizabeth, a Tudor, was related to the Plantagenets through Elizabeth of York who married Henry VII. Thus, through the Plantagenets, I am a 6th cousin, 13 times removed, of Queen Elizabeth-I.

1. John Bacon (1454–1500) + Agnes Cockfield (1457–)

2. Thomas Bacon (1480–1534/35)   2. Robert Bacon (1479–1548)
   + Johanna Wade (1481–1540)   + Isabella Cage (1478–)

3. John Bacon (1507–1556/57)   3. Sir Nicholas Bacon (1509/10–1579)
   + Margaret (1512–1556/57)   + Anne Cooke (1533–1610)

4. Michael Bacon (1535–1615) +   4. Lord Francis Bacon (1560–1626)
   Elizabeth Wylie (1537–1646)

5. Michael Bacon (of Dedham) (1579–1648) +Alice (1588/89–1648)

6. Michael Bacon (1608–1688) + Mary Jobo (1617–1655)

7. Michael Bacon (1638/39–1707) + Sarah Richardson (1640–1694)

8. Mary Bacon (1660/61–1741) + Jacob Fuller (1655–1731)

9. Mary Fuller (1685–1741) + James Whipple (–1766)

10. Mary Whipple (1716/17–1807) + Joseph Whipple (1711–1771)

11. Samuel Whipple (1749–1782) + Lucy Brown (1747–1814)

12. Lucy Whipple (1777–1863) + Barnum Clark (1774–1837)

13. Benjamin Whipple Clark (1812–1880) + Marietta Broadhurst (1820–1890)

14. Alice Whipple Clark (1846–1899) + John Brown Lawhorn (1803–1892)

15. Sarah Edith Lawhorn (1876–1934) + Townley Hannah Bellamy (1873–1959)

16. Orin Ross Bellamy (1908–1974) + Beulah Pearl Zutavern (1918–1998)

17. Joe David Bellamy (1941–)

My grandfather, Townley Hannah Bellamy,
showing off his tobacco in Portsmouth, Ohio

26.

White Slaves

Bellamy is only one of my many names, but it is the one the world calls me by, and it was also the one most shrouded in mystery. No one had ever discovered where these particular Bellamys came from. No one else could give me the answers—I had to find them all myself.

I needed a clue, and it was staring me in the face for decades. My paternal grandfather was a tobacco farmer in southern Ohio, and I should have been asking, "What in the devil was a tobacco farmer *doing* in southern Ohio?" I mentioned this fact to a couple of old South Carolina tobacco farmers at one of the Bellamy reunions in Myrtle Beach, and their response was, "I bet he was growing burley!" and then they laughed derisively. I guess growing burley is the moral equivalent of growing skunkweed if you're from South Carolina and can grow any kind of tobacco you want to. But my grandfather's tobacco looked pretty good to me. It was green and tall and it smelled good, and he sold it for a profit; and, the thing is, he knew how to do it. How did he know all about the relatively elaborate process of growing and curing tobacco in a state where the cash crops were corn and wheat and hardly anyone grew tobacco?

The truth is that he was the last in a long line of tobacco farmers that stretched back into Kentucky for three generations and back into Virginia for two hundred years before that. His English Bellamy ancestor arrived in Virginia in 1634 as an indentured servant and must have gotten a crash course in tobacco farming from his first day on the job—and also must have survived, as few did, and managed to pass on whatever secrets he learned. My grandfather's Scottish Hannah ancestors arrived in Maryland near Port Tobacco in the late 1600s or early 1700s and must have immediately been caught up in the thriving tobacco business there before they moved on into Virginia.

Tobacco was such a part of the lives of these early Virginians that they used tobacco instead of money, so when you read in a court case that someone has been awarded so many pounds, it is usually pounds of tobacco, not pounds sterling. The Bellamys were so entangled in the mystique and vice of tobacco use over 300 years later that my grandfather was still growing it in the 1950s in Ohio, and chewing it, and smoking it—though he lived to be 87 in spite of those habits—and my father can be said to have "smoked himself to death" at the relatively early age of 66.

Once I had made the connection to Virginia, there seemed no other pathway open to me but to go personally to courthouses all over Virginia, to see what I could find. So I did. I went to Goochland, Fluvanna, Albemarle, Powhatan, Cumberland, Bedford, Campbell, Henrico, Chesapeake, Northampton, Northumberland, Norfolk, Virginia Beach, and others—looking everywhere I went for my lost Bellamys; and at every courthouse I encountered other citizens just like me, combing through old records, searching—sometimes desperately—for their missing ancestors. *What possesses these people?* I wanted to ask. *Some powerful human need must be behind it.*

In 1663, Matthew Bellamy was tried in a Lancaster County, Virginia, courtroom, charged with running away from his indenture with Mr. Cuthbert Potter and taking with him two other servants, several "goods," and a boat. The boat would have been his chief means of escape, since transportation by boat on any of Virginia's plentiful waterways would have been the only way to travel far enough, fast enough, to elude capture, which, in any case, Bellamy failed to do. "Several goods" may have been no more than a loaf of bread or a small basket of food or a blanket to help the travelers on their way. And was one of the two servants captured with Bellamy perhaps the young woman Matthew hoped to marry, which his servitude prevented him from doing; and was the other a young boy, Matthew's son with this very same woman perhaps, who, because the boy had been born into servitude, was condemned to serving Mr. Cuthbert Potter until the age of twenty-one (unless he died first)? It's possible.

Matthew Bellamy was sentenced to serve three additional years with Mr. Cuthbert Potter, who was, coincidentally, one of the justices of this particular court, but who recused himself from this case in order to preserve the illusion of justice.

Judging from his other appearances in the Lancaster County records, Mr. Cuthbert Potter was an ambitious, aggressive, dominant, and controlling man—and a cruel master—who used his power to gain enormous wealth and influence. He owned thousands of acres of prime farm land and forest and an enormous stable of "servants" to take care of it for him. In most of the instances when he appears in court documents, other than as Justice or High Sheriff of the county, he is seen wresting thousands of pounds of tobacco (the currency of the time) from his fellow citizens on one pretext or another or responding to humble petitions from several of his servants that they had been treated harshly or unfairly or were denied freedom after their indentures were supposed to be fulfilled and terminated. In every case, the court ruled against the servants.

In one case, however, Lt. Col. Cuthbert Potter was caught selling four hundred acres of land *he did not even own* to one hapless fellow named Nicholas Wren. The court decided that even Potter should not be allowed to go this far—he was forced to pay back the money he had received for the sale plus damages, something Potter probably regarded as nothing more than a timely loan with interest. There was no other penalty exacted for this incredible fraud, and Potter continued in good standing in his gentlemanly role as one of the proprietors of the county and its seats of law, order, and justice, such as they were practiced at that time.

This case and these players might serve to illustrate the nature and condition of Virginia society and hierarchy in the seventeenth century—because in many ways it was typical. Colonial Virginia was a very different place than colonial New England, and I am not speaking primarily of geography and climate.

Whereas the settlements in New England were founded for religious reasons, Virginia was a commercial enterprise from its earliest beginnings, when English investors in the Virginia Company expected to extract gold from every creek and hillock in the new colony in the same plentiful quantities the Spanish had encountered in South America. When this did not happen and the Jamestown Colony foundered, support back home began to wane until the discovery that the tobacco leaf could be another form of gold.

The New Englanders were Puritans who created small towns like the ones they had lived in previously. The Virginians were Anglicans and royalists on the other end of the religious and political spectrum. The New Englanders were mainly middle class and gentry but not aristocrats, and they were family-oriented and owned very few servants. While New England was truly a social experiment unprecedented in the history of the world, Virginian society was even more tyrannical and oppressive for most of its members than old England had ever been (but the same in many ways) because it was dominated by distressed cavaliers, often younger sons of eminent English families, many of them related to one another, who fled England as Parliament flexed its muscles and conditions worsened for them and Cromwell came to power. They created a society in Virginia as much like the one taken away from them at home as they could manage but without the restraints of a more mature social order.

It was a rural conglomerate of manorial settlements and great estates—often tens of thousands of acres in size, some larger than most New England towns—surrounded on all sides by clusters of tiny houses for the slaves, servants, tenants and sub-tenants— almost in the medieval or feudal manner. Virginia was essentially a penal colony! There was a very small and ingrown aristocratic elite and an enormous population of others, and, in the early days, almost nothing in between. You were either a gentleman (or lady) or you were riff-raff; and most people were considered riff-raff, and, in fact, most of the servants were from poor and humble origins. Most remained poor and illiterate and easily victimized their whole lives, and most remained in servitude until they died.

The economy was organized for the production and sale of agricultural products, chiefly tobacco, the main money-maker; and the white slaves, and later, black slaves, were recruited or kidnapped or sentenced and then imported for one purpose alone, for field labor to cultivate and harvest the tobacco crop.

These so-called servants were not at all like the kind who polished stair railings or scrubbed dishes in the scullery or who brought in the tea service for "M'lady" on Masterpiece Theatre, though some were led to believe this would be the case. The terminology was based on a system that had existed in England and whose rules were understood by all. But in actual practice, the lot of these people was far different, the rules were different, and they were deliberately deceived. Most of them slaved from dawn until dusk in the tobacco fields and did nothing else until they died, and many of them died young. In the words of Edmund Morgan, a servant in Virginia was a "machine to make tobacco for someone else" (129). Jordan and Walsh estimate that as many as 300,000 or more whites from Britain were victims of the brutality and abuses of basic humanity we associate with slavery (15).

The system of white slavery euphemistically termed "indentured servitude" developed because England had a problem, and it had a need. The problem was that, for reasons demographers have been unable adequately to explain, the English population expanded very rapidly during the sixteenth and early seventeenth centuries, and the economy failed to keep pace. Prices and rents rose steadily, and wages declined. The price of provisions used by a laborer's family rose twice as fast as wages.

From a quarter to a half of the population lived below the level recognized at the time to constitute poverty. Few of them could count on regular meals at home, and more and more were forced on the road (30). Many starved. Many died of diseases brought on by malnutrition. Many could not feed their children or themselves. Some resorted to highway robbery and their numbers overwhelmed the prisons; some became vagrants and beggars; and English cities were clogged with orphans, vagabonds, and homeless and despondent wretches.

During the seventeenth century, partly because of these economic and social conditions, England had two revolutions within fifty years. Two kings were dethroned, and one was beheaded. There was, of course, a terrible war as well. Following the English Civil War and the domination and then sudden death of Oliver Cromwell, England suffered from continuing religious turmoil, governmental instability, aristocratic decadence, miserable economic conditions for the poor and middle classes, and then the Black Plague.

But the English colonies in America were expanding with the discovery of the economic viability of tobacco cultivation, and there was a huge need for cheap labor—such a demand that the vast majority of the emigrants to the colonies south of New England, both those who came of their own free will and those who were transported, came as indentured or enslaved people. We know from recent experience in the United States in the twenty-first century that big business usually gets its way when cheap labor can be found, and plausible arguments may be brought forth to defend whatever exploitation results, simply because there are profits to be gained. We know that those seeking the labor may not anticipate the consequences.

But the first chapter in the history of British slavery in the New World is even more sordid than is generally known, so ugly that it has seldom been told. The very first of the slaves were not Africans or convicts or "indentured servants," as has often been reported. Perhaps the shamefulness of this act is the reason that the story has so often been obscured, euphemized, neglected, rewritten, or conveniently forgotten. The first slaves shipped to Virginia in any number were English children—many of them orphans!

27.

THE HEADRIGHT SYSTEM, DRIVING FORCE OF SLAVERY

King James exploded in anger following an incident in 1617 when boisterous youths began to make a nuisance of themselves by their disrespectful behavior in his court. The king vowed that they should all be arrested and banished to Virginia! The young men in question were hardly the vagabond poor. They were the bastard sons of royal courtiers with too much time on their hands, and they were eventually sent to the Somers Islands, not Virginia. But the king's reaction was a sign that the idea was growing in high places that one way to cope with the flood of undesirables—whether they were the wandering poor, the pickpockets and prostitutes, the incarcerated who clogged the jails, or the street urchins—was to ship them to Virginia! Laws were hastily rewritten and justifications articulated in order to make such a possibility into a practical policy.

As early as 1615, the Privy Council voted in favor of a decree regarding the transportation of *convicts* that couched their ostracism as an act of clemency by a merciful king, a means of saving them and rehabilitating them. The decree reads as follows:

"Whereas it hath pleased his Majesty out of his singular clemency and mercy to take into his princely consideration the wretched estate of divers of his subjects who by the laws of the realm, are adjudged to die for sundry offences, though hideous of themselves not of the highest nature, so His Majesty, both out of his gracious clemency, as also for divers weighty considerations, could wish they might be rather corrected than destroyed and that in their punishments some of them might live and yield a profitable service to the commonwealth in parts abroad where it shall be found fit to employ them."

Not long after this, the Privy Council made its true intentions slightly clearer when it ordered that all prisoners sent abroad should be "constrained to toil in such heavy and painful works as such servitude shall be a greater terror than death itself."

The shipping of selected convicts was begun slowly and carefully soon after, but the authorities feared that such desperadoes might mutiny aboard ship or, once in Virginia, might prove to be uncontrollable. Therefore, and with the full cooperation and consent of the Virginia Company, the first slaves to be sent in large numbers were the street children, who were far more malleable.

In the first deal, the city of London paid the Virginia Company five pounds per head to remove from the streets one hundred ragamuffins between the ages of eight and sixteen and ship them off to Virginia as "apprentices." As with the arrangement to transport prisoners, the action was fluffed up to appear as if it were a fine humanitarian gesture by all the perpetrators. Hungry children would be given an opportunity to learn a useful trade, to start a new life, and to become self-sufficient. It was "one of the best deeds that could be done," according to one commentator.

Starting in the summer of 1618, the children were quietly arrested and placed in Bridewell Prison, awaiting their voyage to begin forced labor in the Virginia tobacco fields. Three ships carried them during the spring of 1619. Because one of the ships was named the *Duty*, members of this shipment were forever known as the "Duty Boys," but, in fact, one in four of this first group was a girl. When they reached the colony, the ones still living were sold for tobacco.

The following spring one hundred more children were sent, and at the same time, the company was beginning to send so-called "bridal boats" full of exclusively female passengers of marriageable age, which was a strategy to encourage resident male planters to stay, to adjust to the deplorable conditions, and to marry. The women, like the children, were most likely taken from the streets. As an enticement for the colonists to marry these women from the new shipments, the matrimonially inclined were promised an advance opportunity to purchase "an apprentice" for the bargain rate of 20 pounds of tobacco each. The women were considerably more expensive at 120 pounds each. But one currency the more industrious planters could certainly claim was tobacco. Why not spend some of it in order to grow more tobacco at a faster rate—it made good economic sense.

Unfortunately, records show that of the first three hundred children shipped to Virginia between 1619 and 1622, only twelve were still alive in 1624. While some were undoubtedly killed or carried off during the Indian massacre of 1622, and some died of the same diseases that had devastated the Jamestown Colony from the earliest days, many were simply worked to death, forced to perform work that was beyond their capacities, and, when they failed, they were beaten and sent back to the fields. The same fate was true for adults. Of the 1200 newcomers who arrived in 1619, over 800 died before 1621.

While the destiny of a small group of Africans who landed in Virginia a few months later than the first children has sparked great interest from historians, and their arrival in 1619 is often given as the starting date for slavery, the fact is that the pathways to slavery had already been established in England through the institution of indentured servitude and the first Africans joined a flood of indentured whites who were treated more or less the same way.

As Jordan and Walsh point out, after the first Africans arrived, "no flood of Africans followed them. The transaction was a one-off. Although the Dutch and Portuguese were bringing out slaves in the thousands from Africa, for the moment there was no market for them in Virginia...." The fact is that black slaves were more expensive than white slaves, so market forces kept the numbers of blacks low for most of the seventeenth century. "Six years later, in 1625, there were still only twenty-three Africans in the colony.

Many decades later, there were still only a few hundred. That would change late in the century, but for the moment, the poor of England remained the colony's main source of chattel labour" (87).

At the heart of the Virginia vortex of production and service from the earliest days was the headright system, which was a plan devised by Sir Edwin Sandys on behalf of the Virginia Company to encourage settlement. It certainly accomplished its purpose. For each "servant" imported by a wealthy contributor, fifty acres of virgin land was awarded. In essence the land was for sale, and the price was a bargain basement rate—a few pounds to pay the passage of the indentured person—and then that person would be bound to the contributor and the land to work *without wages* for anywhere from three to eleven years, or for life, if they lived beyond eleven years.

The well-heeled and ambitious quickly learned how to manipulate the system. Acquire as much land as possible by importing the maximum number of white slaves—wherever they could be found. Put the slaves to work on the land with the absolute minimum of expenses. If they died from overwork or other causes, there were always more where they came from. Use the profits from the sale of the products they produced to acquire more land and more servants. Keep the cycle going. By this means, some acquired tens of thousands of acres of fertile Virginia land. It was better than a fire sale on Wall Street.

Big promises were made in order to recruit impoverished young people to go to Virginia, including land that they themselves might be entitled to when their indentures were fulfilled, but, in practice, the servants/slaves scarcely ever saw freedom let alone land of their own.

Most of these free-willers had no idea of the hardships they were taking on nor the length of time they would end up serving—often their whole lives—and many of them were brutally exploited simply because they could not read the documents they signed when agreeing to come. The documents did not say what the avid persuaders claimed they did, or the documents were lost en route or considered to be forgeries by any court in the colony, stacked with judges whose main interest was in serving the system.

Even those who were able to pay for their own transportation sometimes ended up in servitude as well. As Morgan points out, "Even if he came with enough to set himself up independently, a bad harvest, insurmountable debts, or Indian depredations might force him into the service of a bigger operator. This was particularly true after the massacre [of 1622], when it was reported that ordinary men who had made a start on their own were obliged, for fear of the Indians, 'to forsake their houses (which were very farre scattered) and to joyne themselves to some great man's plantation'" (116).

Also, according to Abbot Emerson Smith, the practice of "spiriting" was often employed as a method for recruitment: "People of every age and kind were decoyed, deceived, seduced, inveigled, or forcibly kidnapped and carried as servants to the plantations. There were many ordinary individuals of decent substance, and a few even who were entitled by the custom of the time to be called gentlemen" who found themselves trapped in this way (3).

Once on the ground, a "servant," whether a free-willer, a prisoner "rewarded" with clemency, a kidnap victim, or an orphan or child from the streets, was considered to be the *property* of his master. He could be bought and sold freely, without his consent. Upon the death of his master, he could be willed to someone else. He could be loaned temporarily by his master so that his services might pay off a debt, or he could be arrested by the sheriff for the satisfaction of his master's debts. He might even be won or lost in a card game (Smith, 233).

If he misbehaved or misunderstood or showed defiance, he could be beaten, and in Virginia it was provided by law that masters were quite within their rights to whip their servants to compel obedience. Whipping posts were installed widely, and thus masters could punish and humiliate their servants in a public setting; or, if they preferred, they could administer punishment in the privacy of their own plantations—with impunity.

Richard Ligon, an English visitor in the 1650s, gives this account of the treatment of servants he witnessed: If they made any complaint, even in case of sickness, they were likely to be beaten and, if they resisted, their period of indenture very likely doubled: "I have seen an Overseer beat a Servant with a cane about the head, till the blood has followed, for a fault that is not worth the speaking of; and yet he must have patience, or worse will follow. Truly, I have seen such cruelty there done to Servants, as I did not think one Christian could have done to another."

A servant could not marry without the consent of his master, and marriage was discouraged. "The right of free marriage was one which for very obvious reasons would work to the disadvantage and inconvenience of the master, particularly if the marriage was made without his knowledge" (Ballagh, 48). Male offenders who secretly married were condemned to serve their masters for an additional year over and above their regular term, and offending females had their time of service doubled with their master or mistress. Male servants were expressly prohibited from marrying any of the women imported on the "bridal boats." This was a privilege limited to land-holders who could afford the going rate.

A servant could not vote. He was prohibited from engaging in trade on his own behalf, and there were severe penalties in all colonies for freemen who traded with servants, apparently because of the fear that the latter would steal or embezzle their masters' goods and dispose of them to unscrupulous freemen. Even a servant's special abilities, if he had any, were exercised for the benefit of his master. If he earned money in his spare time, it could be taken by his master (Smith, 233-34). If the servant tried to run away, "he was brought back under the auspices of rigorous laws and he suffered heavy penalties" (234).

"The natural desire of the planters to retain their laborers was reinforced, especially in earlier years, by a lively fear that servants would join with Negroes or Indians to overcome the small number of masters. Hence the extraordinary harshness of early laws, the worst being that of Maryland in 1639, which enacted that a servant convicted of running away should be executed.... Legislation on runaways in Virginia began in 1642/43, when they were condemned to serve double the time they had been absent, after the time of the original indenture would expire. For a second offense they were to be branded on the cheek or shoulder with the letter R, have an ear cut off, and were to be deemed incorrigible rogues. In 1658/9 it was provided that the hair of returned runaways should be clipped, for easier identification in case they resumed their wanderings" (Smith, 265).

The likely penalty for any infraction by the servant, in addition to physical abuse, was an extension of the time of the indenture; and it was not unusual to add on time in *years* for relatively minor failings. A female servant who became pregnant, for instance, was routinely sentenced to two additional years of service, even if her master was the father! One can easily imagine the sorts of abuse this led to—it was a virtual invitation to rape.

It is no accident that "liberty" became the watchword of the American Revolution for so many citizens of that time whose immediate ancestors had been the equivalent of slaves, sometimes for generations. Liberty was not an abstraction to them—liberty had an emotional appeal based on deep-seated anger. To them, it was a principle worth fighting and dying for. Little wonder too that in 1776 the British believed America could be easily subdued. Who were these upstart Americans anyway but the dregs of their own lower classes, whom they had regarded and treated as slaves for well over a century and a half.

The oldest brick house in America—Virginia Beach, Virginia

28.

ADAM THOROUGHGOOD BELLAMY

In 1621, 17-year-old Adam Thoroughgood, the seventh son of Rev. William Thoroughgood of Grimston, Norfolk, England, arrived in the Virginia Colony as an indentured servant in the muster of Mr. Edward Waters. Thoroughgood was well-educated and not at all typical. Why he came is anyone's guess, but if he was seeking his fortune, he found it rather quickly.

Adam Thoroughgood's first years in the New World must have been filled with the roughest sort of manual labor—felling trees, digging, plowing, and planting—but after working off his indenture in five years, Thoroughgood rose quickly in the hierarchy of the fledgling colony. Shortly after the time of his release in 1626, he was listed as Captain Adam Thoroughgood, Gentleman of Kiquotan, when he purchased 150 acres on the north side of what is now Hampton Roads, Virginia, later named Norfolk by Thoroughgood himself.

In 1627, Capt. Thoroughgood returned to England, where he took a wife, Sarah Offley of London, whose grandfather and great grandfather had been Lord Mayors of London. Infused with new money, Thoroughgood immediately began carrying out an ambitious plan of sponsoring immigrants to Virginia in exchange for land—under the same terms that he had accepted when he first left home six years earlier: five years of servitude in exchange for passage to the colony and fifty acres of land for the immigrant at the time of his release, plus fifty acres of virgin land per person for the sponsor. Adam Thoroughgood[14] must have been a very persuasive fellow because he was able to convince 105 citizens of England to leave for the wilds of Virginia over the next several years.

By this means, by the year 1635, 31-year-old Capt. Adam Thoroughgood had acquired 5,350 acres in colonial Virginia Beach together with a task force of 105 white English indentured servants to tend to it for him.

During the period of immigration, 1628-1635, Thoroughgood returned to the colony, where his meteoric rise as a mover and shaker continued. By 1628, he was appointed Commissioner for holding a monthly court at Elizabeth City. Soon after, he was elected to the House of Burgesses, the Governor's Council, and as Justice of the Court of Lower Norfolk County, then designated as "the Lower County of New Norfolk," named "Norfolk" by Thoroughgood for his home shire in England.

In 1636, on his newly acquired plantation, Thoroughgood built a substantial brick house for his family. The house was located on the western branch of the Chesopean River, which he renamed the Lynnhaven River in memory of the King's Lynn in his native Norfolk because of its resemblance to the River Ouse that flows through the Norfolk fenland to the Wash and the North Sea. Thoroughgood's house is believed to be the oldest surviving brick structure in America.[15]

When Thoroughgood died suddenly in 1640, he was buried on his own land at the First Church at Church Point on the banks overlooking the Lynnhaven, but, ironically, because of the changing channels of the river over nearly four hundred years, the graveyard and Adam Thoroughgood himself now lie underneath the waters of the river he named. A few years ago, when wealthy residents of Church Point persuaded the Army Corps of Engineers to dredge the river channel so that they could park their

---

[14] In the earliest days of the colony, there is evidence that the rules for indentured contracts were adhered to more often than was the case later on, especially if the indentured servant could read.

[15] Lately, it has been discovered through tree ring dating that this Thoroughgood house is more likely the house of Thoroughgood's grandson.

yachts, there was talk of trying to locate the ancient submerged graveyard and excavating it for archeological purposes. But so far nothing has come of it.

More to the point, among the 105 immigrants who Adam Thoroughgood brought to Virginia Beach were Augustine Warner, progenitor of George Washington, among others, and generations later, of Robert E. Lee; and also, in the same ship in 1634, the ship *Bona Adventure*, one immigrant named James Bellamy. In a show of gratitude, admiration, and respect, and perhaps because of his grief at Adam Thoroughgood's untimely departure from this world, the immigrant Bellamy named his first son born in the New World: Adam Thoroughgood Bellamy. Another of his sons (or nephews) was named Matthew, my ancestor Matthew Bellamy who tried to escape from Mr. Cuthbert Potter in 1663.

James Bellamy was undoubtedly a humble man, an indentured servant, a white slave, and his son Adam was also a humble man, as his will, which is still on file at the Virginia Beach courthouse, makes clear: "In the Name of God Amen. April 18th, 1700. I bequeath my soull unto God Almighty, and my body unto the earth, I, Adam Bellamy doe give unto my son Adam Bellamy one cow and calfe, and one heifer three years old, and one heifer of one yeare old, and one gun, and one Bible.... And unto my son Adam, I give my land to he and his heires forever...." The land was probably the same land his father had received for his servitude, plus whatever he had managed to add in the meantime, not much.

Still it was something! Perhaps because he was the son of a minister, Adam Thoroughgood was one of the few big landholders who faithfully honored the terms of his servants' indentures; and Thoroughgood was also one of the very few who had ever been a servant himself.

An astounding footnote to this story is that—through entirely accidental or coincidental circumstances fifteen years ago and without knowing anything about it at the time—I bought a house and lived for fifteen years on a portion of the land originally owned by Adam Thoroughgood, a tract that was part of the estate that James, Adam, and Matthew Bellamy worked and lived upon nearly 400 years ago!

This is not a very old country, but everywhere I go, I find my ancestors have been there before me. If I were a superstitious person I might believe I was being guided by mystical forces. But the truth of the matter, I think, is far simpler than that. In 400 years, a peripatetic people cover more ground than you might imagine and leave their footprints everywhere. If you look for them, you can sometimes find them—even just beyond your own doorstep.

James Bellamy + Mary

|

Adam Thoroughgood Bellamy & Matthew Bellamy

| |

Adam T. Bellamy   John Bellamy + Unknown

| |

?   John Bellamy (II) + Unknown

|

Benjamin Bellamy + Dorothea Ham

|

John Bellamy + Susanna Bickerton   Elizabeth Bellamy + Townley Hannah

| |

Berry Bellamy + Sally Hannah

|

Townley Hannah "Tom" Bellamy + Sally Jane Miller

|

Berry Stone Bellamy + Elizabeth Jarvis

|

Townley Hannah "Judge" Bellamy + Sarah Edith Lawhorn

Orin Ross "Jim" Bellamy + Beulah Zutavern

|

Joe David Bellamy

My paternal grandparents, Sarah Edith Lawhorn and Judge Bellamy

29.

The Girl Next Door—
Bickertons and Bulkeleys (Again)

Every generation is a love story. When my grandfather Judge Bellamy married my grandmother Sarah Edith Lawhorn in 1890, he probably did not know that his bride Sarah Edith was a descendant of the Rev. Edward Bulkeley through his daughter Sarah Bulkeley who married Mr. Oliver St. John in 1597. It would have meant nothing to him, even if he had known.

I am also quite certain he did not know that he was a descendant of the Bickerton family—any more than Judge's great great grandfather John Bellamy knew very much about the Bickerton family of England when he married Susanna Bickerton in 1796. John Bellamy was the son of a tobacco farmer living in Fluvanna County, Virginia, in the new United States of America; and the marriage bond that survives, misspells Susanna's name rather badly as Becarton or Becanton, though it is written in a beautiful flowing script by a man who was justifiably proud of his penmanship.

In 1796, Susanna probably entered the courthouse and told the clerk in a soft voice that her name was Susanna Bickerton, and the clerk dutifully wrote what he heard—"Be-car-ton"—and he either was too proud to ask for the correct spelling or he did not see the necessity to do so, or perhaps he did ask and Susanna pretended not to hear—because she could not spell the name herself.

I can't tell you how many times, in how many books, for how many years I have searched for the name "Becarton" and never found it, hoping to locate some tidbit of information about my gggg grandmother Susanna. I wish the clerk had been less proud or less illiterate, or that Susanna had been—it might have saved me a lot of time.

Eventually I found out the truth of the matter, which is that Susanna was the offspring of a rather proud Virginia family of Bickertons. She was the daughter of Aquila Bickerton. The Bickertons had been in Maryland and Virginia since 1722, and they had married Winstons, Overtons, Richardsons, and Todds, among others. John Bickerton, who was Aquila's brother, owned over 4000 acres in Hanover and Goochland counties, adjacent to Fluvanna County, in Virginia.

One day, when I finally learned Susanna Bickerton's correct name, I went looking for some evidence of Bickertons in England, and this is what I found. Bickerton is an ancient village in Britain in the county of Cheshire, the famous location of an Iron-age fort named Maiden Castle. A real estate transaction in Bickerton is mentioned in *The Doomsday Book*, which was a survey of the English settlements commissioned in December, 1085, by William the Conqueror. The small village of Bickerton is located perhaps two miles distant from the small village of Bulkeley! There is a Bickerton Hill and a Bulkeley Hill, and if you were to stand on top of Bickerton Hill with a megaphone and call out in a loud voice, it is altogether possible that someone sitting on top of Bulkeley Hill could hear what you were saying. *Members of the Bulkeley family and members of the Bickerton family have been marrying one another in England for at least eight hundred years,* and probably longer.

We are all familiar with the stereotype of "marrying the girl next door," but what about the possibility of marrying the girl next door when it is eight hundred years later and you don't have any idea that she ever was the girl next door? She was just the girl from your small town—in Kentucky—and that was easy enough to understand. But there was something about Sarah Lawhorn that Judge Bellamy never understood. From the moment he laid eyes on her, she was uniquely attractive to him. She had red hair! She was so easy to talk to. He thought she was beautiful in a way that no one else did, and that never changed even after all they went through together in forty-four years of marriage. It was almost as if he had known her for a thousand years!

Sir Richard Bickerton was a naval commander with a long, distinguished career in the British fleet. One of his earliest assignments was aboard the warship *Suffolk*, which was part of an expedition against Cartagena in 1741, where one of my immediate Bellamy ancestors from Virginia was killed in battle. In 1773, Bickerton received the honor of Knighthood, which was bestowed for military achievement, and in 1778, he was created a Baronet, receiving land in return for his service to the Crown. His son, also named Richard, became Rear-admiral and second in command to Lord Horatio Nelson, and later Admiral and General of the Marines, member of Parliament, and was the second Baron of Upwood in Huntington County, England.

In contrast to these illustrious Bickertons, to whom he may have been related, Susanna Bickerton's grandfather, John Bickerton, was tried for highway robbery at the Old Bailey in 1721, found guilty, and sentenced to death! In lieu of the death sentence, he was given a term of fourteen years in prison, which was then commuted to a conditional pardon if he accepted transportation to the colonies. He was transported to Maryland, where he arrived aboard the convict ship *Gilbert* in 1722.

I have examined the original text of the summary of his trial and find it to be quite remarkable: "John Bickerton, of St. Giles in the Fields, was indicted for Assaulting Charles Edwin, Esq; on the High Way, on the 3rd of June last, putting him in Fear, and taking from him a perriwig value 5 pounds. The Prosecutor deposed, that between 11 and 12 a Clock the night aforesaid, he crost Middle Row, and was got into the Broad Place in Holbourn, where he perceived a soldier with a Trull before him, and another Soldier behind him; that not liking to be between such Company, stood to let the soldier that was behind him get before; that he heard a Woman cry out and the prisoner came and told him that there was a Man Murdering his Wife; but he supposing what sort of Cattle they were, walkt on as fast as he could till he got into Monmouth street, then slacken'd his Pace; that his Wig was pull'd off his Head; whereupon he followed the Prisoner, whose Feet flew up in his Flight, but he presently got up again, threw away the Wig, and ran into a Brewhouse-Yard, thence to other places, but he pursued and took him. William Waller deposed, that he took the prisoner, who acknowledged the Fact next Morning, saying that he was drunk, or else he had not done it; and that he was sorry for it. Humphrey Beven confirmed the former Evidence. The Prisoner denied the taking the Wig said that he was drunk, fell down, and was seized. The Jury found him Guilty. Death."

From this evidence, it would appear that, if John Bickerton was guilty of anything at all, it was nothing more than a drunken prank. He claimed that he was drunk, fell down, and was seized, which sounds as if he did not think he had done anything at all, or perhaps could not remember. Yet the constable testified that Bickerton had apologized earlier and said he would not have done it if he had not been drunk. In any case, this John Bickerton does not appear in any other cases within the judicial system of the Old Bailey, so it must have been a first offense. If he, in fact, did do anything, it seems to have been no more harmful than snatching a man's wig and giving it a heave. The incident occurred in town with both victim and perpetrator on foot. Yet the Court saw fit to classify the charge as "Highway Robbery" and to sentence Bickerton to "Death," which seems extremely harsh punishment for an act our system of jurisprudence would probably classify as minor vandalism.

We do not know the age of Susanna Bickerton's grandfather at the time of his arrest, but, according to information provided by the Immigrant Ships Transcribers Guild, the average age of the eighty-two convicts aboard the *Gilbert* in 1722 was slightly over eighteen, and a third of them were women! A Mr. Jonathan

Forward, merchant and notorious slave-trader, provided fare for them and accepted a subsidy from the Government all as a part of his customary business dealings, undoubtedly with the assurance that he would make a profit when the prisoners were sold into servitude in Maryland; and although five of them died during the voyage, my guess would be that Mr. Forward still made out very well for himself after all was said and done, perhaps well enough to continue to grease the palms of those within the system who were probably conducting a well-organized conspiracy for spiriting innocents away to the colonies and justifying it as "leniency" for crimes allegedly committed.

In any case, John Bickerton found himself in Maryland in 1722 and probably knew by then that he had been given a raw deal. The next we see of John Bickerton in the record is in July, 1727, when he serves as a witness for the will of Daniel Brown in Calvert County, Maryland, and in October of the same year when he acquires a parcel of land in Ann Arundell County called "Broughton Ashley." No record of an indenture for John Bickerton has yet been found, nor do we know how he might have managed to acquire enough money to afford to purchase property so soon after his arrival, though there is no necessary reason to believe that he was entirely without means when he landed in Maryland. In fact, in a document from January, 1738/39, in the Proceedings of the Council of Maryland 1732-1753, p. 158, Mr. John Bickerton is listed as one of three "Gentlemen who can prove the Truth of the within Complaint." So he seems to have gone from convict to Gentleman in a relatively short time.

More research might help to explain more fully how he spent the twenty-five years of his life in Maryland, but we do know that he died in 1752, for An Inventory of the Goods and Chattels of John Bickerton, Deceased, dated June 13, 1752, is available for perusal in the Maryland Archives. It shows that at the time of his death his estate was appraised at 173 pounds (not counting his land holdings), that he owned three slaves, various and sundry livestock, including horses, cattle, sheep, and pigs, as well as six leather chairs and a parcel of old books. His nearest kin were listed as Aquila Bickerton and Elizabeth Ross, his son and daughter. His greatest creditor was John Skinner, and his administrator was Joseph Bickerton, who was probably his eldest son.

We know from the death record of Susanna Bickerton Bellamy (from Wayne County, Virginia) that Aquila Bickerton was her father, and all the available evidence about the life of Aquila Bickerton found until then indicated that he lived only in Maryland. So one question that immediately came to mind was, "How did Susanna, a Maryland girl, ever meet her husband John Bellamy, who we know was a Virginian?"

The eminent genealogist, Clayton Torrence, looked into the mysteries of the Bickerton family briefly in his classic *Winston of Virginia and Allied Families*, which includes a chapter on the Bickerton family of Hanover County, Virginia. Torrence concluded that Mr. John Bickerton of Virginia, a man of extraordinary wealth and power, was not related to the Maryland Bickertons because he could find no connection between the two.

According to Torrence's research, Mr. John Bickerton of Virginia acquired over 4000 acres in Hanover, Goochland, and Bedford counties in Virginia between 1740 and 1766. In 1740, he was a Justice of the Peace in Hanover County, and from 1743, continuously until 1765, he was elected and reelected as Vestryman of St. Paul's Parish, Hanover County. From 1737-1747, Bickerton appeared with the title of Captain, and from 1747 onward, as Major.

Bickerton's wife was Mary Todd, daughter of Philip and Anne Day Todd of King and Queen County, Virginia; and his children married into some of the most prominent families in Virginia, including the Winstons and the Webbs. Sarah Winston of Hanover County, for instance, was the mother of Patrick Henry, the firebrand orator of the American Revolution who became first Governor of Virginia after the Revolution and gave his name to Patrick and Henry counties.

Two Maryland wills not found by Torrence provide evidence that Mr. John Bickerton of Virginia was indeed a brother of Joseph and Aquila Bickerton and an unidentified son of John Bickerton of Maryland, the gentleman/convict. The first is the will of Daniel Brown, mentioned earlier, wherein gentleman/convict John Bickerton is listed as a witness. In 1727, Brown wills the north part of "Hambleton's Park" to his son John Richard, executor, and his heirs. This is just a few months before John Bickerton acquired "Broughton Ashley," and as witness to this estate, he was familiar with "Hambleton's Park" as well and apparently acquired that property at some later point.

The second will of interest is that of John Skinner, who, you remember, was listed under "greatest creditor" in the will of John Bickerton when Bickerton died in 1752. Skinner's will is dated 16 February, 1764, and the crucial passage is: "To daughter Ann Rogers, tract, 'Hunt's Chance,' and 'Broughton Ashly,' bought of John and Joseph Bickerton; 'Hamilton's Part,' bought of said Bickertons and John Tucker...." "Hambleton's Park" and "Hamilton's Part" are one and the same, land that John Bickerton, the gentleman/convict purchased after he bought "Broughton Ashley." Then after this John's death, the properties were inherited by his sons John and Joseph Bickerton, who sold them to Skinner. Since John the gentleman/convict was already dead, then the John of record in 1764 in this instance is undoubtedly Mr. John Bickerton of Virginia—since there are no other male Bickertons in either Maryland or Virginia—except John, Joseph, and Aquila—during this period.

Another crucial fact not discovered by Torrence is that in 1754, following his father's death, Aquila Bickerton moved to Virginia, next door to his brother John! The evidence is to be found in a Caroline County, Virginia, court document.

The *Virginia Gazette*—the first newspaper in Virginia—gives a small glimpse into the lives of the Bickertons of Hanover and Caroline Counties, Virginia, from an article dated October 7, 1737: "We have advice from Hanover County, that on St. Andrew's Day, being the 30th of November next, there are to be Horse Races and several other Diversions, for the Entertainment of the Gentlemen and ladies, at the Old Field near Capt. John Bickerton's in that County."

There follows a summary of the "handsome entertainment" promised: "horse racing, violin (fiddling) contest, boys racing, toasts, singing, wrestling, dancing,"...ending with: "And as this Mirth is designed to be purely innocent, and void of Offence, all Persons resorting there are desired to behave themselves with Decency and Sobriety; that Subscribers being resolv'd to discountenance all Immorality with the utmost Rigour."

Since Susanna was the niece of Capt. Bickerton, then, as a young woman, she might well have been a part of the social whirl that attracted eligible young men like John Bellamy to such occasions. In the midst of such gaiety, I wonder if Susanna had any idea that her paternal grandfather had been arrested in London and sentenced to "Death" for threatening a man's wig and had then been banished to Maryland on a convict ship? I also wonder if she knew that the young man showing such interest in her, who would soon become her husband, was the descendant of white slaves?

Convict John Bickerton + Unknown

|

Aquila Bickerton + Susannah Breeding

|

Susannah Bickerton + John Bellamy

|

Berry Bellamy + Sally Hannah

|

Townley Hannah Bellamy + Sally Jane Miller

|

Berry Stone Bellamy + Elizabeth Jarvis

|

Townley Hannah Bellamy + Sarah Edith Lawhorn

Orin Ross Bellamy + Beulah Zutavern

|

Joe David Bellamy

Robert and Townley in Oklahoma near the time of Townley's death

30.

THE OLDEST MAN EVER TO DIE IN OKLAHOMA

I was bedeviled by the idea that there were people living before I was born who I never knew—whose lives were as real as my own—and whose lives made mine possible. My father had eight brothers and sisters, most of them older than he was, and most of them told me stories about the old days. Some of them were even old enough to remember my great, great grandfather, Townley Hannah Bellamy, who was born early in the nineteenth century and lived well into the twentieth. *But where did the Bellamys come from?* I wanted to know. *Where had they lived before the birth of Townley Hannah Bellamy? What sort of people were they?* No one knew! When it came to the important questions, all my Bellamy aunts and uncles showed a tendency to mythologize that was a dead giveaway to me, even as a boy, that they were making it up. But I didn't want phoney baloney. I wanted hard evidence—I wanted the truth.

My great, great grandfather, Townley Hannah Bellamy, was born in 1831 or 1825 or 1818 in a part of Virginia that became West Virginia after the Civil War; and he lived until 1923, which means that he was either 92, 98, or 105 when he died—old enough to be a little bit surprised at himself for carrying on that long. However, he *claimed* to be 105, and as a result of that claim he was described by an obituary writer at the time of his death in Elk City, Oklahoma, as "the oldest man ever to die in Oklahoma." For all I know, he may still hold the record, though it

Townley is at far left next to his pony Maud. Valeria is the woman in the dark dress.

Berry Stone Bellamy, my great grandfather.

seems likely that one of the new crop of centenarians has eclipsed him by now. His parents were married in 1830, according to the record, and he is listed in the 1850 census as age 19, which seems a clear case for the argument that he was born in the year 1831 and died at age 92. However, the fragmentary record that exists from 1850 onward seems to indicate that he aged a little bit faster than normal men the older he became, and that he died more frequently as well—altogether three times.

The first account of his death was in 1881. It followed a report in the Vanceburg, Kentucky, newspaper on April 27, 1881: "The Regulators got after T. H. Bellamy, who lives in the Laurel Country, and after whipping him, fired at and wounded him. He has left the country." May 18, 1881, the same newspaper carried this information: "Tom Bellamy, who was wounded by the Regulators on Laurel several days ago, died last week."[7]

The second account of his death occurred in 1911. *The Vanceburg Sun* reprinted a story from the *Portsmouth Times*: "T. H. Bellamy, who is here from Vanceburg, Kentucky, on a visit to his grandson, Judge Bellamy, of this city was a caller at police headquarters Monday night and entertained quite a crowd with his anecdotes and recitations. Mr. Bellamy is 88 years of age, but is unusually spry for his age. He was born in Cabell County, West Virginia, has 48 grand children, 44 great grand children, and 5 great great grand children. His eldest son Berry Bellamy, lives in Oklahoma and is 60 years of age, while another, William J. Bellamy, lives back of Vanceburg and is the father of 22 children, 19 by one wife, all boys but one, and all staunch Democrats like 'Dad' himself, who boasts that he has a thick layer of moss between his shoulders." The follow-up story, August 17, 1911, reads: "William Bellamy Sr. received word that his aged father Townley Bellamy, who resides in Portsmouth, was fatally injured by a fall."

The third account of his death was when he actually did die in Oklahoma in 1923: "Townley H. Bellamy, known as Grandpa Bellamy, died at 3 A.M., August 4th, at the age of 105 years.... His wife died nineteen years ago. Grandpa lived most of the time at the home of his son, R. S. Bellamy, where he was given every attention. His mind was unusually bright, and up to the time of his death he was a most wonderful conversationalist. When a young man, he taught school and was well-educated for one of that time. We saw some of his writing after he was one hundred years old that was written in a very good hand and every word very

---

[7] Townley Hannah Bellamy was his legal name, but he generally went by the name of "Tom Bellamy."

plain. He was a good Christian man, and his thoughts have been of his Savior and the ones who have gone before. He told us many times he was anxious to go on as all of his friends of younger days, and as many of his loved ones, had gone…. Funeral services were held at the home at Saturday evening at four o'clock, conducted by his friend, Rev. Stanka, of the Church of God. Internment was in charge of Robinson and Son, who believe that Grandpa was the oldest person in Oklahoma at the time of his death."

A May-September Romance

The rest of the information I had for Townley was sparse. On January 22, 1852, he married Sally Jane Miller, the daughter of William Miller and Esther Henderson, and on October 23, 1852, nine months and one day later, my great grandfather, Berry Stone Bellamy, was born in Kentucky. I did not know who Townley's parents or any earlier ancestors were at that time, how long they had been in this country, how they had first gotten to West Virginia or Kentucky, or what their nationality might have been, though the surnames involved suggested English or Scots. I did not know how or why Townley and his son Berry had ended up in Oklahoma, since Townley's grandson Judge, my grandfather, had been born and lived in Kentucky until he moved across the Ohio River to Portsmouth early in the twentieth century, just downriver from Marietta, Ohio.

I posted a generic query concerning Townley on the Bellamy Genforum and received a startling answer: "My grandmother married Townley Bellamy in 1907 in Roger Mills Co. OK. They lived together for only a year. As far as I know, the dates you have of his birth and death are correct. He lived to be very old. Yes, there was more than one Townley Bellamy. I have not researched the line so can not help you more than this. Good luck. –Jo Thrower."

I had never heard anything about such a marriage. There was no record of it on the internet. I had a death date of 1904 for Townley's wife, Sally Jane, so it was *possible*. But I did not know

Jo Thrower and was not sure if her information was credible. We started writing back and forth, and Jo was full of interesting information. She said her grandmother, Valeria Gardner, was the widow of a Civil War soldier, and when Townley met her in Oklahoma she was 48 and he was "quite a bit older." In 1907, he was either 89 or 82 or 76. Jo sent me a copy of the marriage record, where Townley had given his age as 82. If there was ever a time when Townley might have been tempted to lie about his age and claim *he was younger than he was*, this was it. But the man thought he was 82 and said so.

Jo said her mother was a little girl when Townley and her grandmother Valeria were married, and her mother remembered Townley very well because he always took the time to talk to her and she said, emphatically, that Townley Bellamy "was a very nice man." Jo said she never understood why Townley and Valeria drifted apart, but that their relationship was always amiable, and when Valeria died the name they put on her tombstone was "Valeria Bellamy." (My wild guess regarding the reason for this cooling of relations would be that Townley's ambitions regarding a 48-year-old wife—at his age—were larger than his capacity to fulfill them.)

Jo sent me a picture of Townley with the Gardner family taken in 1907, and in it every living creature is named, including the ponies and dogs.

Jo also sent me a photo of Berry Stone Bellamy's gravestone from the Fairview Cemetery in Elk City. The stone is in pink marble. Jo also noted that Townley was buried there too, but he did not have a gravestone

I also have Jo Thrower to thank for helping me make the next step in my pursuit of Townley's history. I had written to the Oklahoma Division of Vital Records for Townley's death certificate, hoping to find a listing for his parents, but the answer had come back that no record for any such person existed. Well, we knew he existed, and we knew he died in Oklahoma, and in 1923 there should have been a record of it! Jo contacted someone who knew the people at the Vital Records office, and they were able to unearth the record, which had been filed under "L. H." Bellamy because the script of the "T." in "T.H." looked like an "L." I received a copy of it shortly thereafter. The vital information had been filled in by Townley's surviving son Robert Sanders Bellamy, and Robert said that Townley died of "old age" and that Townley's father was "Berry" and that he was from "Europe." I thought about those answers for a long time. Could Robert have accidentally written the name of Townley's firstborn son Berry instead of Townley's father? Or had Townley named his firstborn son after his father? And what about "Europe?" Europe sounded like something you might write if you didn't have a clue where Townley's father came from.

I thought about the situation there in Elk City during the year 1923. At the beginning of the year, Townley and his two sons, Berry and Robert, were all living there. The sons were probably living near one another, and Townley was living with Robert by then. Then in January, Berry died at the age of 70 and was buried with his respectable stone. Eight months later old Townley died at the age of 92, 98, or 105, and Robert and his family decided to immigrate to California. They probably sold off everything they couldn't carry and hurried to pull up stakes before something bad happened to them too, or to leave the ghosts behind. But either there was no money for Townley's stone, or in the confusion of their departure it was forgotten, or perhaps they left money for a stone but the stone mason, realizing they would never know the difference, pocketed the money and saved himself the trouble.

Later I met some of the descendants of Robert Bellamy's family from California, and they provided me with a photo of Robert and Townley from Oklahoma, date unknown, but probably near the time of Townley's death. (This photo is at the beginning of the chapter.)

Another cousin was able to produce a copy of a photo of my great grandfather Berry taken in Oklahoma in 1922, a year before he died. I had never seen my great grandfather's face before, but this man looked like he could definitely be related to me. In fact, he looked more like my father than my grandfather did. There is a quality of "I haven't got all day to stand around posing for this damned photograph" about him that reminds me of my father's Type A personality.

At this point, I was teeming with unanswered questions. Why did my great grandfather Berry and his father Townley go to Oklahoma in the first place? Who was the Berry Bellamy who was Townley's father and where did he come from, and what ever happened to him? Who were the Regulators and why did they want to do harm to such a "very nice man" as my great, great grandfather? Where did the name "Townley Hannah" come from in the first place? Was it a family name? Why did Townley Bellamy have to die three times and age so rapidly that he became the oldest man in Oklahoma?

Statue of Stonewall Jackson adjacent to the Albemarle Courthouse,
Charlottesville, Virginia

31.

The Civil War Record

I found mention on the internet that Townley had been a member of the 22nd Regiment of the Kentucky Volunteer Army during the Civil War. That was the Union Army[8], so I wrote to the National Archives, hoping there might be some more information there.

I received a thick envelope from the National Archives. Townley had petitioned for a pension for his war service, starting in 1890. But he had been listed as a deserter. His petition was denied. He wrote again in 1891. That petition was denied. He wrote in 1894, and that petition was denied. He was still petitioning as late as 1913. All denied.

Here is a sample of the correspondence:

> State of Kentucky, County of Carter.
> February, 1890
> Personally appeared byfore me, a notary public in and for the aforesaid County and State, duly authorized to administer oaths, Landisdale L. Taber, aged 63 years, a resident of Olive Hill, in the County of Carter, and State of Kentucky, who, being duly sworn according to law, states that he is acquainted with T. H. Bellamy, applicant for Invalid Pension, and knows the said T. H. Bellamy

---

[8] All of Townley's cousins who remained in Virginia fought for the Confederacy, including Berry, the son of Matthew S. Bellamy, who was undoubtedly named after Townley's father.

to be the identical person of that name who served as a private in Company D, 22nd Regiment of Vols, and who was discharged at Grayson on or about the 10 day of Sept, 1863, by reason of general Disability.

That the said T. H. Bellamy, while in the line of duty, at or near Catlett Burg, in the State of Kentucky, did, on or about the 1st day of December, 1861, become disabled in the following manner, viz: "contracted inflamation of the eyes and disease of lungs through exposure and hardships incidental to army life. Also incured a rupture of left side caused by lifting heavy government wagon from which disabilities he continued to suffer up to the date of his discharge, being unable for duty by reason of same."

That the facts as above stated are personally known to affiant by reason of: "being a member of the same company was with the command when the claiment took sick and was injured [and] observed the weak condition that he was in. He had a bad cough and raised much mucus and phlegm, complained of pains and weakness in the chest and lungs. His eyes looked red and inflamed and sore, causing pain and dimness of sight. He also complained of pains and weakness in groin and left side from rupture. I saw the swollen parts, saw him often, and often heard him complain and saw him in pain as above stated while in the service."

And deponent further states, that he is well acquainted with the claimant, having known him for about 50 years; and further, that his knowledge of the facts above stated was derived from having served as a 1st Lieutenant in Company D of the 22nd Regiment, Volunteers, from 14th day of October, 1861, to the 10th day of December, 1861. And deponent further states, that the claimant was a sound, able-bodied man at enlistment, so far as he knew and could judge, and that he has no interest, direct or indirect, in this claim, and is not concerned in its prosecution.

Landisdale L. Taber
C. H. Ernest, official signature

Oct. 6, 1891
Dear Sir:

There seems to be a mistake in the record of the late war in regard to my service in the U. S. Services. I will give you a true statement of services rendered by myself, which I am able to prove by as good citizens and soldiers as can be produced in Carter and Lewis counties, state of Kentucky.

First, I entered the 4th day of July, 1861, at Olive Hill, Kentucky, and was sworn by a recruiting officer to report at Grayson the 1st day of August, 1861. Col. Garrett, a U. S. mustering officer, swore thirteen into the U. S. service. We were sent to Cattlettburg, Kentucky, to get our uniforms. We got them. I drew from the commissary a suit of blue, cap and overcoat, a blanket, knapsack, cartridge belt, haversack, musket, bayonet, [and] 60 rounds of ammunition. Returning to Grayson, we drilled in Dr. Ellis' company. I received in services in August, thirteen dollars [and] was constantly on the skirmish after John T. Williams and other Rebel bands that was annoying the citizens as well as soldiers. For the month of September I [also] received thirteen dollars.

On the 24th of October, by orders of the Colonel commanding, I was transferred to or adopted by Company D, 22nd Regiment, Kentucky Volunteers, after which I never got no more pay. My service was one of hardship and toil and danger. I was ever ready for duty. I had enlisted in the service of my country in good faith for three years or during the [duration of the] war.

About the first of December, 1861, there came a dispatch for 150 men of our regiment to reenforce Col. Zeigler at Camp Sirredo, West Virginia. I was one who volunteered to go, as Col. Wilson said he wanted volunteers to go—he did not want his men to go who did not have the uniform. We went to West Virginia and then to Guyandott. Then we fell back to Cattlettburg. There was some government waggons that was stalled in the street. I and others was ordered by government officers to assist the teams. While I was lifting at a waggon, I ruptured myself in the left groin [and] was taken back to Grayson [and] put in a house belonging to Allen Duncan. I was left with some thirteen others under the treatment of Dr. Wm. H. Jones of Grayson.

About the 6th of December, 1861, our men was ordered to Camp Swigert to consolidate with the men at the above named camp. Col. Wilson had left us in the care of the doctor named about the 15th of December. The doctor furloughed all home as he was called. I was very bad with the rupture, my eyelids had become inflamed very bad. I had a hemorage of the lungs—I was bleeding when I was seized with a fit of coughing.

[Missing connection here] nothing but justice. The record is certainly wrong in my case. I never deserted as sure as God is in heaven and can prove that I did not. This is all I can do. I know I ought to have something for my services, but if the War Department thinks differently, I cannot help it. It is hard for a man to get injured in the U. S. Service and then be wronged as I have been. The officers of Company D have done a thing that will condemn them in another world by reporting a lie. I can prove what I say.

Give this your special attention, and let me know at your earliest convenience.

Yours with respect,
T. H. Bellamy
Vanceburg

Townley tells the same story in a slightly different form in every one of his petitions, and, over the course of many years, he produced several witnesses who testified to the truth of his claims. I have two different photos showing him on crutches late in his life, indicating that he was perhaps still suffering from the injury received in lifting the government wagon. Also, it does not seem unlikely to me that, given war conditions and the number of transfers he made from troop to troop, that the paper work (if it was done at all) might not have caught up with him. It also seems possible that the doctor who treated him, Dr. William Jones, who was no doubt busy and overworked, might have failed to report the furloughs he made. In spite of the evidence that he was not beyond stretching the truth, I have to say I do believe my gg grandfather in this case. If he was lying, he told the same lies with remarkable persistence over the years, and the lies are surrounded by very convincing details. If he was lying, I think he believed the lies he was telling. I think he suffered more from the fact that he was listed as a deserter and that his Government did not believe him than from the denial of his pension.

The Regulators Capture Townley Bellamy

An article in the *Lewis County Herald* by Dr. William M. Talley entitled "An Era Of Disorder Followed End of Civil War" gave me more information to chew on concerning Townley's life. Dr. Talley describes the conditions in Kentucky that led to the formation of the Regulators. Since Kentucky was a border state between the North and the South during the Civil War, the citizens were quite divided in their loyalties. Not only were counties and towns divided against one another—some standing firmly for allegiance to the Union, others opting for succession and fighting on the side of the Confederacy—but even different members of the same family sometimes chose to support opposite sides in the conflict.[9] As a result, a great deal of hatred and animosity was created that

---

[9] In fact, as noted earlier, Townley's first cousins who remained in Virginia (which was soon to become West Virginia) fought for the Confederacy. His cousins in Kentucky fought for the Union.

lingered for decades after the war was over. People who had grown accustomed to violence and lawlessness as a way of settling scores during the War found it difficult to change their ways after the war was over, and old grievances for acts committed during the war often festered into full-blown feuds that included gun battles and bush-whackings, house and barn-burnings, beatings, harassment, and murder.

The Regulators were a splinter group of the original Ku Klux Klan, which had been put out of commission by President Grant. Until the Ku Klux Klan was revived, the Regulators reigned in this part of Kentucky and their wrath was directed at anyone—white or black—who they thought needed "regulating." One early case reported in the newspaper was of a man named Jarvis who was beaten and whipped because he had not paid his doctor bills, and the editor reported that the doctor was among those who whipped the man! The brave editor had gone on to comment: "We hope the business of whipping for refusing to pay doctor bills will stop just where it is, as we don't want it down here."

In May, 1881, the newspaper carried a story about the Regulators whipping several women in the southern part of Lewis County, one of whom was a young woman named Anne Smith who was severely handicapped. Both of her hands had been nearly burned off in a childhood accident. Her mother was also beaten. The crusading editor commented: "We think the Regulators have gone too far in this matter. The idea of a party of stout men whipping old and crippled women is a little too small for those who claim regulating to be essential to the welfare of the moral condition of the country." The Smith family had apparently come under the scrutiny of the Regulators when the father, John Smith, joined a political group called the Greenback Organization, a type of Labor Party that supported farmers and other laborers. Smith was suspected of having revealed some of their secret business. Also, Smith was accused of going "to dances and then refused to confess his sins." Going to dances was apparently considered injurious to the moral fabric.

Soon after the whippings of Mrs. Smith and her crippled daughter Anne, a house and barn belonging to a neighbor burned, and the suspicion for who started the fires fell upon John Smith. A member of the Bloomfield family claimed that while riding by the Smith home they had been fired upon by someone inside the house, and soon after that the barn of Reuben Bloomfield was set afire and burned to the ground. No proof was ever presented, but the Smiths were blamed. A group of Regulators surrounded the Smith home and whenever any member of the Smith family became visible, the

Townley "Tom" Bellamy with Maud in Oklahoma in 1907

crowd would fire upon him or her. One of Smith's sons, age 17, was shot through the leg, just above the knee, and Mrs. Smith was nearly killed.

Constable A. G. Brewer and a posse of deputies left Vanceburg with warrants for the arrest of three of the Regulators and rode to the Smith home. When the constable and posse arrived, the Regulators listened as he read the warrants and then informed him they had better things to do than to be arrested. They told him if he was through with his job he should just go home. In the conversation that followed, the Regulators decided that if the Smiths agreed to leave the area, they would let them go. Constable Brewer negotiated with the Smiths, and they agreed to move to Vanceburg. The constable sent for a doctor to treat Smith's wounded son, but the doctor was afraid to come to the scene. After the Smiths vacated their home, the Regulators burned it to the ground.

Even more appalling was the end of the Smith story, which reveals just how extreme the vindictiveness of some of the Regulators remained and how long it continued. John Smith and his wife Nancy Jane (Davis) raised their children and lived out their modest, peaceful lives in Vanceburg. Their daughter Anne, whose hands had been burnt off at the wrists except for two or three withered fingers, grew to adulthood and married. She had a reputation as an excellent cook and housekeeper in spite of her crippled condition. One summer day in 1904, nearly twenty-five years after the Smiths had been driven out of their home by the Regulators, Anne's body was found floating in Heath's Hole of Salt Lick Creek near Fly Branch, one crippled hand sticking out of the water. She was still clutching her apron in which she held

William Jackson Bellamy (far right) with two of his seventeen sons together with the midwife, with whom they must have been well-acquainted. William also had three daughters.

vegetables she had picked in preparation for dinner. It appeared that she had fallen into the water and drowned, but several years later a man in the neighborhood in his seventies called some of his relatives to his bedside and made a deathbed confession. He and other former Regulators had murdered Anne and thrown her body in the creek. But he would not name any of the others, and no one was ever prosecuted for the crime.

The family of Townley Bellamy was another target of the Regulators. The record is not clear about what my gg grandfather or some member of his family may have done to aggravate them, but it does seem that the Regulators, like most bully groups, enjoyed picking on cripples or people who were too weak to fight back; and after his war injury it seems likely that Townley was either still on crutches or walked with a decided hitch in his gait. It is also possible that some earlier grievance—Townley's fighting for the Union army, for instance, or even something his father might have done—may have been at play.

For whatever reason, in April, 1881, the Regulators captured Townley Bellamy in one of his fields, knocked him down, and standing above him in their hoods, began whipping him with hickory switches. After they had beaten and cursed him for some time, until he was bleeding and exhausted, the story goes that he asked if he could have a drink of water. His torturers agreed to allow him to get up and limp to the nearby creek to get a drink. But after he was a certain distance away, Townley made an attempt to save himself by running as fast as his gimpy legs would carry him. The Regulators drew their guns—which was perhaps their intention all along—and they yelled, "Stop." But when Townley didn't stop, they fired in unison and the bullets spun him around and he fell hard into the corn stubble from last year's harvest, bleeding and unconscious, and at first presumed dead. You will remember that the Vanceburg newspaper reported in May, 1881, that Townley Bellamy had died from his wounds. This was perhaps a rumor that Townley had instigated in an effort to save himself from further harassment.

By August of 1881, however, it was clear that Townley was not dead. Perhaps he had been spotted by one of the perpetrators, limping along a back country road or ducking inside a barn door as someone rode past his house. "That son-of-a-bitch is still alive," they must have said. So they burned down his house! Unfortunately for them, however, Townley was not living there anymore. He had rented the house on Buffalo Creek to a preacher's family named Sizemore, and the Sizemores barely escaped the conflagration with their lives.

The incident called attention to the recklessness of the Regulators, and finally the law came down on their heads. A man named McClure, who had boarded with the John Smith family, was able to identify several of them, though he died soon afterwards. (The editor of the Vanceburg newspaper stated that McClure had been living out in the woods from fear of the Regulators, and his health was destroyed by bad weather and exposure.) The Bellamy family filed suit against the Regulators, alleging libel, slander, defamation of character, and a charge that they had started rumors to destroy Townley's business. (Never mind aggravated assault and attempted murder!) Even without McClure to testify, several of the Regulators were sent to the penitentiary, including one who claimed he could not have been guilty of regulating the Bellamys because the same day his wife gave birth and he had not left the house except to fetch the midwife. The jury did not believe him.

Most of the Regulators who were convicted received only one-year sentences, however. One may imagine that some of their colleagues who were still under cover and living in the area were not happy with the Bellamys, and that the ones returning to Lewis County after a year in prison were even less hospitable upon their release.

The record is not clear as to exactly when Townley and his first born son Berry, my great grandfather, left Kentucky for Oklahoma. But in 1881, Berry was twenty-nine, and my grandfather Judge (whose legal name was also Townley Hannah) was already a boy, eight years of age. I do not know whether Berry or Judge were ever involved in old Townley's dispute with the Regulators, but they could have been. Let's put it this way, given the forces marshaled against the Bellamys in that region of Kentucky at that hour of the world, it was a good time to leave.

Sooners or Laters

Townley and Berry, and later Townley's son Robert, all went to western Oklahoma, a place whose recorded history began in 1541 when the Spanish explorer Coronado ventured through that region on his quest for the Lost City of Gold. In 1803 it had officially been acquired by the United States of America under the auspices of Thomas Jefferson as part of the Louisiana Purchase. But the Oklahoma region was essentially a barren wasteland populated mostly by Indian tribes that had been relocated from other, more populated areas.

During the 1880s land-hungry frontier farmers agitated to obtain the unassigned lands in the western section—the lands not given to any Native American tribe. This agitation succeeded, and a large strip was opened for settlement in 1889. Land was offered to settlers through a series of "Land Openings," where newcomers initially competed for the land in horse races. Prospective settlers lined up on the territorial border, and at high noon they were allowed to cross on a run to compete in finding and claiming the best allotments. Those who illegally entered ahead of the set time were nicknamed the "sooners." Later other strips of territory were opened, and settlers poured in from the Midwest and the South. The Homestead Act of 1862 provided that a legal settler could claim 160 acres of public land, and those who lived on and improved the claim for five years could receive title. The land was free, but compared to the garden paradise of fertile and densely wooded Kentucky, it was surely a disappointment to some who hoped to farm there. Oil had not yet been discovered.

Whether Townley, Berry, and Robert were "sooners" rather than "laters," I have no way of knowing. But these Bellamys did settle in the Oklahoma territory and made a life for themselves there. Occasionally, Townley would travel the long road back to Kentucky to visit his relatives and friends, but something always caused him to return to Oklahoma. Judging from his elaborate stratagem in 1911 to claim that he had died from a fall, I suspect that someone back in Kentucky was still after him; and there is ample evidence that the Regulators had a long memory.

Another tragedy in the Bellamy family begins to seem like a pattern of intimidation. According to a story in the *Vanceburg Sun*, January 18, 1917, with the headline: BURNED TO

DEATH: "Two boys of William Bellamy [Townley's son] burned to death when their house near Clarksburg burned Sunday night. Mr. Bellamy carried out the baby sleeping with him, and his wife rushed upstairs to awaken the five little boys and one girl sleeping there. She succeeded in getting the girl and four of the boys downstairs and out of the building, but two boys, Orville, age 11, and Eugene, age 7, perished in the flames. The mother was badly burned about the face while trying to rescue them, and Mr. Bellamy had his mustache burned off. Russell, age 14, was severely burned about the face, ear, and hands, and all his hair was burned off. The family was taken to the Tim Carrington home. Inez, the 15-year-old daughter, sprained both ankles when she fell down the stairs. The family lost everything and a relief fund was set up. Mr. Bellamy said when they got outside the building they saw a young man standing in front of the house and when they asked him to help he ran away. He thought it was Ray Hall, age 23. Hall was held on $200 bond. . . . Mr. Bellamy is the father of nineteen children."

Twenty years later, William Jackson Bellamy, the father of this large family, was run over and killed by a hit-and-run driver as he was crossing a quiet street in the middle of summer.

Thus, the Bellamys were apparently still the object of a vendetta as late as the 1900s. However, the next stage of my search for the early Bellamys raised the possibility that a feud against the Bellamys had been going on from a much earlier period. It started with the discovery of a marriage record in Greenup County, Kentucky, for the Berry S. Bellamy who was old Townley's father. This early Berry (my ggg grandfather) shows up on census records in 1830 and 1840, and then he vanishes from the census and the tax records. In 1843 there is a deed showing Berry acquiring land in Greenup County from his father-in-law Townley Hannah, but then Berry disappears from the face of the earth. Berry was not yet forty years old.

Another clue that the family was under duress turned up in the record a few years later. Sally Hannah Bellamy, Berry's widow, remarried in 1850 to a man named James Savage, and thus she became Sarah Savage. The 1850 census shows her living with James Savage, and the children she had from her marriage to Berry Bellamy are living there as well, including my gg grandfather Townley, aged 19. Then in 1852, when Townley's son Berry Stone Bellamy (my great grandfather) is born nine months and one day after Townley's marriage to Sally Jane Miller, the county record shows the father's name as Savage! Yet I have DNA evidence[10] that Berry was Townley's son, as everyone in the family has always supposed. (If I was actually a Savage, I wanted to know!)

Townley and his son Berry (named for Townley's missing father) were not only father and son, they were very close their whole lives. I suspect that listing Mr. Savage as the father was an early attempt by Townley to conceal the fact that an heir of his father, Berry Stone Bellamy, named, in fact, Berry Stone Bellamy, had just come into the world! Someone had a serious grudge against the first Berry Stone Bellamy and possibly that someone was involved in his early demise. I think Townley wanted to protect his new son against a similar fate.

Considering the stress Townley must have been under for most of his life: the early death of his father under mysterious circumstances, his bodily injury during service in the Civil War, the refusal of the Government to accept his claims concerning his pension, the insult of being charged as a deserter when he was not, the continual threats from the Regulators which culminated in his beating and wounding, his disability, his effective banishment to faraway Oklahoma, the loss of his dear wife, the failure of his second marriage, it seems a miracle he lived to be such a very old man. Stress is supposed to kill people. Whenever I begin to feel a little stressed out, it helps me to think about my great,

---

[10] The Y-chromosome, which always passes from father to son, has been helpful to genealogists because it mutates, on average, only once every five hundred generations. Thus, it is possible to ascertain the chromosomal identity of any male line simply by testing any living member and comparing the results to any other living member who is descended from another line in the same descendancy. Through the Bellamy DNA Project at FamilyTreeDNA.com, we have now tested twenty-four male Bellamys, sixteen of whom spring from the Virginia family described here—with lines divergent as far back as 1710—and they have all been matches.

great grandfather Townley Hannah Bellamy and what he went through. Nothing I have to face compares to it. Yet he slogged on and kept his wits about him and lived a long and fruitful life to the very end.

Berry S. Bellamy + Sally Hannah

|

Townley Hannah "Tom" Bellamy + Sally Jane Miller

Berry Stone Bellamy + Elizabeth Jarvis

Townley Hannah "Judge" Bellamy + Sarah Edith Lawhorn

Orin Ross "Jim" Bellamy + Beulah Pearl Zutavern

|

Joe David Bellamy

HOPEWELL FURNACE

In 1824, William Ward built here
a bloomery forge, converting it,
1832-33, to a blast furnace, also
known as Camp Branch Furnace. Air
blast was water-powered. In 1850,
this stone stack made 600 tons of
iron, consuming 1500 tons of ore,
and burning 165,000 bushels of
charcoal fuel. Operations ceased
in 1844.   See other side.

32.

Pig Iron

The records I discovered for Townley's missing father, Berry S. Bellamy, were spotty at best. They consisted of some dim-to-undecipherable Xeroxes made from old records a friend had unearthed for me in Greenup and Carter counties in Kentucky, where Berry had lived before he disappeared. I went over them with a magnifying glass and tried to decipher them, but I was still not certain of what they meant. One of them said: *the heirs* of Berry S. Bellamy were sued by a man named John Cagall in 1849. That must have meant that Berry was dead by then. But since he was born in 1806, he would have been a man in his early forties by 1849, much too young to die from natural causes. How did he die? Maybe Berry died in a cholera outbreak or was killed in a farm accident. Or maybe he was murdered in a feud. Some of the events in Berry's son Townley's life certainly indicated that dying as the object of vicious revenge in a feud was not unheard of in that part of Kentucky during those years.

Another set of papers showed that in 1841, a man named William Ward sued my ggg grandfather Berry Bellamy in Carter County court, alleging that he had seized "by force and arms" 50 tons of pig iron! How could a person steal 50 tons of pig iron without several giant teams of oxen and an army of men to help load the wagons? What would a person *do* with that much pig iron? Whatever it was, he could hardly plan on making a fast getaway. What in the world *was* pig iron and why did Ward have so much of it?

Would you believe that during a sixty-year period, from 1815 to about 1875, there were 79 iron furnaces built in the Hanging Rock Region, which included Greenup, Carter, and Boyd counties in Kentucky, and extended north into Hocking County, Ohio, in the area surrounding Ironton. Because of its huge deposits of iron ore, the Hanging Rock region has the honor of being the site of the first major expansion of iron manufacturing in the United States; and because it was the best cash crop of the time, most of the male population of these counties was engaged in it in one way or another, as a full-time job or as a sideline to agriculture.

Because the furnaces produced such quantities of iron, the molten iron was cast into bars, called pigs, for easier transport and later remanufacturing. The pig iron could be made into everything from tools, farm implements, and cooking utensils to guns and ammunition for the U.S. Government on the verge of a war with Mexico.

As early as 1824, William Ward built what was called the Hopewell Furnace in Greenup County, which is described on-line as a "bloomery forge." In 1832-33, he converted it to a "blast furnace" with a "water-powered air blast." In 1838, Ward's stone stack made 600 tons of iron, consuming 1500 tons of ore, and burning 165,000 bushels of charcoal fuel. The charcoal was made from hardwood timber, which the region had in abundance.

When my ggg grandfather Berry Bellamy moved from Greenup to Carter County after 1843 and near the time of his death, he began buying up land at a rapid rate, borrowing heavily to do so. He had acquired about a thousand acres by the time of his death in early 1846, and it does not seem likely that he would have expected to farm that much land in the 1840s without the benefit of tractors and mechanized equipment that would not have been available to him.

Berry Bellamy was most likely engaged, from at least 1841 and onward, in the timber business and, most likely, had provided hardwood lumber for the charcoal for Ward's furnace. Further, it seems probable that Ward might not have been in any hurry to pay Berry for the privilege of burning great quantities of wood extracted from the forests on Berry's land with gut-busting effort.

Ward must have been something of a fat-cat by 1841, and he probably thought he could get away with stiffing the smaller operators, of which there would have been a great number: iron makers, stone masons, charcoal makers, blacksmiths, carpenters, teamsters, and millwrights, not to mention the men like Berry providing the raw timber. In fairness to Ward, it might not have been an easy matter to keep the books for such an enterprise in balance. He probably had a large payroll to meet, and the checks from the sale of his iron might have been a long time in coming, especially if he was selling to the U. S. Government. His lawsuit against Berry might simply have been trumped up in order to buy time to pay for the timber Berry had supplied or to scare him off altogether.

Berry seems to have been a very ambitious man, however, and it's certainly possible, especially if he was under pressure from creditors and Ward was intractable, that he might have felt it necessary to seize a quantity of pig iron equal to the debt he was owed. Certainly by the time of his land acquisitions in Carter County, he must have felt he knew what he was doing and he must have expected to earn a profit fast enough to pay for all that land; and those who sold their land to him and those he borrowed from in order to pay for the land, must have felt he was capable of paying them back, that he was a man who would honor his debts.

Another Ward lawsuit that I uncovered in Greenup County gives a hint of why Ward might have filed his suit against Berry in a different county. This suit was almost simultaneous with the one that Ward had filed against Berry Bellamy in Carter County and continued for most of the year of 1841. Judging from his treatment by the Greenup Court, Ward himself must have understood that he was persona non grata in Greenup.

In Ward's 1841 lawsuit against one John McAlister in Greenup, a March entry indicates that Ward had to post bail of fifty dollars and security of two thousand dollars worth of land at Lost and

Sand Creek, and he was the plaintiff! In May the same Court ruled in favor of McAlister, that Ward had to "prove the account filed by the appellor in this cause" [i.e. Ward] or that his security would be forfeited. By November of 1841 Ward agreed to drop his suit and the cause was dismissed, each party paying his own court costs. The air of peeved impatience with Ward by the Greenup Court seems to suggest that he might have been a man who had a reputation for filing frivolous lawsuits.

That seems to have been the case with his suit against my ancestor in Carter County as well. The case in which Ward had accused Berry Bellamy of armed robbery of fifty tons of pig iron and to which Berry had pleaded "not guilty" was put before a jury of twelve men on April 2, 1842, and Berry Bellamy was exonerated. He was innocent of the charges. William Ward received nothing on his complaint except "mercy" for his "false claim."

The estate papers of Berry S. Bellamy reveal that Berry was alive on December 31, 1845, when he signed an I.O.U. to James Savage, and dead by March 16, 1846, when his widow Sarah paid a debt in his behalf and he is listed as deceased.[11] That may be as close as anyone will ever come to learning his actual date of death. The estate was in disarray and in and out of court for years while Sarah and her children (Townley, Julia, and A. J.) struggled to pay all the debts from people who came out of the woodwork to file claims, and there are several pages in the estate settlement showing plats of how the land was divided to satisfy the creditors.

As to the cause of Berry's death, that remains a mystery. The cause of death is not listed in the estate papers. It could have been anything from a falling tree to a shot in the back from one of Ward's gang.

---

[11] The Administrator for the estate of Berry S. Bellamy was one Robert Henderson, who was the Constable for Carter County. When Berry's son Townley married Sally Jane Miller in 1852, he was marrying the daughter of Esther Henderson, who was Robert Henderson's sister. Robert and Esther's father, also named Robert Henderson, was one of two Henderson brothers who settled Carter County in 1803. The elder Robert Henderson was a Justice of the Peace and Big Sandy Judge until his death in about 1818. He was my great great great great grandfather.

One touching detail that is mentioned, however, is that in December of 1845 Berry paid seventy-five cents as an installment on a bill to Dr. Thomas Williams for "schooling two scholars." The scholars in question were undoubtedly his two eldest children, Townley and Julia, and the fact that Berry was willing to invest in their educations as one of the last acts of his life—in spite of all his other debts and cares—probably explains why his son Townley was a literate man, why Townley's son William Jackson was a school teacher, and why Townley's great great grandson Joe David was a writer who became a genealogist. Sometimes seventy-five cents spent in the right way at the right time can reap unexpected dividends. The charge for educating these two scholars in 1845 and 1846 was $3.75 per scholar. Apparently teachers were paid even more poorly in the 1840s than they are today. Sarah paid most of this bill in 1846 together with a $1.00 charge to Dr. Williams for his work completing Berry's coffin.

❧ ❧

John Bellamy + Susanna Bickerton   Elizabeth Bellamy + Townley Hannah

Berry S. Bellamy + Sally Hannah

Townley Hannah Bellamy + Sally Jane Miller

Berry Stone Bellamy + Elizabeth Jarvis

Townley Hannah Bellamy + Sarah Edith Lawhorn

Orin Ross "Jim" Bellamy + Beulah Pearl Zutavern

Joe David Bellamy

33.

Open Heart

Each day, when I visited my father at the cardiac-surgical-unit of the Texas Medical Center, I used to pass Dr. Cooley's car in the doctor's lot on my way from the Tides Motel across the street. It was a customized Cadillac, black as an undertaker's limousine, and with a private nameplate that read Denton Cooley, M.D. It made me think of the mountains of money Cooley must be raking in from desperate and dying people like my father.

In a book about Cooley I had bought at the airport on my way in and read from each night at the Tides, while my mother leafed through magazines and tried to watch TV, I learned that several other doctors would precede Cooley and perform the surgery for opening up the chest cavities. Then, at the crucial moment, Cooley would enter the operating theatre, moving briskly from room to room, and on each table he would find a patient whose open heart was glistening and wobbling and he would immediately seize the heart and do what had to be done.

He was the medical equivalent of a star quarterback—the operation truly started as soon as the ball was in his hands. But it wasn't as if he was mass-producing open-heart operations for purely pecuniary reasons, I told myself. It was because there were so many seriously ill people who needed his care and because he was the best. A man of his skills and stature deserved to be well-paid. I think I wanted to admire Dr. Cooley because I knew my father's life was in his hands.

In the late afternoon, I used to drive over to a track I had located on the campus of Baylor University and put in some laps. The day before the operation I got in a conversation there with one of the other runners, a pleasant-looking, bald-headed man—he had noticed my Duke T-shirt and wanted to know if I had done my medical work at Duke—and I said no, that I was just an English professor from upstate New York, and that I had only been an undergraduate at Duke and that I was in Houston because tomorrow my father was going to have a heart operation.

"Cooley?" he said, and I nodded. It turned out that he was an obstetrician who happened to have been Dr. Cooley's college roommate. At first, I thought he was joking. He said Cooley had been an incredible athlete as a young man, a gifted basketball player. I thought of Cooley's large, delicate hands, his spatulate fingertips with enormous moons, cradling the ball. The bald-headed obstetrician wanted to talk about Cooley's nobility and his success with women. He said my father was in good hands—none better. I decided he probably had been Denton Cooley's roommate, and although I am the world's least superstitious person, I wondered what it meant, if anything, that I had met him under such circumstances.

Neither my mother nor I slept well that night at the Tides. Early the next day, we ate a light breakfast and plodded across the parking lot past Cooley's Cadillac to the huge beige hospital building. There is a special room where the families of Cooley's patients await news from the staff on that morning's operations. Quickly, the room filled up with worried-looking people. We spent the morning crowded together like passengers in an airline departure zone who expect to hear the plane has crashed upon arrival—reading, looking at one another, and trying to block out the sounds the bored children were making.

Finally, in mid-afternoon, Dr. Cooley himself appeared and began talking to one of the families. A wave of energy and expectation washed across the room. Cooley said a few words, smiled in a controlled, noncommittal way, and moved on to another group. It was evident that he intended to report personally on each patient. We could hear the music of his soft Texas accent as he moved from family to family but not what he was saying. He was a tall man, a commanding presence among us, still wearing the pale green surgical gown and the cap like some sort of priestly or extraterrestrial visitor conducting a somber communion ceremony, and everyone in the room was extremely attentive.

The waiting was painful. Already, other families were filing out, the relieved rumble of their talking and occasional laughter echoing back down the hall. My mother and I were among the last to hear. Cooley placed his hand on my shoulder, and I was conscious of the nearly empty room surrounding us.

"Your father didn't have an easy time of it, Mr. Bellamy," he said, "but he seems stable at present. He experienced arrhythmia and heart failure on the table while they were wheeling him into the operating room and several times during the operation as well, which made the operation rather difficult and long. The valve was severely-damaged, only a flap really, and the heart very weak. We replaced the valve and performed a bypass operation in two locations, using veins from his legs, as we had described. I don't know how he made it to that room, but we'll hope for the best now."

"Thank you so much, Dr. Cooley," my mother said. Cooley hesitated a moment, eyes downcast towards the carpet as if searching for words to say something else. Already I began to feel an ominous sense that he was spending too much time with us, and the tone was pessimistic. Cooley nodded matter-of-factly and I could feel the pressure of his hand leave my back as he turned to go and I regretted that we had so little time to discuss the situation. But he was so obviously a tired man with other important work demanding his attention. I hugged my mother and we walked out into the hall in a daze and on out into the blinding Texas sun.

Later that afternoon, after I had taken my mother back to the motel, I drove to the Baylor track and ran lap after lap until darkness descended, and then I just kept running around the pitch dark oval, the distant streetlights weaving spools of light around my head, until my heart was pounding as furiously as his might have been on the operating table, and I imagined my strength, my fresh blood, somehow feeding into his heart and his blood, making him well again. Then I collapsed on the stiff bleachers and watched the shadows of the tackling dummies in the infield and the stars and UFOs wheeling in merciless profusion across the night sky.

I remembered that as a high school sophomore in Ohio, my father, Orin "Jim" Bellamy, who weighed in at 140 pounds in those days, had played first-string tackle at Portsmouth High School—if you know what that means—before Depression conditions forced him to quit school and he eventually took up sales work. That section of south-central Ohio has some of the most brutal football of any region of the country. That was where Woody Hayes used to come looking for his linemen, to Massilon and Ironton and West Portsmouth. Even in the twenties, a 140-pound lineman must have been an anomaly. He would have had to be quick, strong, and willing to take incredible punishment.

When I returned to the Tides, my mother was propped up on her bed watching the late movie. Her cheeks were shiny and her eyes looked suspiciously red. She said it was just about the saddest movie she had seen since *Gone with the Wind.*

The room at the funeral home in Cincinnati was so large that I was certain, when I first saw it, that we would stand there for hours staring at the white walls and the coved ceilings, casting an occasional blurry glance in the direction of the silver casket at the far end and feeling embarrassed and miserable, but an overwhelming number of people began arriving and soon the room was bustling with guests. Most of them I had never met, though many of the names were familiar. It should have been no surprise to me that my father had been an extremely popular man, whom many people admired or credited with helping them in business or with personal problems, but I was surprised nonetheless.

The body in the coffin was that of a thin man who bore only a passing resemblance to my father. But I tried my best to appreciate the truth of the matter rather than the appearance. At the conclusion of visiting hours, several obese volunteers from the local Masonic Lodge lined up and read stupidly from a prepared ceremony. After everyone had gone, I spent some time alone with him. The funeral director had to ask me to leave.

In the church the next morning, along with a core of relatives and friends from the day before, half a dozen Marines in full dress uniform were present and accompanied us to Oak Hill Cemetery. Perhaps because he had decided at the end on a military funeral, my mother had been spending every spare second sorting through old papers and boxes, searching frantically for his Honorable Discharge, which she could not find. She was so businesslike, so distracted, so tuned out, that she nearly succeeded in repressing what was happening to her.

The sort of pomp and circumstance that would have embarrassed my father as a younger man must have seemed necessary in the end to shore up his weakening grasp on his identity. He wanted to be remembered as a man whose life had counted, and, I suppose, when he looked back over his life, his time as a Marine must have seemed the best proof of actions that had made a difference in the world.

I thought of the print on the wall above his desk, which he dutifully took down and nailed up again in every new house we moved into: the Marines raising the flag at Iwo-Jima and the inscription: "Here Marine courage and skill were put to the supreme test."

My mother and I stood at his graveside in Ohio in the drizzle while the Marines fired three shots into the grey sky and lifted the flag from his coffin and folded it. "By order of the Commandant of the Marine Corps and the Secretary of the Treasury," one said, "we present you with this flag on behalf of a grateful nation."

The main house and barns at the Zutavern farm in Bloomville, Ohio.
All-in-all it was 240 acres.

34.

Last Trip to Bloomville

The day my father taught me to drive the tractor, we were alone together in a freshly plowed forty-acre field in Bloomville. He often let me sit between his knees on the front edge of the tractor seat and put my hands on the wheel and pretend to drive while his larger, surer hands did the actual steering. This day, he showed me how to make large circles with the grater attached on the back, chopping all the large clods of earth into smaller and smaller lumps. After he had done it several times, he let me sit by myself in the big tractor seat and he hung on behind and I could feel the pressure of his hand on the seat as I made a wide circle the way he had done, steering carefully and overlapping with the previous swath. After I had completed a round or two, my father stepped off the back of the tractor without my knowing it and I made one complete pass alone, thinking he was still there, and, when I looked up, I was astonished to see him standing in the field ahead of me, grinning and congratulating me.

I prepared for fifteen years for his dying—from the time of his first heart attack—and yet I was caught off-guard by his death and, even now, in some way, I am not ready to accept it.

He believed in the American dream with an innocence and fierceness that, at twenty, I took to be corny and mindless. Yet, by middle age, I could see it was the well-earned patriotism of a man who had made brutal, verifiable sacrifices in the name of national honor and for the sake of values about which no civilized person would quarrel.

He had navigated the Depression as a young man and subsequently feared unemployment all his life, especially after forty, yet he quit enough good jobs to have kept a small army happily employed. He worked his way up several avenues of business and having reached a kind of pinnacle or dead-end in each instance, quit and moved on to something new. He made and spent two or three fortunes during his lifetime and died a poor man, so poor he was afraid he could not afford the heart operation he needed to stay alive for a few more years.

He loved me with a kind of helpless, unselfconscious paternal devotion that was like a protective mantle, a powerful light always flowing around my shoulders.

When I was a boy, we visited the farm often; and although the houses and towns we lived in and the schools I attended from year to year changed and were, in a sense, interchangeable, eventually becoming a blur in my memory, the farm was the only location that was always the same, a constant, dependable corner of the earth that I felt I could always refer back to and call my own. The extent to which I made use of this connection was not apparent to me until I visited Bloomville for probably the last time—to attend my grandmother's funeral.

I took an early morning walk down the narrow, humped-back country road that bisects our land, and I began to notice how many of the sites I passed already existed in my imagination as vivid and detailed locations for dreams, stories, and novels I had read, and automatic reference points to place. This ditch beside the orchard was where I had imagined Sarty Snopes huddled to elude Major DeSpain's horses in "Barn Burning." This small outcropping of trees was where I had imagined the old woman in "Death in the Woods" frozen to death with the sack of food on her back and where the frightened dogs had danced in circles under the moon. For me, I began to realize, Bloomville was Winesburg, Ohio, and Yoknapatawpha County and parts of Updike's Pennsylvania and Flannery O'Connor's Georgia. It was also Cranford and Middlemarch and all of eighteenth and nineteenth century rural England.

When we were very small, I remembered, my cousin and I used to dress up in musty old clothes we found in a big trunk in the woodhouse, mainly elegant old lacy dresses and shawls and the silliest hats, and we would come knocking on my grandmother's door, pretending to be old ladies from Bloomville; and my grandmother would welcome us as if she too believed we were old ladies and great good friends of hers and she would sit down and pretend to gossip with us.

Both before and after our actual residency there, my father used to invite the men of his family, his brothers and his father, Judge (when he was still alive), and various business acquaintances to visit the farm around Thanksgiving time for the hunting of pheasant and rabbit. I remembered those hunting trips vividly that morning on my walk, possibly because I was looking at some of the same woods and fields they had tramped through so avidly and because I was thinking about final things; and all the members of my father's large family were dead and gone by then, every one of them. But his brothers, my uncles, were a fine bunch of men, stalking the farm in plaid jackets and yellow and fluorescent slickers and heavy boots, shotguns slung under their arms, setting out at daybreak and hunting all day as if their lives depended upon it.

As a small child too young to go along, I remembered wandering out into the summer kitchen and being astonished by three large rabbits, their yellow eyes still clear and open, piled on the wooden deck waiting to be cleaned. I had never seen a dead creature of any kind before that moment, and I remembered staring into their eyes for a long time and feeling an unfamiliar heaviness and sense of anguish. Later on, as I grew older, I was allowed to join in the hunting. I enjoyed the responsibility of carrying the weapon and the camaraderie, but I identified too closely with the animals to ever enjoy the killing. By then, it seemed, there was not much left to kill anyway. The object seemed to be to tramp for hours across frozen corn stubble or quietly through the trees, to avoid complaining or shooting one another, and to return in the late afternoon to a sumptuous dinner that the women had been cooking since breakfast. That we returned empty-handed did not seem to matter.

Gram's funeral was held on a perfect spring day. Seeing her there, I thought of the irony of my father's oft-repeated remark about her: "She'll probably outlive us all." Well, she was 89 when she died and she did outlive quite a few, including my father. Most of the comments at the funeral from my mother and her sisters were about the flowers, how beautiful they were, as if to avoid the awesome fact of what they surrounded. After hearing the flowers mentioned so many times during the visitation, I noticed during the funeral that the flowers formed a huge grotesque frame for the casket, and this frame was so unnaturally bright that it almost seemed to be moving towards us like an event in a film, as if to engrave itself and this scene forever on our memories.

In death, I've learned, people resemble themselves somewhat imperfectly. The undertaker, I believe, must have taken it upon himself to smooth out some of Gram's wrinkles. The result was, oddly, that, lying there that day, her most recognizable features were her ears and her arthritic forefinger. Something about that gnarled finger was especially touching—because it reminded us that she had suffered pain? Upon seeing it, my Aunt Dorothy was moved to remark, somewhat guiltily, that she had once called Gram "old crooked finger" to taunt her.

Several of the citizens present remembered Jim Bellamy very clearly and with considerable enthusiasm. A number informed me that they knew I was Jim Bellamy's son the minute they laid eyes on me. One wanted to know if I was going to come to Bloomville now and be a farmer, but I said no, I was afraid not. The only furrow a professor is likely to plow is down the middle of a page.

They kept the casket open during the visitation and funeral, and I was dreading the moment during the ceremony when they might close the lid, but, of course, they spared us that and did it after we had left. Similarly, at the cemetery, the ceremony was handled in such a way as to deflect strong emotional response.

The grave was not even visible. The casket was mounted above it in an imposing metal chassis and so surrounded by flowers that the only evidence of loam at all was the rich smell of it. The entire grave sight was covered by a bright green awning, as if pitched for a festive lawn party, and the grounds were well-manicured for Memorial Day and bright with flags and fresh flowers dotting several of the graves.

While the minister gave the eulogy, I thought of how Gram had spent the last forty years of her life protecting and defending the farm against all intruders, as generations of the Zutaverns and Spaldings had done before her, how she would sometimes mention proudly that the original deed had been signed during the presidency of James Monroe. I could see the land in my mind's eye as it had looked when I was a child and my father had stopped the car and pointed eagerly across the marsh and the orchard and the green alfalfa fields to the silver-roofed barns gleaming in the sunlight. Somehow, even then, I came to understand that my own destiny was to be committed to that piece of the earth. But it was only an illusion.

Gram had understood the call of the land, that to work the land and to defend the land and to cultivate the harvest is a calling. But my grandmother was too possessive and short-sighted. Having borne no sons who might naturally have taken over, nor daughters who wanted to, she made a mistake in driving away the only heir in the next generation who loved the farm the way she did, who had a vision for it and the capacity to carry it through and the will to pass it on.

My father's instinct during that year—during what today we would call a mid-life crisis—was to retreat from the chaos of civilization, to return to the simpler ways of his ancestors, who had also once worked the land, in order to perpetuate a legacy and an honorable tradition of husbandry, to leave something to his children that was worth inheriting. He failed at that. Instead, he was swept along by circumstances and by the electric and electronic revolutions of the mid-twentieth century and became, in a sense, their handmaiden. Now that he is gone and his brothers are gone, now that my mother and Gram and the farm are gone and all that the generations of my mother's family worked to preserve, I sometimes wonder if there is any evidence left on the face of the earth that any of them ever existed? But of course there is, all around me, and I am a part of it. Without them, I would not be who I am. For now at least, I'm still here, and my children are still here; and their children are still being born.

The night after Gram's funeral, I had a strange dream: It had been raining for days—severe conditions—the sky would blacken suddenly, and windows would be blown out. I was on my way to have an electrical cord repaired, a part of the electrical system of the house that had been damaged by the storms. My wife Connie and the kids were in some danger. The repairman in the shop looked familiar, but I couldn't place him. He was wearing a brightly polished silver space-helmet. Later, I realized it was Cooley's former college roommate from the Baylor track—somehow he had found his way into my dream.

On my way home, I got hopelessly lost and I stopped the car along the highway next to this out-of-the-way roadhouse or tavern with the idea of locating someone to ask directions. The building was painted dark green and seemed boarded up, but a large faded sign near the door read: BLOOMVILLE. The place looked abandoned from the outside but, once inside, I could see a tremendous crowd of people in the dining room, eating and talking, smoke rising and glasses clinking and loud laughter.

As I was passing through an aisle near the bar on my way to try to flag down the cashier, I saw a man who bore an uncanny resemblance to my father, sitting at one of the tables. I couldn't resist walking a little closer and looking at him intently. Just as I was passing quite close to him, he turned and looked at me. His light eyes and the shape of his cheeks were unmistakable. His eyes focused on me and instantly he recognized me—it was my father, very much alive (he looked about fifty—and was clean shaven and healthy). My father was sitting with a woman, quite young and pregnant, who was obviously with him. I was shocked. He seemed somewhat surprised and embarrassed but immediately said, "Hello, pal," and welcomed me, introducing me to the woman. He was glad to see me, it seemed, though it wasn't going to be easy to explain how he had gotten here, why he hadn't really died, and why he had kept himself concealed from my mother and me for such a long time. He was getting ready though, evidently, to tell me what had happened and it was going to be a good story: who the woman was, where he had been for the last several years and why, how his health had improved so markedly.

Then suddenly we were out beside the road, and I could see him running along the shoulder up ahead, running unbelievably well for his age, and I was frightened that my mother might see him. How would he ever explain to her what he was going to explain to me? And how had he been living here all this time, so near us, and we hadn't chanced upon him before? But then I began to notice that he was outdistancing me. I ran harder to catch up, but I kept falling farther behind. I wanted so much to talk to him, to hear his incredible story. I found I was locked in an all out sprint, gaining on him slightly but gasping for breath. But he disappeared up ahead around a bend in the road, his arms pumping smoothly, his feet rising and falling in perfect cadence along the sloping highway.

My wife Connie and daughter Lael in 1966

35.

Epilogue—There's my Blimp!

Salt Lake City—Mecca! The air is crisp. The sky is lighter blue than I am accustomed to seeing—is it something about the altitude, the latitude, or just the glamour of Mecca? We find the library, and we go in and go straight to work. In the huge, high-ceilinged room, I immediately stumble upon a series of books about the Mayflower that I could easily spend all day reading from and taking notes.

At some point, after writing feverishly and losing track of time, I raise my head up and look around me and take a deep breath. A grey-haired woman is inquiring about something to one of the librarians: "She was my grandmother!" I hear her say, somewhat petulantly, as if the librarian might be persuaded by that fact. All around us, and as far as the eye can see, middle-aged, mostly graying-headed white people—fellow Americans like me—are bent over tables and squinting into computer screens and open books and stalking up and down between high rows of shelving, all searching with a kind of desperation for their own origins.

I do mean desperation. Desperation sets in almost immediately when one arrives in Mecca. Mecca is expensive, and one's time there is always too brief. Of the two hundred unanswered questions one hoped to answer conclusively, there will be time to examine parts of only three. *Which three?* With so many records and so little time, it is difficult to focus. The excitement itself is distracting, and then the day wears on and hardly anything worth knowing has yet been found and one's spirits begin to sag, and then the anxiety felt is even keener. *Must push on—forget about eating. The reading room closes at 8 PM!*

I am thinking about my mother and father: they both had ancestors who were officers in Cromwell's Army. They both had Puritans, and Bulkeleys, in their trees, going back nearly four hundred years in this country and at least a thousand years in England. They both had ancestors who had been farmers in Virginia as early as the 1700s. They both were close relatives of the Adams family of Braintree, Massachusetts. They both had ancestors who fought and died and some who played starring roles in the American Revolution. They both had ancestors who strongly opposed slavery, who served in the Underground Railway, helping indentured blacks escape the South, or who moved their entire churches and congregations from Virginia to Ohio to escape slavery. They both had a number of ancestors who became prolific and influential preachers. They both had ancestors who adhered to unconventional religious beliefs in spite of the threat of torture, mayhem, and death. Whether I like it or not, this is my legacy.

I will say this about the genes that I may have inherited from the Adamses, the religious martyrs, and the revolutionaries in my family: I have a gut-level, fierce, stubborn resistance to any form of bullying, no matter how small and inconsequential, that has sometimes made my life more difficult than it needed to be. I understand that it would be much easier for me if I could become more compliant, but I cannot help myself.

I doubt that I could ever have been as socially responsible as my Adams cousins during the Revolution, though they were hardly men who caved into bullies either. But, given the provocation, I could have thrown bricks through windows or dressed up as an Indian and dumped tea into Boston Harbor. I would have been good at that. No doubt I would have been one with the Sons of Liberty—in spite of my pacifist Mennonite genes. I fear I would have been much better as a revolutionary than I would ever have been as a patient nation-builder like John Adams, who believed so devoutly in the law and in the importance of the legal process and in the writing of constitutions—too many hot-headed Puritan preachers in my background or too many members of Cromwell's army, pious men who liked to bash aristocrats over the head with their heavy swords and then retire to the chapel for a few prayers before dinner.

How could all the family lore I've collected here ever have been lost? How was it lost? Someone died too soon? Someone thought it was too trivial to mention. Someone mentioned it and it was forgotten? Pictures were not labeled and after a time no one living knew who the people in the pictures were. Someone was too busy simply making ends meet or keeping their lives together to worry about it.

Great grandparents need to find a way to communicate with their distant offspring even if they do not live long enough to see them and talk to them personally. We need to find a better way to communicate from one generation to another—because who our ancestors were is part of who we are, and if we do not know the one, we cannot possibly know the other.

After my immersion in genealogical research, I now see exactly why I made so many of the decisions that defined my life. My family tree is chock full of preachers and even some intellectuals, from Puritans educated at Cambridge to fire and brimstone back-woods evangelists educated in the school of hard knocks, and somehow their genes descended to me. I wish I had known sooner just where I came from and, therefore, who I was "meant" to be.

I felt like a character who enters the action in the last chapters of a long novel and suddenly realizes he has not read the rest of the book and desires to go back and start reading from Chapter One in order to find out what the book is about. Which is to say: the best result of this genealogical journey I've been taking is not that I have found an illustrious background for myself—though parts of it are far more illustrious than I ever imagined—but that my history, such as it is, is now not simply a blank. Now I know what the book *I am in* is about, and that knowledge is liberating. Now I know what the book is about, and what an amazing story it is!

Once, when my father was still alive, he and my mother visited us in Mansfield, Pennsylvania, where I held my first teaching job. I remember that we were all out in the backyard of the small house we were renting then, trying to take pictures in order to memorialize the visit.

My wife is always very impatient at picture-taking time, and I have never been the swiftest of photographers, partly due to perfectionism and partly to ineptitude. We have had some of our worst crises at these moments when I try to make everyone stand still long enough, and Connie (and then my daughter Lael, as she grew older) becomes so exasperated with me that she is soon scowling at the camera or stomping off to do something else, refusing to be photographed at all.

My daughter Lael, who was then about five years old, was upset about something. I don't remember what it was, but I remember trying to blot it out of my mind so that I could concentrate on making the proper adjustments to the camera before Connie threw one of her classic exit scenes. Then Lael began to cry, and I told her to please shut up and try to be a good girl, and of course that made her cry all the harder. My father rushed over to Lael and swept her up in his arms and started to coo into her ear, and within a matter of seconds he had her smiling ecstatically and deep in some intimate conversation about matters I could not imagine. I began to realize then that there was a special bond between them.

Years later, when Lael was performing on stage in a musical when she was about sixteen, she was amazingly good, and I registered the fact that Lael is a lot more extroverted than her parents, but also, for the first time, I was struck by an actual physical resemblance to my father in Lael's face. It shocked me because I was still mourning his death (though it had been years earlier), and I thought I might be merely imagining it. But I blinked and I kept searching for it, as Lael cavorted on the stage like an old pro, and, yes, it was there—a certain expression, something in the cheeks and the smile—it was my father's face, smiling down on me, while Lael did high kicks. I might add that Lael resembles pictures I have seen of my grandmother as a young woman, and she has Gram's indominable presence and self-confidence.

When Lael was in law school at Emory, she lived briefly in a damp, cheap basement apartment in Atlanta, and on a visit I noticed that one of the photos she had prominently displayed was a framed 8 X 10 of my father. This quite surprised me because she had been only about eight years old when he had died and I supposed that she hardly remembered him.

"Why do you have that one out?" I said. "Do you remember him at all?"

"Not really," she said. "I just think he looks like a terrific man."

Incidentally, Lael eventually married a young man who resembles my father in both physical appearance and in occupational orientation.

Lael finished law school and her first job was working as in-house counsel for a small printing firm. When I visited her in 1996 just before the Atlanta Olympics, we were driving back from the airport up Interstate 85, approaching the skyline of downtown Atlanta, and Lael pointed up over the distant landscape and said, "There's my blimp!"

I noticed an enormous blimp hovering over the distant horizon, but I didn't know what she was talking about. "What do you mean, *your* blimp?" I said.

"Kroger is one of our clients, and they wanted to do something big for the Olympics. Someone had the idea of renting a blimp, but the City and the Olympic Committee control the airspace over the area, and they wanted $2-million a week. So I came up with this idea. We rent a blimp a month *before* the rates go up, and it has Kroger painted on the side. The blimp flies all over Atlanta, and then during the Olympics we sublet the blimp to the Atlanta Police, so people look up and they see the same blimp but now it says Atlanta Police and they think, "Look what they did to the Kroger blimp!" and Kroger still gets some spin out of it, and the Atlanta Police get a blimp too. But it doesn't cost as much for them and Kroger helps pay for it."

"And they bought the idea?'

"They loved the idea. Everyone loved it. I told some of my friends that I rented this blimp for Kroger and the Atlanta Police, and they were like, 'Sure, Lael. Maybe you could rent a blimp for us some time.' Then the same friends were at Braves Stadium when the blimp first appeared over the field and they called me on their cell and they were like: 'Lael, your blimp is here! We were just sitting here, and all of a sudden this enormous *blimp* came over! This is the biggest blimp we've ever *seeeen*, Lael.'"

"What did it cost?" I said.

"Only about $400,000 a month."

"How did you know where to get it?"

"I went to the Law Library and looked it up. There are thirteen blimp companies in the world, and I called them all—to get the best price. The company I chose wanted to give me a $45,000 commission, but of course I couldn't accept it. Then they tried to hire me."

I said, "You wouldn't have to rent very many blimps at that price to do pretty well for yourself." But I was thinking, *My God, the spirit of Jim Bellamy is alive and well—and living in Atlanta!*

I spent several years and enormous effort trying to find pictures of my family's ancestors. I wanted to have photos of everyone back through at least my great grandparents. I had written to total strangers and coaxed them into their attics. I had made impossible phone calls to distant cousins I had never met who were dying in nursing homes and begged them for help. I had finally gotten all of them but one.

Before my children's visit, I had carefully laid out all these ancestor photos on the dining room table—everyone before us going back to my great grandparents and including that old rogue Townley Hannah Bellamy, my great, *great* grandfather, and Samuel Dunham Spalding, a great *great* grandfather on my mother's side—a strikingly handsome man, I thought. It was a wonderful face—I was grateful to be descended from such a man. I did not have a photo of Alice Whipple Clark, that genetic paragon, so I substituted a picture of Olive Clark, a near cousin who, I imagined, might have resembled her. It was the first time I had laid out the photos all together—even for my own perusal—and I was amazed and pleased by it.

To me, it was like a DNA print of who we were—only better—because instead of abstract patterns, we could examine the actual faces of our predecessors and see something of ourselves in the blending of features.

I was determined not to mention these photos to my children but rather to let Sam and Lael discover them on their own. They had often expressed impatience with my genealogy obsession, and I was determined to be low key. But I thought their curiosity would get the better of them, and they would want to know more.

Instead, for two days they walked by the photos quickly, as if they didn't notice them at all. On Sunday, the day for leaving, Lael made an effort to humor me by asking a series of pointed questions about the pictures, but, obviously she was just being polite. Sam felt obligated to glance over her shoulder for a few moments, but then he fled into the living room and blurted out: "How can you expect us to care anything about all those *dead people*!" He seemed to think it was macabre!

"But these aren't just any dead people," I said. "These people are our ancestors. They made our lives possible."

"But they're dead now," he said, "aren't they?"

"So will we *all* be," I said, "and sooner than you think." Not the most reassuring comment I could have come up with…especially since I think Sam's reaction may have been, in part, because if anyone was about to join those already in the cemetery it was most likely going to be me—his rapidly aging father! I think he had already imagined my demise as a nightmare he wanted to avoid. He called once after seeing a drug ad on TV that featured a father dropping dead during a backyard basketball game with his son. Sam wanted to know how I was feeling. He's a good son—I certainly didn't want to worry him.

"I don't think of them as dead people," I said. "I don't think of them as *dead*. I think of them as . . . kindred spirits." What I should have said is: "When you begin to realize how many lives it takes to make one person's life, you begin to realize something of human value and worth. Each of us is a community, the meeting point for hundreds and hundreds of lives and aspirations. Each of us is a community *within*."

I *am* Hannah Siple in her grief and John W. Kagy, dying too soon. I *am* the Bulkeley sisters. I am Rolla Zutavern, dedicated to the land of my fathers. I *am* illiterate Matthew Bellamy, captured while trying to escape a life of drudgery and humiliation. I am pious Peter Bulkeley and fatherless John B. Lawhorn. I belong to Cromwell's Army and to George Washington's and to Dwight Eisenhower's. I am John Bickerton, sentenced to Death for a trifle. I am part of John and Samuel Adams and a fraction of Francis Bacon. I am Berry Bellamy and Rudolph Kagy, cutting my way through an endless forest. I am Townley Bellamy, driven out of my home because of something my father might have done. I *am* Philip Von Gemmingen and his jilted milkmaid, the mother of his child. I am King Edward the First and Charlemagne. I am a persecuted Mennonite and a Magna Carta baron and a Pilgrim and a slave, yearning to be free.

Appendix

New England Ministers' Letter in Response to Cromwell:

"Right Honorable,

As the state of England hath bene pleased to call you to cheife place of civil and military Command in Ireland, so hath the Lord in admiration prospered your undertakings there and made you a glorious Instrument of the execution of his just Vengeance upon those bloody monsters of mankinde, and therein heard the cries of his dyeing and liveing people in Ireland, together with those of his Saynts in both Englands, who have cryed in his eares for vengeance against the inhuman murtheres of his poore people in Ireland; and what can the remnant left of his people there, or the rest of their bretheren in both Englands doe lesse, than thankfully acknowledge amongst all other wonders of God's grace done for you, and by you, that he hath there also compased you about with his favor as with a shield, and crowned you with renowned victories over these bloody rebels and enraged enemies of his name and saynts; nor can we doe other than thankfully acknowledge this as a superadded mercy to all the rest, that by his grace he hath kept it in the frame of your heart amidst all the glorious victories which under God you have gotten, thankfully to ascribe the glory thereof to him alone, who is the King of Glory, the Lord of Hoasts, mighty in battel, and your pious care in abaseing men and meanes to exalt the Lord in all your victories as it hath not a little honoured you in our eyes; so have we looked at the same as a speaking pledge that God will yet goe on to perfect his admirable worke by you; now therefore Redoubted Worthy, thinke with yourself, "What shall I render to the Lord for all his benyfits towards me, what further service hath the Lord to use me in, whoe hath done soe great things for me and by me."

Yea you are studying (thrice noble Sir) which way to lift up the name of Jesus Christ there when it hath beene most vilely trampled upon, and where you are called to cheife place of rule, there to take effectual care that Jesus Christ alone may reigne, and that desolate Ireland which hath been drenched and steeped in blood, may be moistened and soaked with the waters of the Sanctuary, for which end your Honour is pleased to cast your eyes, as upon godly people and ministers in England, soe upon such like in America also, whose hearts the Lord may moove to soe blessed a worke. We therefore whose names are underwritten doe, in behalfe of ourselves and some others here in New England humbly returne to your Honour many thanks for your noble offers respecting us also, and since your Honour hath so large a heart given you of the Lord as to desire to build him a Temple amidst the ruinous heaps in Ireland, and so royal a spirit as to be ready soe nobly to befriend the friends (even in America also) of any such workes, soe far as to impose your uttermost interest for their furtherance in removing thither and for their safe and confortable habitation there, together with like care had of their injoying the Lord in his ordinances there, we know not but we may attend this providence of the Lord soe far also as to observe what further of the minde and counsel of God may appeare to us in your seasonable prosecution of your noble proposals, hopeing that as we came by a call of God to serve him here, soe if the Lord's mind shall cleerly appear to give us a sufficyent call and incouragement to remove into Ireland, to serve the Lord Jesus there we shall cheerfully and thankfully imbrace the same. Thus commending your Honour's weighty occasion to the Lord's guidance and blessings, we humbly take our leaves resting.

Your Honours to serve you in the Lord,

Peeter Bulkeley, min.
Samuel Whiting, min.
John Knowles, min.
Thomas Cobet, min.
Danyel Denyson
John Tuttell."

Bibliography

Anderson, Robert Charles. *The Great Migration Begins: Immigrants to New England 1620-1633*. Boston: New England Historic Genealogical Society, 1995.

Anderson, Robert Charles; Sanborn, George F., Jr., and Melinda Lutz. *The Great Migration: Immigrants to New England 1634-1635*. Boston: New England Historic Genealogical Society, 1999.

Anderson, Robert Charles. *The Pilgrim Migration: Immigrants to Plymouth Colony, 1620-1633*. Boston: New England Historic Genealogical Society, 2004.

Baker, Sir Richard. *A Chronicle of the Kings of England from the Times of the Roman Governments unto the Death of King James*. London: George Sawbridge, 1679.

Baldwin, Thomas W. *Michael Bacon of Dedham, 1640, and His Descendants*. Cambridge, Massachusetts: Press of Murray and Emory Company, 1915.

Ball, Edward. *Slaves in the Family*. New York: Ballantine Books, 1998.

Ballagh, James Curtis. *White Servitude in the Colony of Virginia: A Study of the System of Indentured Labor in the American Colonies*. Johnson Reprint Corp, 1973.

Bartlett, J. Gardner. *Henry Adams of Somersetshire, England, and Braintree, Massachusetts, His English Ancestry and Some of His Descendants*. New York: privately printed, 1927.

Bearr, David W. C., ed. *Historic Fluvanna in the Commonwealth of Virginia*. Palmyra, Virginia: Flvanna County Historical Socity, 1998.

Bellamy, Madge. *A Darling of the Twenties*. Vestal, New York: The Vestal Press Limited, 1989.

Brookhiser, Richard. *America's First Dynasty: The Adamses, 1735-1918.* New York: The Free Press, 2002.

Brown, Alexander. *The Cabells and Their Kin.* Boston and New York: Houghton Mifflin and Company, 1895.

Brown, Carol Willits. *William Brown: English Immigrant of Hatfield and Leicester, Massachusetts and His Descendants.* Baltimore, MD: Gateway Press, 1994.

Bulkeley, Peter. *The Gospel Covenant or The Covenant of Grace Opened.* London: Matthew Simmons, 1651.

Coffin, Robert P. Tristram & Witherspoon, Alexander M. *Seventeenth Century Prose and Poetry.* New York: Harcourt, Brace & World, 1957.

Deetz, James and Patricia Scott. *The Times of Their Lives: Life, Love, and Death in Plymouth Colony.* New York: W. H. Freeman & Company, 2000.

Dodd, Alfred. *Francis Bacon's Personal Life-Story.* London: Rider and Company, 1949, 1986.

Dorman, John Frederick, ed. *Caroline County, Virginia, Order Books,* 1732-1740, 1740-1746, 1746-1754. Washington, DC: Dorman, 1971-72, 1976-77.

Emerson, Ralph Waldo. *The Journals of Ralph Waldo Emerson.* New York: Modern Library, 1963.

Fischer, David Hackett. *Albion's Seed: Four British Folkways in America.* New York & Oxford: Oxford University Press, 1989.

Fischer, David Hackett & Kelly, James C. *Bound Away: Virginia and the Westward Movement.* Charlottesville & London: Univerisity of Virginia Press, 2000.

Friesen, Steve. *A Modest Mennonite Home.* Good Books, 1990.

Hastings, Lansford W. *Emigrant's Guide to Oregon and California* (reproduced in facsimile from the original edition of 1845). Princeton: Princeton University Press, 1932.

Jacobus, Donald Lines. *The Bulkeley Genealogy*. New Haven, Ct: The Tuttle, Morehouse & Taylor Company, 1933.

Jordan, Don & Walsh, Michael. *White Cargo: The Forgotten History of Britain's White Slaves in America*. Edinburgh and London: Mainstream Publishing, 2007.

Keagy, Franklin. *A History of the Kagy Relationship in America from 1715 to 1900*. Harrisburg, Pennsylvania: Harrisburg Publishing Company, 1899.

Leeson, Michael A. *History of Seneca County Ohio*. Chicago: Warner, Beers & Company, 1886.

Ligon, Richard. *A True and Exact History of the Island of Barbados*, 1659, 1673. Reprinted London: Frank Cass, 1970.

Lockridge, Kenneth A. *A New England Town: The First Hundred Years: Dedham, Massachusetts, 1636-1736*. New York & London: W. W. Norton & Company, 1985, 1970.

Maurois, Andre. *A History of England*. New York: Grove Press, 1937, 1958.

McCullough, David. *John Adams*. New York: Simon and Schuster, 2001.

Miles, David. *The Tribes of Britain*. London: Weidenfeld & Nicolson, 2005.

Morgan, Edmund S. *American Slavery, American Freedom: The Ordeal of Colonial Virginia*. New York: W. W. Norton & Company, 1975.

Nachfolger, Albert Kobele, ed. *Deutsche Ortssippenbucher: Ortssippenbuch Eppingen im Kraichgau*. Lahr-Dinglingen, 1984, 2003.

Neal, Daniel. *Neal's History of the Puritans: Or, The Rise, Principles, and Sufferings of the Protestant Dissenters, to the Era of the Revolution.* London: Longman, Hurst, Rees, Orme, and Brown, 1811.

Nugent, Nell Marion. *Cavaliers and Pioneers: Abstracts of Virginia Land Patents and Grants.* Richmond, Virginia: Virginia State Library, 1977,

Palmer, William. *The Political Career of Oliver St. John, 1637-1649.* Newark: University of Delaware Press, 1993.

Parramore, Thomas C. et al. *Norfolk: The First Four Centuries.* Charlottesville & London: University of Virginia Press, 1994.

Pearson, John. *Blood Royal: The Story of the Spencers and the Royals.* New York: HarperCollins, 1999.

Philbrick, Nathaniel. *Mayflower: A Story of Courage, Community, and War.* New York: Viking, 2006.

Pond, Rachel Adams Cloud & Clifton Ray. *John Adams of Plymouth, Massachusetts (1621) and His Descendants.* New York, 1963,

Pope, Charles Henry. *Pioneers of Massachusetts.* Bowie, MD: Heritage Books, 1991.

Powell, Allan. *Forgotten Heroes of the Maryland Frontier.* Baltimore: Gateway Press, 2001.

Price, David A. *Love and Death in Jamestown.* New York: Alfred A. Knopf, 2003.

Purkiss, Diane. *The English Civil War: Papists, Gentlewomen, Soldiers, and Witchfinders in the Birth of Modern Britain.* New York: Basic Books, 2006.

Ripley, Edward Franklin. *Shepherd in the Wilderness: Peter Hobart 1604-1679.* Lanham, New York, Oxford: University Press of America, 2001.

Robert, Eunice Byram. *Bryam-Crawford and Allied Genealogy.* Nortex Press, 1976.

Roberts, Gary Boyd. *The Royal Descents of 500 Immigrants to the American Colonies or the United States Who Were Themselves Notable or Left Descendants Notable in American History.* Baltimore: Genealogical Publishing Co., 1993, 2001, 2002.

Schrag, Martin. *The European History of the Swiss Mennonites.* Swiss Mennonite Cultural & Historical Association, 1974.

Scudder, Horace E. *A History of the United States of America With an Introduction Narrating the Discovery and Settlement of North America.* New York: Sheldon & Company, 1897.

Smith, Abbot Emerson. *Colonists in Bondage.* Gloucester, MA: Peter Smith, 1965.

Spalding, Charles Warren. *The Spalding Memorial: A Genealogical History of Edward Spalding of Virginia and Massachusetts Bay and His Descendants.* Chicago: American Publishers' Association, 1897.

Sparacio, Ruth & Sam, eds. *Lancaster County, Virginia, Order Book, 1656-1666, 1666-1680.* Arlington, Virginia: The Antient Press, 1993.

Spencer, Jack Taif & Edith Woolley. *The Spencers of the Great Migration.* Dekalb, Illinois: Spencer Publishing.

Stratton, Eugene Aubrey. *Applied Genealogy.* Ancestry, Inc., 1988.

Stratton, Eugene Aubrey. *Plymouth Colony: Its History & People.* Sale Lake City, Utah, 1986.

Shoumatoff, Alex. *The Mountain of Names: A History of the Human Family.* New York: Simon and Schuster, 1985.

Sykes, Bryan. *Saxons, Vikings, and Celts.* New York & London: W. W. Norton & Company, 2006.

Sykes, Bryan. *The Seven Daughters of Eve.* New York & London: W. W. Norton & Company, 2001.

Strickler, Harry M. *Forerunners: A History or Genealogy of the Strickler Families, Their Kith and Kin.* Athens, Georgia: Iberian Publishing Company, 1998. Reprinted from the 1925 edition.

Tilden, William. *History of the Town of Medfield, Massachusetts, 1650-1886.* Medfield: Medfield Historical Society/George H. Ellis, 1887, 1975.

Torrence, Clayton. *Winston of Virginia and Allied Families.* Richmond, Whittet & Shepperson, 1927.

Usher, James. *History of the Lawrence-Townley and Chase-Townley Estates in England.* New York, 1883. Reprinted by Higginson Book Company.

Van Braght, Thieleman J. *The Bloody Theater or Martyrs Mirror of the Defenseless Christians Who Baptized Only Upon Confession of Faith, and Who Suffered and Died for the Testimony of Jesus, Their Savior, From the Time of Christ to the Year A.D. 1660.* Translated from the Original Dutch or Holland Language from the Edition of 1660. Scottdale, Pennsylvania: Herald Press and Mennonite Publishing Company, 1660, 1886, 1950.

Weis, Frederick Lewis. *The Magna Charta Sureties, 1215: The Barons Named in the Magna Charta, 1215, and Some of Their Descendants Who Settled in America During the Early Colonial Years.* Baltimore: Genealogical Publishing Co., 1999.

Whitelaw, Ralph T. *Virginia's Eastern Shore: A History of Northampton and Accomack Counties.* P. Smith, 1951, 1968.

Wills, Gary. *Henry Adams and the Making of America.* Boston & New York: Hougton Mifflin, 2005.

Index

About the Author

Joe David Bellamy was Whichard Distinguished Professor in the Humanities at East Carolina University and has taught at several colleges and universities, including George Mason University and the University of Iowa. He won the Editors' Book Award for his novel *Suzi Sinzinnati,* and he is also the author of fifteen other books, including *Atomic Love, Literary Luxuries: American Writing at the End of the Millennium,* and *The New Fiction.* He is a voting member of the National Book Critics Circle and served as Director of the Literature Program of the National Endowment for the Arts. His essays, fiction, poetry, and reviews have been published in: *The Atlantic, The Nation, Harper's, Paris Review, Saturday Review, The New York Times Book Review, Ploughshares, The Washington Post Book World,* and some seventy others.